Looking for Blackfellas' Point

AN AUSTRALIAN HISTORY OF PLACE

MARK McKENNA

Looking for Blackfellas' Point

AN AUSTRALIAN HISTORY OF PLACE

UNSW PRESS

an Exploring Breakfast

A UNSW Press book

Published by
University of New South Wales Press Ltd
University of New South Wales
UNSW Sydney NSW 2052
AUSTRALIA
www.unswpress.com.au

National Library of Australia
Cataloguing-in-Publication entry:

McKenna, Mark, 1959– .
Looking for Blackfellas' Point: an Australian history of place.

Bibliography.
Includes index.
ISBN 0 86840 644 9.

1. Aborigines, Australian — New South Wales — Social conditions — History. 2. Aborigines, Australian — New South Wales — Government relations. 3. Aborigines, Australian — New South Wales — Treatment — History. 4. New South Wales — Race relations — History. I. Title.

994.40049915

Design Di Quick
Printer Everbest Printing
Page i Towamba Valley, NSW. *Mark McKenna 2001*
Page iii Percy Mumbler at Shoalhaven, late 1970s. *Lee Chittick*
Page iv 'An Exploring Breakfast', Oswald Brierly, 1842. *A535, Mitchell Library, State Library of New South Wales*
Cover Beach walkers, Narooma, NSW south coast, 1987. *Mark McKenna 1987*

In memory of

Hilda Dymphna Clark 1916–2000

and

Nancye Eileen McKenna 1927–1999

This then, I thought, as I looked round about me, is the representation of history. It requires a falsification of perspective. We, the survivors, see everything from above, see everything at once, and still we do not know how it was.

WG SEBALD,
The Rings of Saturn[1]

The Aborigines … who saw in the English nothing but an invading enemy, were calling out 'Warra! Warra!' ['Go away! go away!'] … [Their land] had recently been invaded, their means of livelihood had been reduced, and there was still no recognition that these two grievances were, in the eyes of the Aborigines, the greatest of possible wrong … The Aborigines mounted reprisals and the Europeans maltreated them in turn, and this gave rise to terrible acts of vengeance, which more than once brought trouble and terror to the colony.

LOUIS DE FREYCINET,
Reflections on New South Wales 1788–1839[2]

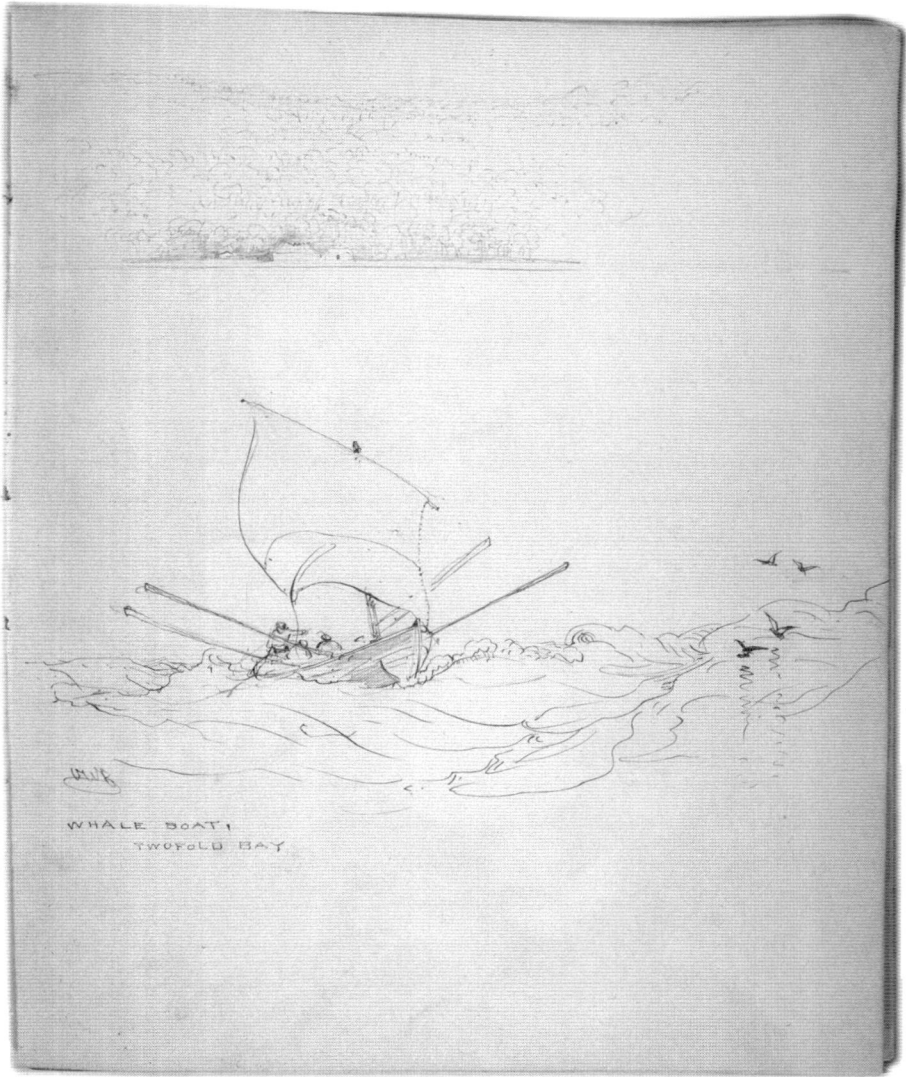

'Whale Boat, Twofold Bay', Oswald Brierly, 1843
[A536, Mitchell Library, State Library of New South Wales]

contents

contents

'Camp Beermuna, Twofold Bay, 13 December 1842', Oswald Brierly, 1842
[DGD19.f.4, Dixon Galleries, State Library of New South Wales]

'Natives, Twofold Bay', Oswald Brierly, 1842
[A535, Mitchell Library, State Library of New South Wales]

ILLUSTRATIONS

ACKNOWLEDGMENTS

For advice, assistance, criticism and encouragement. With many thanks to:

Bain Attwood, Bega Valley Family History Museum, Tim Bonyhady, Carl Bridge and the Menzies Centre for Australian Studies in London, Nicholas Brown, Betty Buckland, John Carrick, Bernard Cohen, Kate Clery, Beryl Cruse, BJ Cruse, Martin Dwyer, Rene Davidson, Robin Derricourt and UNSW Press, Ray Gardaya, Tom Griffiths, Wayne Hudson, Jeff James, Catherine McGrath, Geraldine McKenna, Mary Mitchell, Robert Morrell, Ellen Mundy, Sue Norman, Tim O'Rourke, Susan Pfisterer, Peter Read, Edwin Ride, Tim Rowse, James Warden, Sue Wesson, John Williams, George Winterton, and my family, Fiona, Siobhan and Claire McKenna.

1 cm = approx. 15 km

Canberra

Queanbeyan

ACT

Michelago

KINGS

Bungendore

River

HWY

Braidwood

KINGS

HWY

ARALUEN

ROAD

Batemans Bay

Murrumbidgee

SNOWY

Adaminaby

MOUNTAINS

River

Lake
Eucumbene

HWY

MONARO

Shoalhaven

Moruya

SOUTH

PACIFIC

OCEAN

Cooma

River

Berridale

Jindabyne

Tuross

Narooma

Cobargo

PRINCES

Wallaga Lake

Bermagui

Nimmitabel

SNOWY MOUNTAINS HWY

Snowy

River

Bega

Wapengo

Candelo

HWY

Tathra

Cathcart

Bombala

MONARO

Wyndham

Pambula

Merimbula

NSW-VIC STATE BORDER

Delegate

HWY

VICTORIA

Towamba

Eden

PRINCES

NSW

Nungatta

TASMAN

SEA

Green Cape

Disaster Bay

Cape Howe

GEOGRAPHICAL TERMS

This book focuses on the history of the far south-eastern corner of Australia. This is the southern portion of Eden–Monaro, in the state of New South Wales, the vast area that comprises the federal electorate of the same name. Although towns such as Cooma, on the Monaro, and Batemans Bay, on the south coast of New South Wales, feature in this book, my main focus is on the southern part of Eden–Monaro. This is the area which includes the far south coast, from Cape Howe on the New South Wales–Victorian border, north along the coast to Eden, Pambula, Merimbula and Tathra, and inland, from Bega in the north to Bombala in the south-west. Towamba, the village in which my own land is situated, lies in the coastal hinterland, near to Eden.

introduction

Looking south from Blackfellas' Point, Towamba River, NSW, 2001. [Mark McKenna]

LOOKING FOR
BLACKFELLAS' POINT 1

In early 1993, I bought 8 acres of land on the far south coast of New South Wales. Three months earlier, on a warm summer's afternoon, I was walking along the banks of the Towamba River with Tim O'Rourke, a friend who had lived in the area since the late 1980s. After walking for an hour or more, we came to a point where the bush was so thick we were unable to continue. Tim knew the way back to the road, so we left the riverbank and climbed up a short hill covered in tea tree and black wattle.

From the top, about 20 metres above the river, we stopped to catch our breath. Looking south-west at mid-afternoon, through the scrub and distant peppermints, I could see the snake trail of the river, backed by cleared farmland and state forest, winding slowly away. Across the river I could see an arc of tall gums standing on a point of land wrapped tightly by the river's arms. Turning north-west, I could hear the sound of the water as it rushed over the rapids less than 500 metres away. I was immediately entranced by the view, captivated by the natural beauty of the place.

Having found the land before I discovered it was for sale, I was convinced it was my destiny to become the new owner. Clearing the tea tree away from the front gate weeks later, I could just make out the name written on the top fence post: 'Eureka'. For a historian then writing a book on the history of republicanism, this was too much of a coincidence to bear. Eureka indeed. Over the next three years, in an initial burst of enthusiasm, I planted trees and shrubs, spent long nights making poor sketches of house plans, and probably exhausted the patience of friends and family with my visions of bucolic bliss.

Like many urban Australians, I had long dreamt of escape from the city to the bush. Escape from traffic, pollution, queues, constant din and the property ladder to silence, peace and the pleasures of a more natural environment — the city slicker's rural idyll. I wasn't planning on living in my new-found paradise immediately. Perhaps this was because I understood the terror in the eyes of friends who drove down to 'the block' from Sydney in their gleaming sedans on long weekends. After 24 hours of communing with nature they would look at me in a deeply puzzled way and say, 'It's beautiful but what will you do down here?

'Down here' — the 'far' south coast — was as far away from civilisation as most of my friends preferred to travel. Hanoi, London, New York and Barcelona posed no threat, but Towamba in the coastal hinterland behind Eden, 50 kilometres from the Victorian border and roughly equidistant from Sydney and Melbourne, was a bridge too far, a wilderness without lights.

I tried to listen to the advice of Cecil Poole, a traveller who passed through Towamba in 1894, and who wrote an account of his journey for a local newspaper entitled 'The Towamba River'. Poole reassured his readers that 'although Towamba looks dull it isn't … after all Towamba and the Thames both begin with T'.[1]

The same fears of social isolation and the absence of city distractions that concerned my friends when they stepped from their cars onto 'the land' were inside me too. I remember the day I first trucked boxes of my possessions down from Sydney. Frantically stacking the boxes in a shed — I had to get back on the road with the rented vehicle as soon as possible — one box burst open, my precious books falling onto the muddy earth. Stopping to pick up the books, I suddenly realised I had not

Towamba River, Blackfellas' Point, Towamba, NSW, 2001 [Mark McKenna]

even had time to appreciate the beauty of the scene around me. Late-afternoon autumn light after rain, every colour of the land and bush aglow, Welcome swallows darting across the western sky, all else still — the only sound the river flowing. I looked down at the books on the ground and for an instant saw myself as just another colonist arriving in a distant land — stacking my books and belongings up against the silence of the bush. The truth was that I felt more at home on a street corner in inner Sydney than I did 'down here'. Although I was in love with the aesthetics of the land, I was still a stranger, still waiting to feel at home.

When I bought the land in 1993, it had been owned by a succession of people over the previous two decades, all of whom had their plans to develop it. For various reasons, they had sold up and moved on. I could see the evidence of their plans all around me — fenced paddocks, cypress pines, oak trees, Tasmanian gums, an orchard of plum, apple, pear and almond, and tracks leading down to the river. But there had been no shed. So far as I could tell, nothing had been built on the land, and it had probably not been farmed since the turn of the century.

Looking south from where the house now stands, I could see only the river and distant farmland, to the west across the river an arc of peppermints and, behind me, more bush stretching for almost 100 metres until it met the road. Much had changed since the first squatters arrived in the 1830s. Most of the land had been cleared, fenced, and infested with blackberry, rabbit holes and tussock grass. After every clearing the forest struggled to return — first the tea tree, then the black wattle, before the peppermints finally towered above them all. The clearing of the land over a century or more, often down to the riverfront, had only served to wash tonnes of silt into the river, whose banks were now swollen with sand. The majestic forest that lined the banks of the river only 150 years ago would probably never return. A hundred and fifty years — a mere fifteen decades — had wrought an eternity of change on the land; and my presence was part of that change.

By 1996, my mudbrick fantasy had finally taken shape. The house was to sit on the knoll above the river, looking across to an outcrop of peppermint gums and granite boulders strewn on white sand — the point where the river turned sharply before winding its way another 30 kilometres to the sea.

Visiting the site at dusk one winter's day, I was admiring the view across the river when Ray Gardaya, my friend and builder, noticed me gazing across the water and asked, 'You know what that point on the river is called, don't you'? 'No', I replied. 'It's Blackfellas' Point', he said. When I asked Ray who had told him about the name he said he wasn't sure. Apparently 'Blackfellas' Point' was one of the names it had been given over the years, a name which on first impression was all that remained of a presence that stretched back thousands of years. My white-fella Eureka was a blackfella Eureka too.

I recalled a conversation I'd had with BJ Cruse, an Aboriginal officer with the local land council in Eden. 'If you want to know where our sites are just look around you', he said, 'we like the same spots you do'. Blackfellas' Point had been an Aboriginal camping place, a meeting point, and a place for cooking, feasting and dancing. Later, I would discover a document in the National Library which contained a description of a corroboree that had taken place near Blackfellas' Point in 1847. For longer than I could imagine, Aboriginal people had been there before me. My view across the river looked into a past so deep, so out of reach.

I found it difficult to grasp that in the relatively brief time since the arrival of the first squatters in the 1830s, one civilisation seemed to have so utterly displaced another. I looked in vain for stone tools or grinding grooves in the rocks along the banks of the river, and I asked many of the locals if they'd heard any stories or found any artefacts. Some remembered finding stone tools at Aboriginal campsites in the bush, or on the river flats, but these had been lost long ago, together with much of the oral history of the early colonial days. With few exceptions, there was little local knowledge of the 'distant' past — whether the indigenous past or the pioneer past. For many people I spoke with, the past was something that began when they were born.

We have probably all wondered at one time or another what the land was like before the fences and the bitumen — we have all sighted a bridge to another time. But when I walked the land, it seemed as if I had only my imagination to conjure up the past. At other times I felt that the past was there but that I had no way of reaching it, as if I had to learn a new language before I could understand what had happened. But if I was to understand my own place in this part of Australia, I felt I had to know more about the lives of those who had walked before me on the same ground.

I wanted to know something of the Aboriginal societies that once thrived on the land I now owned. Less than a hundred years after they experienced contact with the first wave of colonists, they had been forced off the land — perishing in violent confrontation, falling prey to diseases to which they had no immunity, or moved onto Aboriginal reserves on the coast. Initially, I could only see their story as one of oppression and betrayal.

When I began my research, I discovered that the few scholars who had made an attempt to understand the local indigenous societies had observed that the area around Twofold Bay was 'the most poorly described of all culture areas in the region'.[2] For an area that had been occupied by Europeans since the late eighteenth century, there seemed to be a dearth of knowledge concerning its indigenous past. Yet the far south coast also represents one of the most concentrated areas of Aboriginal placenames in south-eastern Australia. On the coast and in the hinterland, the Aboriginal presence lives on every time the name of a town or village is mentioned: Bega, Cobargo, Bombala, Mallacoota, Narooma, Merimbula, Tathra, Bermagui, Pambula, Towamba, Burragate and Wolumla — similar names for the same places, before and after 1788.[3]

Early in 1997, I had begun work on a book on the politics of history in Australia. At that stage, I imagined the book as a history of the public and professional debate over the moral legitimacy of the nation-state — 'black arm-band history' or 'white blindfold history'? pioneers or land grabbers? to apologise or not to apologise? I wanted to explain the genesis of this debate from the nineteenth century to the present, but in particular to focus on the last three decades of the twentieth century.

As I wondered about the Aboriginal presence at Blackfellas' Point, and tried to discover more about the interaction between the first wave of settlers and Aboriginal people on the far south coast, I began to appreciate how this history might speak to the politics of reconciliation on a national scale. It occurred to me that my personal quest to discover more about the history of Blackfellas' Point and my professional interest in understanding the politics of history in Australia were closely related. The personal, regional and national journeys invited by the knowledge of colonial history and Aboriginal culture and dispossession are intimately connected.

'Blackfellas' Point' was most probably a whitefella name for an Aboriginal camping place. 'Blackfella' is a word used by many people in the area today, both Aboriginal and non-Aboriginal, to describe Aboriginal people. For local indigenous leaders such as BJ Cruse, the term 'Blackfella' carries no pejorative overtones. I liked the title *Looking for Blackfellas' Point* because it described my personal search to discover more about the indigenous history of south-eastern New South Wales. It also seemed to me as useful a metaphor as any for describing Australia's current search for reconciliation — sharing a perspective and a sense of place, journeying towards a future meeting point where Australians might find a history that explains what they have become and why some now wish for reconciliation.

The more research I did on the south-eastern corner of New South Wales, the more the shape of the book changed as a result. If someone had suggested to me in 1997 that I would soon write a history of south-eastern New South Wales, I would have reacted with disbelief. But the more I uncovered about the 'local', the more I came to see that the best way of explaining the 'national' was to focus on the 'local'. Through the history of one area, I could perhaps explain how Australia had come to be so deeply divided over the history of Aboriginal dispossession and European settlement.

Through researching and writing this book over the last three years, I have learnt much about the writing of history. I have come to appreciate more fully how national politics can reconfigure local communities, yet I have also come to see how the politics of local communities can impact on national politics. I have learnt how the debates in the federal arena throughout the 1980s and 1990s, particularly those concerning the Bicentenary in 1988, the *Mabo* decision in 1992, and the Stolen Generations in the late 1990s, have all touched the everyday lives of ordinary Australians. Political debates over the question of an apology to indigenous Australians are not merely the symbolic theatre of Canberra politics. They are not simply an abstract discussion among opinion-makers and the political class in the major cities. They matter at a grassroots level, in councils, clubs, churches, schools and public meetings. They affect not only national identity, but also the identity of individuals, homes, streets, suburbs, towns and 'communities'. The struggle of each community to come to terms with the past mirrors the national struggle. That this is true is testament to the power of history to alter the political and social landscape in which we live.

In her 1999 Boyer Lectures, *True Stories*, Inga Clendinnen pleaded for a different kind of history:

> We need history: not 'black armband' history and not triumphalist white-out history either, but good history, true stories of the making of this present land, none of them simple, some of them painful, all of them part of our own individual histories.[4]

When I asked myself what such a vision of 'history' might look like, I saw I had the opportunity to write a book that might show how history could become a conversation of hope. I knew that if I could include some of the 'true stories' of human contact on the frontier of the far south coast of New South Wales, both settler stories and indigenous stories, in an area that I knew personally, I might be able to follow Inga Clendinnen's advice. Perhaps I could not only show how the history of one region in Australia reflected the tensions and struggle in the national story, but also show the richness of history — a canvas that reveals much more than a singular tale of darkness or light.

In taking this approach, I do not want to suggest that this kind of history has never been attempted before. Don Watson's *Caledonia Australis*, first published in 1984, in which he manages to explain the motives and limitations of Scottish settlers in East Gippsland, and tells the tragic story of the dispossession of Aboriginal people that followed in the wake of the settlers' arrival, is probably the finest example.[5]

Looking For Blackfellas' Point explains what happened on the frontier in southeastern New South Wales and how settler culture came to forget what happened. It tells the story of Aboriginal dispossession in the nineteenth century and the revival of Aboriginal culture in the late twentieth century. It explores the relationship between Aboriginal and non-Aboriginal political activists in the period between 1970 and 2000. Influenced by the critical histories of the 1970s and 1980s, together they created a new form of politics, a politics founded on the exposure of historical injustice and oppression which ultimately proved to be the catalyst for the increasing politicisation of Australian history in the 1980s and 1990s.

Finally, in an effort to understand the deeply held beliefs of non-indigenous Australians which impact on Australia's path towards reconciliation, I have also explored the historical identity of non-Aboriginal society on the far south coast. Much of this history has cast the settlers as victims of forces beyond their control, and in the telling of that history there is a profound sense of incompleteness, absence and melancholy. Visions of 'civilisation' and development have often remained unrealised.

At the start of most chapters, I have written a brief introduction which attempts to explain the broader national issues that have led me to focus on that particular aspect of the 'local' story. Throughout the book, more visible on some occasions than others, is the story of my personal relationship with the history I have researched and narrated. Although I own Eureka, I live and work in Canberra, visiting the property when 'time' allows.

Eureka is 'my place' but it is not my place of abode. I am neither a genuine local nor a complete outsider. In this way, I suppose my situation reflects that of many Australians today. I have not lived my life in one town, city or country. I grew up in the western suburbs of Sydney, lived in Germany for two years, travelled in Europe, Russia and Africa, returned to live in inner Sydney for ten years, and in the last four years I have lived in Bega, Canberra and London. My sense of belonging is divided, varied and unpredictable. I can feel I 'belong' on a particular street in Sydney or London, as I can on the south coast of New South Wales, though for different reasons. I am not one who believes 'the land' is the only source of spiritual belonging in Australia. Nor do I believe that non-Aboriginal Australians can or should seek to appropriate an Aboriginal way of belonging to the land. We should try to understand, but we should also accept that there are some things we do not understand. This is part of learning to accept cultural difference.

In writing about the far south coast of New South Wales, I also realise that I am writing about a place that, for me, is elsewhere. Most of my writing time has been spent at the Menzies Centre for Australian Studies in London, and the National Library in Canberra. Regardless of whether 'elsewhere' is a person, place or imagined reality, there is always a danger of creating an idealised image. But in writing history which does not pretend that my view of the past can be detached from my personal life, I hope I have avoided that pitfall, without losing the ability to convey the deep attachment I have developed to Eureka and Blackfellas' Point over the last decade.

When I ask myself what has motivated me to write this book, I am aware that, like many other Australians, I feel I cannot understand the place in which I live without first understanding something of the history and culture of Aboriginal people, and their interaction with settler Australia. If I remain unaware of this past, I feel as if I am living in one room of a house, in which all the other rooms remain closed. In this sense, my own experience in writing *Looking For Blackfellas' Point* reflects the concerns of time in which I live.

I was born in 1959, a time when Australians did not feel the need to know about the indigenous past. Since the early 1990s, I have been influenced by the work of many of my colleagues over the last three decades. After reading the work of Australian historians such as Henry Reynolds, Ann Curthoys, Peter Read and Heather Goodall, I have come to believe it is necessary to understand the history of indigenous Australians if I am to live in this country with my eyes wide open. But my interest has also been prompted by the fact that I purchased 8 acres of land on the far south coast, the place I now call Eureka, the place which looks across to Blackfellas' Point. Coming into close contact with one small piece of land, uncluttered by the landscape of urban Australia, probably created the space and opportunity for me to ask questions I might not have asked had I remained in Sydney or Canberra. It also allowed me to have the experience of living in rural Australia. One image in particular from my time there has stayed with me.

I remember driving south from Canberra, along the Monaro Highway towards Cooma, in late December 1999. Turning off the highway after an hour or so, I travelled along a narrow dirt road, climbing slowly through dry scrub and the cleared paddocks of nearby farms. Searching for the name of the property I was visiting, I slowed down at each rusted tin drum mailbox, eventually finding the right address. As I turned the car into the driveway, I could see a farmhouse in the distance.

It was just before dusk, and the last rays of the sun showed up the stark white lines of a large flagpole that stood in front of the house. As I came closer, I could make out the colours of the flag. There, in the front garden, rising up above the bottlebrush and grevillea, was the Australian flag, flying at least 7 metres high. Surrounded by farmland and bush, with no other house in sight, the flag seemed to turn the farmhouse into a fort — a bush outpost of the conquering settler, an assertive act of possession which seemed all the more naked for being planted on the land.

I had seen Australian flags flying on countless occasions in suburban front yards. But seeing one on a rural property for the first time reminded me how the urban environment in which most Australians live disconnects them from the history of dispossession — as if dispossession was something that happened only in the bush or the outback. In rural Australia, the dust of frontier history is more easily touched. It is there in the old farmhouses and colonial streetscapes, and it is there on the land and in the names on our maps. Rural Australia is still a frontier, a point of contact between indigenous Australians and the history of their resistance to those who took their land.

From the beginning of Australian history, the physical distance between the frontier and the metropolitan engine behind its expansion has always been vast. The distance between London and Sydney was mirrored on a smaller scale in the distance between Sydney and the outer limits of the colony. Physical frontiers created imaginary frontiers.

In the early colonial period, the distance between the heart of the Empire and the frontier contributed to the development of different attitudes towards Aboriginal people — the greater the distance from the frontier, the greater the concern for the protection of indigenous rights. Responsibility for what happened on the frontier was usually passed to those on the front line of contact. In the nineteenth century, unjust treatment of Aboriginal people might be blamed on convicts or the lower classes, while in the late twentieth century urban Australians could blame the continued manifestation of racism on 'rednecks' — usually without risking tautology by applying the adjective 'rural'. The widening gap between rural and urban Australians today has its origins in the history of these physical and imagined frontiers.

The history of colonialism in Australia, and the aggressive expansion of a global capitalist economy, also reveals a complex web of connections. Just as some of the finest buildings in England were built from the profits of the slave trade or the opium wars, investors in Britain reaped huge profits from the pastoral industry in the Australian colonies. Many of Australia's finest 'heritage' buildings were built on the back of profits made possible by the taking of Aboriginal land and the assistance of Aboriginal labour.

View from the Bridge, Towamba River, 1994. [Mark McKenna]

On the south coast, whale oil from Twofold Bay was exported to England, China and America. The 'fingernail like substance from the upper jaws of baleen whales' was used in corsets, knife handles and brushes. European dressmakers sewed it into their clothes to provide the necessary support.[6] When the fashionable women of London stepped out on Sundays to stroll in Kensington Gardens, many of them carried whalebone from Twofold Bay with them. Meat and dairy products from Eden–Monaro ended up on the dining tables of English homes, just as Australian wool was used in clothing all over the world.[7] There may have been a front line of contact on the Australian frontier, but the economic frontier behind it was boundless. Every British citizen was a colonist — everyone was implicated, directly or indirectly, in the dispossession of Aboriginal Australia.

The political challenge of reconciliation today is related intimately to our understanding of this history. More than helping us to understand the past as if it was a time and place entirely detached from our experience, or available for selective embrace, I hope that by telling both the whitefella and blackfella stories on the south coast of New South Wales, I might make a small contribution to the process of achieving reconciliation through a better understanding of our shared past.

As someone who now owns land in the area, I also see this book as one way of giving something back to indigenous people, and giving life to histories that might not otherwise have come to light. In 1999, I attended a small exhibition in Bega. It offered a brief survey of the cultural history of indigenous people in the Bega area. One comment in a report that accompanied the exhibition stood out:

> The Aboriginal people who lived in this area had a very rich culture and history at the time European settlers arrived. Unfortunately most settlers thought that the Aboriginal people were just animals who weren't fit to live, let alone have a culture with its own laws, marriage systems and religion. Because so many of our elders have died over the last years, a lot of this cultural information has been lost, some things have been lost forever … The situation has now reached a critical point where our culture will collapse unless a concerted effort is made now by all people.[8]

Reading this remark was one of the reasons I came to believe that writing a national history of place might be more illuminating than writing an exclusive analysis of recent political debates over Australian history. My research could perhaps offer something of real value for Aboriginal and non-Aboriginal people in the community in which I live.

The best way to begin is to ask the question I have asked myself many times when gazing across the river from my verandah. What was this land like before the Europeans arrived? Before the ships and the horses, before the sealers and the whalers, and before the squatters and the settlers? What can I glean of the indigenous past?

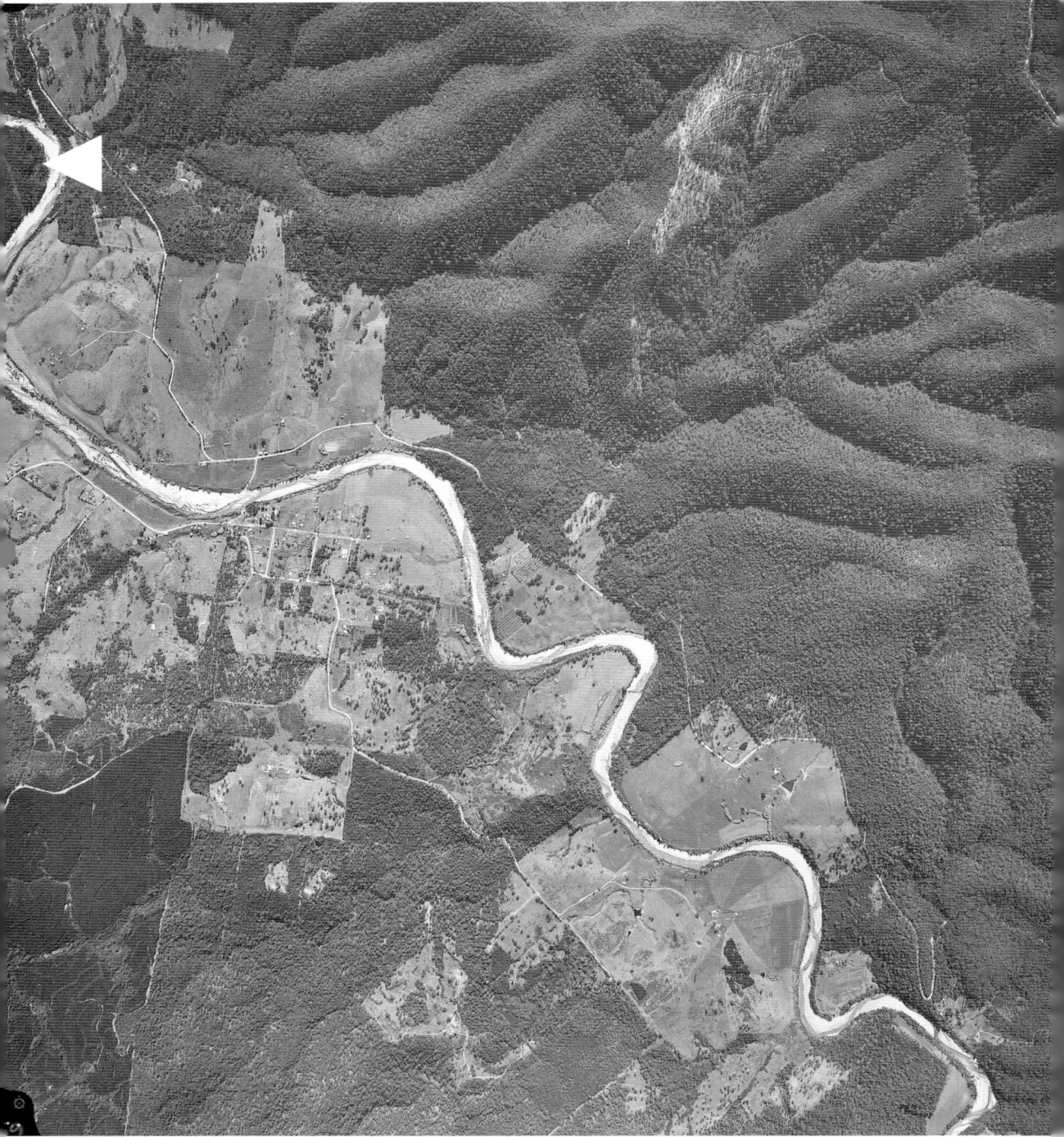

Aerial view of the Towamba River, 1994. Blackfellas' Point is on the top left-hand corner. [By permission of Land and Property Information, Bathurst, NSW]

LOOKING FOR
BLACKFELLAS' POINT II

'WHEN THE SALLY WATTLE BLOOMS'

If it were possible on a clear day to look down from a small aircraft flying from the Monaro plains to Eden on the far south coast, you would see the Towamba River, one of the quickest draining in New South Wales, winding its way through one of the deepest and narrowest river valleys that dissect the Great Dividing Range. From its source at Cathcart on the Monaro plain, 1000 metres above sea level, the river falls sharply as it cuts through forested hills, steep ridges and occasional alluvial flats, before reaching the tidal waters within 8 kilometres of Twofold Bay.[9]

From above, most of the land that stretched out beyond the river below would appear thickly forested — a mixture of vacant and leasehold Crown land, freehold, state forest, national park, nature reserve, and Aboriginal places. At first sight, the land might appear like many other areas of the east coast of Australia — relatively undeveloped, underpopulated and undiscovered, a cruising strip for holidaymakers on parole from Sydney or Melbourne.

On the coast, the hills of the Great Dividing range often seem to force their way out into the sea, the result of geological events long ago, when the opening of the Tasman Sea was accompanied by the formation of the steep slopes that now line the south coast. Like much of the far south coast, sandy beaches, small coves and rocky headlands mark the rugged shoreline of Twofold Bay, the thin strip of land between the Great Dividing Range and the sea broken intermittently by estuaries, lagoons and coastal lakes. Choose any cliché from a tourist brochure and it would probably apply — as you move through the landscape beauty is the first word that comes to mind.

From the Bega Valley, which extends as far as 45 kilometres inland, to Mallacoota on the north coast of Victoria, there is an extraordinary range of forest environments, from dry eucalypt to pockets of rainforest. Silvertop ash, coastal grey box, Maiden's gum, peppermints, stringybarks and woollybutt are among the most common species of trees. Up on the Monaro, towards Bombala and Dalgety, the plateau rises gradually until it reaches the Great Australian Alps, 2300 metres above sea level. Here, the vegetation moves from open grassland to cypress pine and subalpine woodland. In all, the climb from the sea to the Monaro is a mere 50 kilometres — from the azure stillness of Twofold Bay, through dense forest, to windswept grasslands.

The stretch of coast and hinterland between Eden in New South Wales and Orbost in Victoria is one of the most thinly populated and isolated areas of south-eastern Australia. When the early settlers spoke of 'coming down' to Twofold Bay, the words suggested more than a journey south from Sydney — they also implied a descent into a land still waiting to be civilised. Even in the term 'the far south coast', there is a suggestion of an area distant, remote and left behind, pristine yet still somehow beyond the reach of civilisation.

There is always a place nearby that people consider to be too far away, and for every frontier reached there is another in waiting. Some people who have lived all their lives in Bega or Eden have never ventured 20 or 30 kilometres inland. Like many Australians in the major cities, they prefer the coast to the bush. When I first inquired about buying property inland from Eden, several estate agents in town looked at me aghast. 'Why would you want to live *way out there*?' they asked. 'Way out there' was a mere 25 kilometres by road from the coast. But for many people in the area, the distance from the coast to the hinterland is not measured in kilometres; it is imagined, a psychological frontier beyond which civilisation is left behind.

Everywhere today in the small communities throughout Eden–Monaro, there is a feeling of being detached from the imaginary heartland of the state — one that is liberating but also leaves many feeling vulnerable. Perhaps this explains why colonists have imagined Eden–Monaro as a separate region from the first moment they arrived. Mavericks have long dreamed of making Eden–Monaro a separate state. In Victoria today, many refer to north-eastern Gippsland as 'the forgotten corner'. In the early nineteenth century, 'Twofold Bay' referred not only to present-day Eden but to the vast area between Eden and Moruya, 170 kilometres to the north, and the coastal ranges to the west as far as the Monaro plains.[10]

In the land use patterns of both indigenous societies and European settlers, the southern Monaro and the far south coast were intimately linked. Just as Aboriginal people moved to and fro between the coast and the Monaro at particular times of the year, the settlers moved their flocks and herds from one area to another to take advantage of the complementary climates. Before they drew the first lines on their maps, they imagined the area as one region.

In 1903 and 1904, the Senate voted for Eden–Bombala as the preferred site for Australia's capital. Like the first squatters who dreamed of pastoral empires in which the produce from the grazing lands of the Monaro would be shipped from Twofold Bay, many federal parliamentarians were attracted by the idea of a capital with a subalpine climate with ready access to a major port. But lying halfway between Sydney and Melbourne, the area has always suffered from the fear of both cities that another major port might emerge as an economic rival. As a result, Eden–Bombala has often been seen as a region 'in between' more important centres — an area waiting to be developed, ever hoping for its promise to be fulfilled.[11]

Yet despite the region's relative lack of development — tourism, for example, is still in its infancy compared to the north coast of New South Wales — and unlike many other areas of the New South Wales and Victorian coast, the region still gives the overwhelming impression of natural abundance. Looking south along the coast from Green Cape Lighthouse, 40 kilometres south of Eden, the forest meets the sea for as far as the eye can see. From here, it is easy to imagine the land as it must have appeared in the late eighteenth century.

Like many other areas of Australia, most people who live in the region today have little or no idea of the indigenous societies which inhabited the land for

Where the forest meets the sea. Disaster Bay, south-west from Green Cape Lighthouse, NSW, 2001. [Mark McKenna]

thousands of years before their own brief tenure began with the arrival of sealing and whaling gangs in the 1790s, or the squatters in the 1820s and 1830s. Instead, they live like their colonial forebears, residents in a 'new country' with a brief history surrounded by antiquity. Aboriginal people may inhabit the whaling stories of the far south coast, but popular understanding of their traditional culture and their relationship with the land is restricted to a small minority.[12]

In one sense, this ignorance of the indigenous past is understandable. So much has been lost, so much allowed to pass without a thought for its future importance. Knowledge of traditional society is limited to the surviving indigenous oral history, and a small number of anthropologists, linguists, and amateur and professional historians. Relative to the complexity of the indigenous societies that once inhabited the area, even this knowledge is threadbare. Early settlers often died without writing down or passing on their memories of the colonial period. Those that did often did so in a manner that could not be easily verified.[13]

Many of the first attempts to observe and detail traditional indigenous culture in the area took place in the late nineteenth century. By then disease, frontier conflict and the dispossession of land that followed in its wake had already altered or destroyed the richness of the culture that had existed a hundred years earlier. The finer details of population, movement, trade, spiritual beliefs and the kinship systems of indigenous societies were by the 1880s already a subject of conjecture. With each step of the colonist, one history was created as another struggled to survive.

But there is still much we can know about the indigenous societies that inhabited the Eden–Monaro region. This knowledge comes to us from the existing diaries and records of colonial officials, travellers, artists and settlers. The remaining details come from the oral history of local indigenous people that has been recorded by writers, linguists, anthropologists and historians, a process that did not begin in earnest until the 1960s and is by no means comprehensive. Brian Egloff, an anthropologist who was responsible for some of the first attempts to understand indigenous society in the far south coast, has pointed out that the 'dynamics and complexity of Aboriginal territoriality' have been only recently understood.[14] Yet this recent understanding extends beyond territorial knowledge: it includes every facet of indigenous society. More than two centuries after the first contact between Europeans and indigenous people took place, the colonisers are finally looking over their shoulder in an attempt to understand the indigenous culture they dispossessed.

Aboriginal people have lived on the far south coast for over 50 000 years. They arrived during the last ice age when the coastline was much further east than it is now. To try and describe the changes that took place in indigenous societies between this time and 1788 is like gazing into the night sky and seeing a distant galaxy — we can only wonder and speculate.

Based on the evidence we have at our disposal — oral history, coastal middens, tools, artefacts, surviving records — we can be certain that indigenous societies were not static. Like all human societies, they changed and adapted as the climate and environment changed around them. They also had an enormous impact on their environment — their constant burning, for example, gradually restricted rainforest to more inaccessible sites and affected the habitats of flora and fauna.[15]

The society encountered by Europeans in the late eighteenth century on the coast near Twofold Bay had probably existed in much the same form for 5000 years.[16] Archaeological evidence suggests that the indigenous population increased at this time, largely due to climate change. A warmer climate and the formation of new lakes and waterways resulted in a greater supply of food on the coastal fringe.

The population on the coast was almost certainly greater than it was in the hinterland. Yet there is no doubt that both the Bega and Towamba river valleys would have been well populated in 1788, especially within 20 kilometres of the coast.[17] Any attempt to map Aboriginal territories is understandably complex and speculative. But thanks largely to the work of one person, Sue Wesson, over the last eight years, we can now be reasonably sure of the approximate linguistic and territorial boundaries of indigenous societies in the Eden–Monaro region. Unlike earlier descriptions provided by Alfred Howitt in 1904, Norman Tindale in the 1970s, or more recently, the *Encyclopedia of Aboriginal Australia*, Wesson relies heavily on the evidence of George Augustus Robinson, the Protector of Aborigines in Tasmania and a humanitarian, who passed through the region in the winter of 1844.

Within the vast territory that comprised the far south coast, which included the Towamba river valley, there were divisions between those who lived on the coast and hinterland, and a further separation between groups who lived at various points along the coast. Robinson, for example, observed that Aboriginal people on the coast, the Kudingal, who subsisted predominantly on seafood, were distinguished from those who lived in the river valleys, the Pyender, who used tomahawks to climb trees in search of koala and possum.[18]

From Twofold Bay, north to the Bega River, south as far as the Genoa River at the eastern entrance of Mallacoota Inlet, and west as far as the lower reaches of the Towamba and Bega river valleys, lay the territory of the Kudingal people. The word 'Kudingal', as recorded by Robinson, describes the fishing livelihood of the Aboriginal people who lived within these boundaries. Therefore 'Kudingal' is not the name of a tribe or group, of which there were several in the area. (The 'names' of particular groups often varied depending on who was speaking, 'us' or others.) But it does provide a means of describing the Aboriginal societies who lived in the area through an important and shared cultural practice. By 1844, the year in which Robinson passed through Bega and Twofold Bay, many Aboriginal people on the Monaro had already moved to the coast. 'Kudingal' was a word that then described the livelihood of the vast majority of Aboriginal people in south-eastern New South Wales.

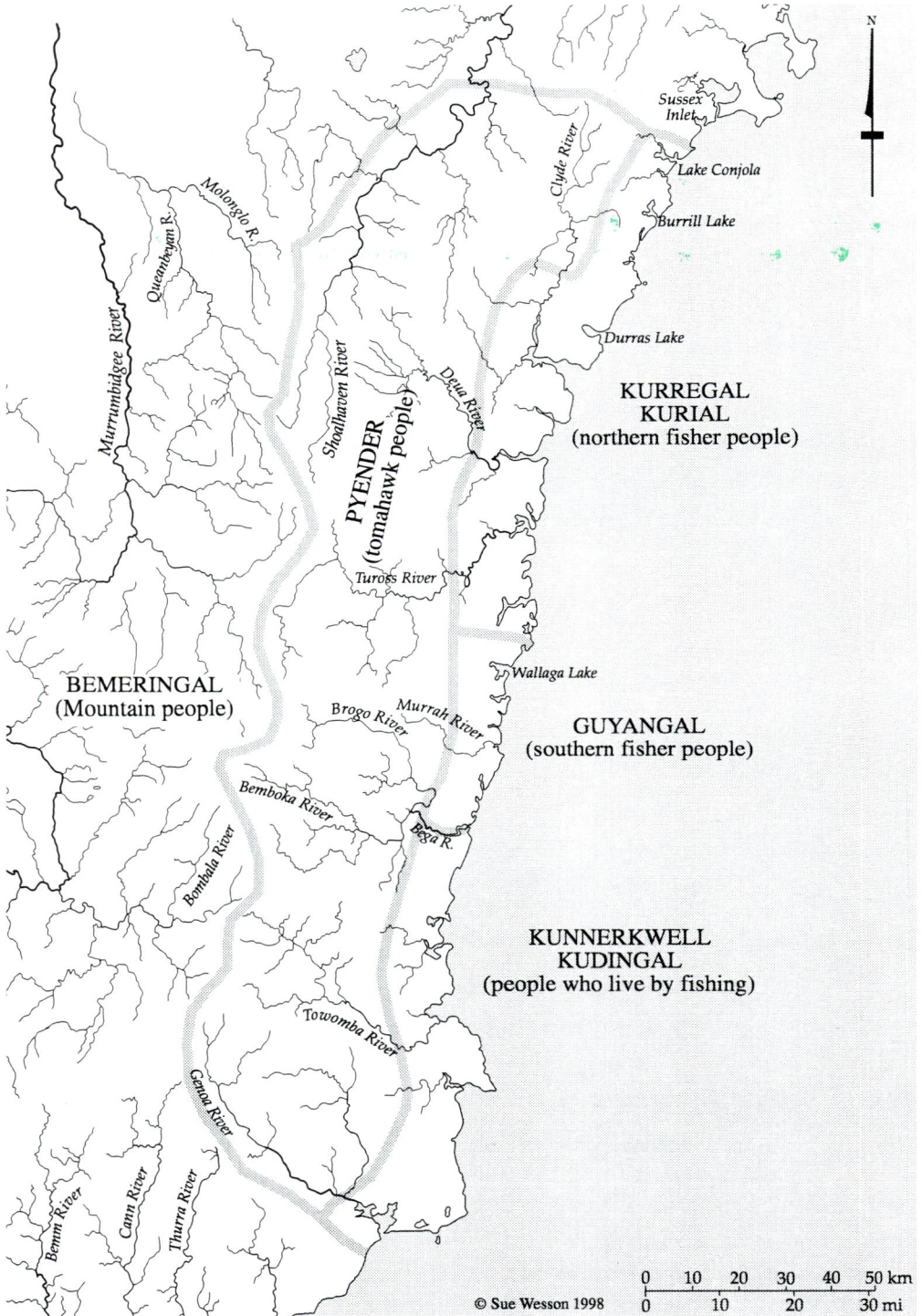

Murrumbidgee River

Queanbeyan R.

Molonglo R.

Shoalhaven River

Clyde River

Sussex Inlet

Lake Conjola

Burrill Lake

Durras Lake

KURREGAL KURIAL
(northern fisher people)

PYENDER
(tomahawk people)

Deua River

Tuross River

Wallaga Lake

BEMERINGAL
(Mountain people)

Brogo River

Murrah River

GUYANGAL
(southern fisher people)

Bemboka River

Bega R.

Bombala River

KUNNERKWELL KUDINGAL
(people who live by fishing)

Towomba River

Genoa River

Bemm River

Cann River

Thurra River

© Sue Wesson 1998

| 0 | 10 | 20 | 30 | 40 | 50 km |
| 0 | | 10 | 20 | | 30 mi |

South Coast Functional Names. Sue Wesson, 1998. [By permission of Sue Wesson]

About the movement and alliances of Aboriginal people in the Eden region we know considerably more. In the oral history of local Aboriginal people, there are many references to seasonal changes in location and the extent of intermarriage and relations with neighbouring tribes north at Bega, south in Gippsland, or on the Monaro plains. The material and sensory changes that accompanied the shift from coast to grassland plain is embedded deep in cultural memory.[19]

In the summer months, the Kudingal would travel to the Monaro plains to trade weapons, tools, baskets and possum skins, and feast on the Bogong moth — the plump oily creatures which today sometimes descend on suburban backyards in Sydney when they are blown off course by strong winds. There they would join people from northern Victoria and the Monaro, as early as late October, where they would smoke the moths out of the rents in the rocks and catch them in nets made of fibre from the Kurrajong tree and kangaroo skin, before roasting the bodies on hot ashes, sifting the dust off them, and finally rolling them in their hands. These sweet morsels of flesh with a distinctly nutty taste would then be eaten immediately or pounded in a wooden vessel 'into masses or cakes resembling lumps of fat'. For months on end, they would be preserved, and either consumed or traded as delicacies.

Oswald Brierly's watercolour of an Aboriginal canoe at Twofold Bay, 1843. 'Sketches Made in Australia', 1842–44. [PXD81f.8, Mitchell Library, State Library of New South Wales]

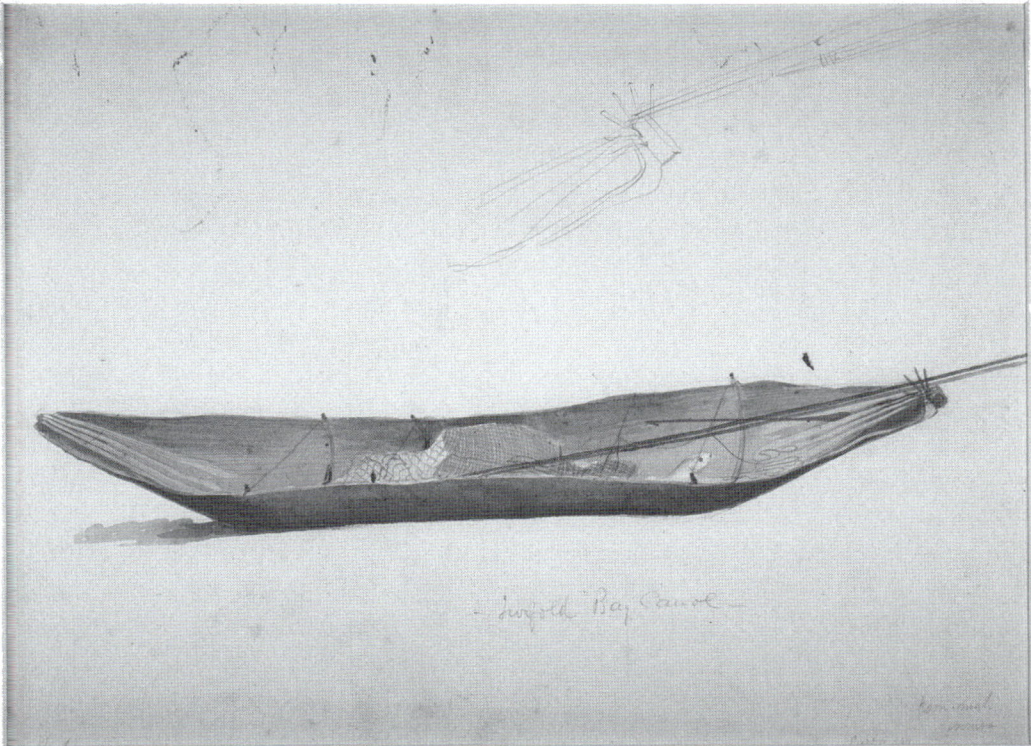

The feast sometimes involved the killing of the black crows that had been feeding on the moths. As the crows entered the hollows of the rocks to feed, they were quickly clubbed to death, affording another nutritious meal. Some Aboriginal people apparently amused themselves by distinguishing between the 'fatfella' crows (Arabul) who managed to eat their fill, and the 'poorfella' crows (Worgan) who merely existed on leftovers.[20]

In the winter months the Monaro people from Bombala, Delegate and nearby areas would journey to Twofold Bay, travelling along the Towamba river valley, where they would meet with the Kudingal and perform corroborees, sometimes on the river flats, before journeying to the coast. Once there they would trade for shellfish and pick the reeds used in the weaving of their baskets in the area now occupied by the Bega racecourse.[21] Freshwater mussels at the mouth of the Towamba River would have been one of many enticements.[22]

The oral tradition of Aboriginal people in the Monaro tells how they travelled to the coast for the whaling season, the whales and fish herded into the bay by the killer whales being harvested by Aboriginal people long before the Europeans arrived with their harpoons and ships.[23] Europeans often reported seeing Aboriginal people feeding on the carcasses of beached whales along the south coast.[24] At Twofold Bay, a traditional calving site for several species of whales, the Kudingal believed their departed souls would live on in the body of the killer whale. So strong was their relationship with the killers that when spearing the fish in the bay they would call to them or smack the water to get their attention, and the killers would respond. If the evidence of the anthropologist RH Matthews is to be believed, the Kudingal heralded the arrival of killer whales in the bay with a degree of ceremony.

> When the natives observe a whale … near the coast, pursued by [the] killers … one of the old men light[s] fires at some little distance along the shore to attract the attention of the killers. He then walks along from one fire to another pretending to be lame … leaning on a stick in each hand. This is to excite the compassion of the killers and induce them to chase the whale towards that part of the shore in order to give the poor old man some food. He occasionally calls out … 'Heigh Ho … that fish upon the shore throw ye to me.' If the whale becomes helpless from the attack of the killers, and is washed up on the shore, some other men who have been hidden … make their appearance and attack the animal with their weapons. A message is sent to all their friends and fellow tribesmen in the neighbourhood inviting them to attend and participate in the feast … [They then cut through the blubber and eat the flesh, and after the intestines are removed] any persons suffering from rheumatism or similar pains go and sit [in the body of the whale] and anoint themselves with the fat.[25]

The image used by Aboriginal people to signal the beginning and end of the whaling season is redolent with the poetry of their relationship with the environment — when the sally wattle blooms whaling begins, when the big fly comes whaling ends.[26] By the early nineteenth century, this brief period from winter to early spring would see the waters of Twofold Bay turn red with the blood of the Southern Right Whale, their bloated and stinking carcasses hanging on blubber hooks around the shores of the bay.

The movement of the Kudingal was naturally not confined to the journey from the coast to the Monaro. They also had 'traditional alliances' to the north at Bega and to the south in present-day Victoria, alliances which no doubt shifted between animosity and affiliation. Message men would move with impunity between territorial boundaries, while tribal elders would meet at particular times on common ground, arranging marriages and festivities or settling disputes.[27] Although it is difficult to be certain, the available evidence indicates that the Kudingal were on largely friendly terms with the Dyirringan people at Bega and the Maap people to the south beyond Mallacoota. If they feared any enemy it was probably the people further north from Canberra and Yass and to the west at Omeo. But many details of the Kudingal's traditional enmities and the intricacies of their alliances and social interactions will remain lost.[28]

While we do know something of the complex social institutions and territorial boundaries that emerged in the area over the previous 5000 years, we will probably never know more than the thread that now connects us to the Aboriginal past. Today, in the area previously inhabited by the Kudingal, there is no surviving speaker of Kudingal languages. Given that the Kudingal spoke at least three languages, and probably understood several others, this is a tragic loss. Thawa, the language spoken south of the Bega River, at Twofold Bay, and as far south as the Mallacoota Inlet, is today represented by a vocabulary of less than 200 words.

Changes in the movement patterns of Aboriginal people wrought by colonisation altered the patterns of language use. At Twofold Bay, because of the large influx of Aboriginal people from surrounding areas during the whaling season, the Thawa language was already under threat in the mid-nineteenth century and was probably not in use after 1880. Robinson, when he passed through in 1844, recorded three separate vocabularies, two from Twofold Bay and one from Cape Howe, and even drawing on these imperfect phonetic transcriptions is like trying to construct a symphony from a score barely begun. With the disappearance of the language goes a whole world of seeing — and so much of the cultural inheritance. But this is the story of Aboriginal Australia after 1788, resisting, cooperating, adapting, and yet managing nonetheless to survive in the face of enormous loss.[29]

'DISCOVERING ONE ANOTHER'?

Season upon season of smoke followed. Billows rose from
that cup of land around the bay and drifted inland, carrying
like incense. We wandered, seeing the smoke from afar as
a mushroom on the horizon; or from the edge of the scarp
smelling it mingled with seasalt on the wind; or as we
returned stepping through patches of it caught among
vines and star-flower bushes.

RODNEY HALL
The Second Bridegroom, 1991

The journals of the first Europeans to sail along the Australian coast frequently noted the sight of smoke from Aboriginal campfires. Smoke was usually the first sign of human habitation, an indication that someone else occupied the land and irrefutable evidence that Europeans were not the first to 'discover' the Great South Land.

When British naval officers and their crew stepped ashore from their longboats in the late eighteenth century, they smelt the smoke of the Aboriginal fires, often their first physical sensation of an Aboriginal presence. At this point, whatever had been was about to be shattered; whatever would be, would be on the invader's terms — the smoke of some was more civilised than the smoke of others.

On 10 October 1798, the English naval surgeon, George Bass, and Matthew Flinders, the man who first charted the Australian coast, visited Twofold Bay as they sailed south along the coast from Sydney en route to Tasmania.

The journey of the two friends Bass and Flinders, both in their early twenties, can only be described as inspirational. In the twelve weeks allotted to them by Governor Hunter, sailing in the sloop *Norfolk* with a crew of eight, they managed to establish the existence of Bass Strait, chart the south-eastern coastline of the mainland and Tasmania, and return with valuable botanical specimens and a raft of information on the natural history of the area. Like many educated men who sailed in the front line of the British Empire, they were fired by scientific endeavour and the joy of discovery — the hunger for knowledge and the sensation of the new.

On the afternoon of 9 October 1798, bad weather forced Bass and Flinders to bear up for Twofold Bay. Like many vessels that would later seek shelter in the bay from storms off the coast, the *Norfolk* was moored in Weecon (Snug Cove) the next morning. Once there, they were keen not to waste the opportunity. As Flinders said in his journal, they had to 'make some profit of this foul wind'. After mooring, they immediately they set about the tasks of the explorer — hunting and gathering. While Bass walked off to explore the country nearby, Flinders collected his instruments and walked over a small headland, before descending to Aslings

Aslings beach, Eden, from the vantage point Matthew Flinders would have first seen it in 1798. [Mark McKenna]

beach. As he walked along a well-beaten track, he was seen by a small group of Aboriginal women and their children. When they saw Flinders they screamed in terror and ran. Kudingal women had probably already encountered sealers at Twofold Bay.

Shortly after the women and children disappeared into the bush, Flinders was followed by a middle-aged Aboriginal man carrying a waddie. The man approached Flinders with 'careless confidence'. Flinders offered him a biscuit, and in return he offered Flinders 'a piece of grisly fat, probably of whale'. An exchange of gifts had now taken place.

As the man began to eat the biscuit, Flinders placed the piece of whale fat in his mouth. He found the taste so sickening he watched immediately for an opportunity to spit it out when the man wasn't looking. At the moment Flinders turned his head to spit the meat to the ground, he caught sight of the man doing the same with his biscuit.

The encounter on Aslings beach is of two radically different cultures colliding, determined initially not to give offence. Matthew Flinders and the Aboriginal man who trailed him were curious yet wary, both shaking their head in disbelief at the habits of the other, culinary or otherwise. Just as Flinders was ignorant of the Kudingal culture and territory he had entered, the Kudingal man was ignorant of Flinders' culture and intentions. For both men, there was much to learn.

One of Oswald Brierly's first sketches of an Aboriginal man at Twofold Bay, 1843. Brierly Journal, 1842–43. [A535, Mitchell Library, State Library of New South Wales]

Afterwards, the man walked on with Flinders to Aslings beach. As Flinders commenced his trigonometrical observations he noticed that the man reacted 'with indifference if not contempt' and decided quickly to leave, 'apparently satisfied that, from people who could thus occupy themselves seriously, there was nothing to be apprehended'.

Flinders was sensitive to the encounter of discovery. He understood the mixture of 'good will', 'curiosity' and 'apprehension' that existed on both sides. But Flinders and Bass were passing through. They had not come to settle the land with sheep, cows and guns or to take Aboriginal women by force, although their maps and measurements were undoubtedly preparing the way for all of these.[30]

Over the next 200 years, colonists would encounter every possible reaction from the Aboriginal people of Twofold Bay: hostile aggression, shock, help, curiosity, courtesy and laughter — discovery was an unpredictable experience.

The initial phase of contact was one of watching and confronting difference — discovering one another. On some occasions this resulted in violent conflict and death, at other times it involved Aboriginal people offering assistance to the white intruders. But it also meant curiosity and mirth. If the Europeans found many Aboriginal habits disgusting, Aboriginal people often found the habits of Europeans hilarious.

When the *Sydney Cove* was wrecked on the shores of Cape Howe after a violent storm in March 1797, seventeen survivors undertook a desperate trek, attempting to walk along the coast from northern Victoria to Sydney. Only three managed to reach their ultimate destination, the remainder perishing of thirst and hunger, or killed by Aboriginal men. George Bass was sent by Governor Hunter to search for survivors, Matthew Flinders to retrieve the *Sydney Cove*'s cargo.

A description of the walk to Sydney by one of the survivors, William Clarke, described 'the natives of Twofold Bay' who assisted the party in crossing the waters of the Towamba River. Clarke recalled his initial disgust:

> Their hair is long and straight …it serves them in lieu of a towel to wipe their hands as often as they are daubed with blubber or shark oil, which is their principal article of food. This frequent application of grease to their heads and bodies renders their approach exceedingly offensive … upon the whole they present the most hideous and disgusting figures.

He then speaks of their curiosity: 'they viewed us most attentively. They opened our clothes, examined our feet, hands [and] nails, frequently expressing their surprise by laughing and loud shouting'. Later when they were seen by a group of Aboriginal women, Clarke remembered hearing their 'cries and laughing' through the bush. The women found the white men strangely comical and seemed 'astonished' at their appearance.[31]

In the first instance, discovery involved the sighting of a ship by Aboriginal people — either seen or reported. For those on the ships it may have been the sight of smoke curling above the forest canopy, or of Aboriginal people standing on the beaches or headlands of the coast. Around Twofold Bay, it is possible that stories of passing ships existed in local communities long before Friday, 20 April 1770 when James Cook's *Endeavour* sailed past the bay. The previous day Cook had seen the Australian coastline for the first time at Point Hicks, only 100 kilometres to the south. The Kudingal people of Twofold Bay were probably among the first Aboriginal people to see the *Endeavour*. They may also have seen or heard of Portuguese ships passing in the sixteenth century, or of Abel Tasman's journeys of exploration for the Dutch East India company in the early 1640s, and they almost certainly knew of the French ships passing in the early 1800s.[32]

Long before Europeans stepped ashore at Twofold Bay in the late eighteenth century, in the caves on the coast south of the bay, and on the trees and rocky headlands along the shore, there were almost certainly drawings of European ships — harbingers of an unimaginable future.

When the French explorer Dumont d'Urville sailed into Twofold Bay in November 1826, he looked longingly from his 'floating prison' at the land 'covered with beautiful trees and carpeted with green grass'. The following day he stopped further north at Jervis Bay and saw 'the drawings of cutters and launches' that Aboriginal people had made on the sandstone rocks. That night he accepted the offers of fish from the local 'Aborigines', and some of them slept on board. Later, when one of his officers picked up a wooden ruler he had left behind on the beach, he found it 'decorated with similar drawings' of European ships.[33]

In Kudingal oral history, there are stories of the first appearance of ships in Twofold Bay: 'how the blackfellows retreated to the hills — how a few first ventured out — and finally how they began to carry bark for the white fellow'. These stories are echoed up and down the coast. Aboriginal communities remember seeing the first 'white man ship', 'a monster bird of some unearthly kind'. At Twofold Bay they first believed Europeans to be the spirits of their departed ancestors who had 'jumped up again all white'.[34] This impression would not last for long.

For both Aboriginal people and their invaders, discovery was an ongoing experience — the process of confrontation, learning, and finding a way to live together continues on the south coast today. But from the moment Matthew Flinders and his Aboriginal companion turned away from one another in polite distaste in 1798, Aboriginal culture was forced to change and adapt far more than the culture of the invaders. This was not simply because the Europeans were bent on conquest. It was also because of the way Europeans saw the land and its Aboriginal people when they arrived. They came from a distant and foreign world equipped with a limited range of strategies for dealing with cultural and environmental difference. They could only discover what they were able to see.

PART ONE

dispossession

1

'WITHOUT TREATY, BARGAIN OR APOLOGY'

We hold [the land] neither by inheritance, by purchase, nor by
conquest, but by a sort of gradual eviction. As our flocks and
herds and population increase ... the natural owners of the soil
are thrust back without treaty, bargain or apology ... depastur-
ing licenses are procured from government, stations are built,
the natives and the game on which they feed are driven back
... the graves of their fathers ... trodden underfoot.

GODFREY CHARLES MUNDY
1852[1]

In nineteenth-century Australia, observers of colonial society — historians, newspaper editors, letter writers, humanitarians, governors, politicians, bureaucrats, and
Aboriginal Australians — all voiced their concern about the ethics of colonisation.[2]
While these voices were never significant in number until the late twentieth century, they represented an undercurrent of resistance to the Australian story. From the
beginning of the colonial project, there was considerable disquiet regarding the possession of Aboriginal land. Given the wealth of evidence concerning the frontier
encounter between Europeans and Aboriginal people, it is clear that the settlers did
not find themselves 'in quiet possession of [Aboriginal] country'.[3] As Henry
Reynolds and other historians have shown, the land was neither quietly possessed nor
quietly ceded; rather it was seized.

In the early nineteenth century, colonial politicians had tabled in Parliament the
most fundamental complaint of Aboriginal people: they had 'no country to call their
own'.[4] When the Austrian diplomat Baron Charles von Hugel travelled to Australia
in 1834, visiting Tasmania and New South Wales, including Twofold Bay and the far
south coast, he saw the 'annexation of New Holland for the British Crown' as resting on a 'scandalous ... law' which assumed 'that the whole of the earth is the inher-
ited birthright of Europe'. The fate of the 'Aborigines' was, he said, 'England's ...
brand of shame that nothing will ever efface'.[5] Reflecting on the colonists' desire to
convert the indigenes to Christianity, von Hugel made a telling observation:

What effect can the Christian religion possibly have on these peoples? The first principle is: 'Thou shalt love thy neighbour as thyself', but they see the whites gorging themselves and in possession of immense flocks and herds, while they themselves are frequently on the verge of starvation. They must have the idea ... that this religion is for the white people and not for them, for if Christ had come into the world for them, they must surely have heard of it earlier.[6]

In the light of von Hugel's comments, the pathos of the Aboriginal people's contact with the civilising mission of the God-fearing colonisers becomes all the more apparent. When George Augustus Robinson instructed his group of 'remaining' Tasmanian Aborigines on Flinders Island in 1837, he had them sit Sunday school examinations. A selection of the questions and answers offers an insight into the tragedy wrought by colonisation.

Who made you? — God
Who made the white man ? — God
Who made your country? — God
What did Jesus Christ do for us? — He died on the Cross
Which is the best book? — The Bible
Where will the wicked be sent to when they die? — To hell
Whose place is hell? — The devil's place
What sort of place is it? — Plenty of fire and sickness
Do you wish to live as white people live? — Yes
Is the bush a good place to live? — No Sir
Do you like to live on Flinders Island like white people? — Yes Sir.[7]

The God who made their country told them the bush was a bad place to live. The only answer for the Aboriginal person was to live like the white man or dutifully confirm his expectations and die quietly. There might be solace in heaven.

For colonists who read the journals of those who had travelled widely throughout the frontier, and the many reports of atrocities and violence in colonial newspapers, there was ample opportunity to reflect on the process of invasion and settlement.

John Dunmore Lang, founder of the Presbyterian Church in Australia, republican, and one of Australia's most widely travelled politicians in the colonial period, was frank when he reflected in 1847 on the process of land acquisition in the colonies. The squatter, said Lang, 'takes possession of the native country ... without permission and without compensation, and calling it his run, orders the native off, because ... his cattle ... do not like black men'. Then come 'disease', 'vice' and 'a war of extermination', as the blacks fall 'like ... leaves in autumn' before the 'dogs and guns of the squatters and their stockmen'. With great difficulty, Lang brought himself to acknowledge the 'too extensively practised' poisoning of flour or porridge or bread, a 'horrible practice' which he saw as 'disgraceful to the British name'.[8]

1887

Four decades later, the popular historian of bushranging in Australia, Charles White, wrote his *Story of the Blacks,* which was serialised in the metropolitan and regional press. In plain and detached prose, White's history told the brutal tale for all to see. The fourth chapter of his story was entitled 'The Racial War Begins', the last, 'Decimation and Extinction'.[9] Here, in a history published and read widely, was prose that acknowledged the reality of Aboriginal dispossession.

> The story of European settlement is the story of Aboriginal decay, decimation and death … The meeting of the Aborigines and the white pioneers … invariably led to war … unequal war … and the fighting was at times fierce and extended over a lengthy period.
>
> Where the natives succeeded in killing one white man, the white man killed scores of natives … the organised slaughter of the blacks in disturbed districts [was] not infrequent … No sadder story was ever written … the Aborigines have been practically civilised off the face of the earth which was their inheritance, and those who occupy the land once theirs … like to forget that ever a black man walked upon the soil.[10]

White's description of European settlement did not attempt to place a 'veil' over frontier violence. Historian Ann Curthoys has written of the manner in which nineteenth-century histories frequently acknowledged the reality of frontier war — in the words of John Rusden in 1883, 'a sin crying aloud to the covering heavens … the stars the silent witness'. But, like other historians who have chronicled the 'Great Australian Silence', Curthoys shows that these truths went largely unmentioned between the 1920s and the early 1970s.[11] It was not until the last three decades of the twentieth century, with the emergence of a new school of critical history which exposed the violence on the Australian frontier, together with an increasingly politicised Aboriginal resistance, that Australians were confronted with the story of Aboriginal 'decay, decimation and death'.

Frontier violence could be acknowledged without political tumult in nineteenth-century Australia because it was widely believed that Aboriginal people were inferior to the settlers and destined for extinction, a view that prevailed until the 1940s. Since the demise of the White Australia policy in the 1960s, Australians have claimed to believe in racial equality. Their historical identity, especially in the twentieth century, has been built on images of their own reasonableness and benevolence, such as the fair go and the peaceful progress of stable democracy. Confronting the fact that the nation was founded on the violent theft of

Aboriginal land, and that Australian governments oversaw the forced removal of Aboriginal children from their families as recently as the 1960s, is for many Australians a threat to their own identity and right to belong. For many Australian conservatives, it poses a more serious threat, undermining the moral legitimacy of the nation-state.

From the time of the Bicentenary in 1988, until the centenary of federation in 2001, the acknowledgment of Aboriginal dispossession has been labelled by Australian conservatives and the far Right as the work of a national 'guilt industry', 'black armband' historians, or those who would besmirch the national honour. Most recently, conservatives have focused their attention on two issues: the Human Rights and Equal Opportunity Commission's 1997 report into the Stolen Generations, *Bringing Them Home*, and the accuracy of estimates concerning the number of Aboriginal people killed in violent conflict on the Australian frontier. Through much of the conservative offensive there is a consistent argument. I would summarise it as follows.

Although there are occasional 'blemishes' in Australia's history, particularly in its treatment of Aboriginal people, by and large the Australian story is a story of heroic achievement in the face of extraordinary odds. A balanced perspective is the key to understanding our history. As Geoffrey Blainey argued in 1993, the pendulum has swung too far towards the 'black armband' view of history. But if we must deal with the 'blemishes', it is necessary to look at the evidence. After all, history is what can be verified from documentary evidence — writing history is like pushing the beads of an abacus. Therefore, if Henry Reynolds' figure of 20 000 Aboriginal war dead on the frontier can be shown to be doubtful, the history of the violent dispossession of Aboriginal land can be called into question. Relations between settlers and Aboriginal people were predominantly peaceful. If only twenty-five Aboriginal people died in a punitive expedition instead of 145, this does not constitute a 'massacre'. If, as the Commonwealth Government claimed in its submission to a Senate Inquiry in April 2000, only 10 per cent of Aboriginal children were removed from their parents between 1910 and 1970, then there can be no 'stolen generations'. If the courts rejected a claim for compensation by Aboriginal Australians claiming to have suffered psychological and physical abuse after being separated from their families and placed in institutions, as happened in the Gunner-Cubillo decision in August 2000, this proves that the history of the 'stolen generations' is a myth. The intention of government policy towards Aboriginal people was mostly one of concern and compassion. What's more, there is no need for the Commonwealth Government to apologise to Aboriginal people, first, because there was no policy of 'genocide', as stated in *Bringing Them Home*, and second, because the present generation cannot be held responsible for the actions of previous generations.[12]

Regardless of whether these arguments have merit, their apparent focus, the all-encompassing sweep of words such as 'massacre', 'stolen', 'generations' and 'genocide' becomes much wider in a political context. What ostensibly appears to be an argument about numbers and semantics is disseminated in the mass media with an underlying yet slowly cumulative message: 'The history of Australia is largely benign. While there may have been a few "blemishes", talk of frontier war and the "stolen generations" is absurd'.

Under the guise of arguments over historical method, much of the conservative offensive is an attempt to undermine the effectiveness of Aboriginal legal and political resistance and stave off legal claims for compensation. Henry Reynolds is one of the most frequently quoted historical authorities for Aboriginal leaders, and the moral basis for their political struggle is built on the recognition of historical injustice. Therefore, if conservatives succeed in undermining Reynolds' credibility, or that of any historian who has written on frontier war, they potentially weaken the legitimacy of Aboriginal leaders' political demands.[13]

Unfortunately, the ongoing legal and political controversy over terms such 'as 'genocide' and 'stolen generations' serves to create a new myth concerning Australian history: namely that historical understanding is achieved by testing the past against the language of contemporary politics. By constantly pushing our interpretation of the past through the narrow prism of words such as 'genocide' or 'the stolen generations', we seem to be asking, does history fit? Perhaps this is because we are less intent on historical understanding, and more interested in legitimising or discrediting a particular political viewpoint. There is a constant tension in using terms such as 'genocide'. On the one hand they offer a means of looking at history anew; on the other they sometimes suggest closure, as if there is nothing more to explore in our past, as if all the questions have been answered.

When the history of the colonial frontier has become so politicised, as it clearly has in Australia since the 1980s, it is helpful to look at one region about which little has been written. In south-eastern New South Wales, the history of the colonial frontier demonstrates that three decades after the first wave of critical histories of the Australian frontier emerged, there are areas in Australia where the culture of silence and forgetting has not been broken. In this sense, the questions asked by historians in the 1970s still need to be asked today. What happened to Aboriginal people when the Europeans arrived? What was the nature of relations between the settlers and Aboriginal people? How did Aboriginal people react to the invasion of their soil? How did dispossession occur?

Answering these questions in south-eastern New South Wales reveals that there is a fundamental truth concerning the colonial project which is still denied. Equally, it reveals how a much deeper understanding of the frontier can be gained by looking not only at what can be known through documentary evidence but also at the broader cultural memory of the frontier.

'QUIETLY, THE
ABORIGINES
SUBMITTED'

Time the destroyer is time the preserver,
Like the river with its cargo of dead negroes,
cows and chicken coops

TS ELIOT,
The Four Quartets

What is frail falls away; stories that take root become like
things, misshapen things with an illogical core, which pass
through many hands without wearing out or falling to pieces,
remaining in essence the same, adjusting here and there at the
edges, as families or forests produce ever changing appearances
of themselves; the geology of fable.

MURRAY BAIL,
Eucalyptus 1998[14]

Sealing was one of the first large-scale industries in the Australian colonies,
much of the export going to China. The initial activity occurred on the far
south coast of New South Wales and Bass Strait. So intense was the harvesting that
seals had already become scarce by 1802. The industry was competitive. French,
American and British ships ploughed the South Pacific in search of profit and
adventure. Crews were made up of convict bolters, American, French and British
seamen, and Maori, Aboriginal and Tahitian men.[15]

At first, the Aboriginal people of Twofold Bay did not so much encounter
another civilisation as a ragbag of European and American entrepreneurs in competition with one another, their ships manned in part by indigenous people from
other areas of the South Pacific whom they had managed to cajole into coming
aboard. In some ways, the sealing industry represented the lawless vanguard of
European imperialism. Gangs of men carrying guns, knives and clubs, often
accompanied by packs of dogs, would come ashore to hunt, sometimes for weeks
on end. Violent confrontation with Aboriginal people was common. The rape and
abduction of Aboriginal women by men of all ethnic backgrounds became a
renowned feature of the industry. Along the coast, from Twofold Bay to Tasmania,

sealing gangs were responsible for the spread of venereal disease among Aboriginal people, and their theft of Aboriginal women severely affected traditional lifestyle. Stories of the cruelty of sealers pervaded the memories of Kudingal people and exist today in the local and regional history of Eden–Monaro.[16]

While the impact of sealing on Tasmanian Aboriginal communities is well documented, the effects of sealing at Twofold Bay are less well known but equally troubling, not least because contact with sealers represented the Kudingal's first impression of their intruders. For a period of twenty-five years, from 1803 to 1828, the Sydney papers carried intermittent reports of clashes between visiting ships and 'Aborigines' at Twofold Bay.[17]

In July 1803, His Majesty's armed tender *Lady Nelson* sheltered in Twofold Bay and indulged in gunnery practice, firing cannon balls into the cliff faces around the bay. Some of the cannon balls were later found and reside now in the Eden

Char-ree-ueroo at Twofold Bay, watercolour by Oswald Brierly. 'Sketches Made in Australia', 1843. [PXD81f.6, Mitchell Library, State Library of New South Wales]

museum — reminders of an event that must have struck terror into the hearts of Kudingal people.[18]

By that year, the Kudingal had already suffered severe dislocation at the hands of sealing gangs, and over the next two decades they displayed an understandably hostile reaction to visiting ships. Within four years of the First Fleet arriving at Sydney Cove, the Kudingal's perception of the men who sailed on the monster birds shifted greatly. At first they imagined the invader as part of their own kinship system, their own spirits returned. Yet within a few years of their first contact with the sealers, they were in open warfare with the crew of any vessel that stopped at Twofold Bay. Until the late 1820s, they fought to defend their land and people from invasion. Ships that were forced to take shelter in the bay during the first decades of the nineteenth century received a hostile reception. Kudingal men surrounded and attacked ships or crew who came ashore. Their spears were answered with musket fire, sometimes resulting in the death of Aboriginal men.

In April 1806, a sealing vessel bearing the name of the Roman goddess of love moored in Twofold Bay. Sealers came ashore and made camp, only to find themselves under the constant threat of attack. On one occasion Kudingal men advanced 'en masse' throwing spears. The sealers responded with musket fire, killing nine. To intimidate the Kudingal, they hung the bodies of the nine Aboriginal dead from the branches of trees nearby, only to find at first light that they had been taken down. The crew of the *Venus* had left their mark.[19]

One month later, Kudingal men surrounded the crew of the sloop *George*, another vessel 'laden with seal skins'. After the sealers had fired twenty-seven rounds of ammunition into the bush, killing several men, the Kudingal set the grass on fire, threw spears, and 'rushed like a torrent' on their assailants. The crew only narrowly escaped death, clambering into their boat just in time to see all they had left behind 'destroyed'.[20] This state of warfare continued for many years.

When Governor King wrote to the Colonial Secretary in March 1806, he acknowledged that the Kudingal had 'suffered some wrong from the worthless characters who are passing … the different places on the coast'.[21] But King's understatement made no reference to the extent of the Kudingal's resistance. Over the next twenty years, at first sight of a ship, they would often run along the headlands of the bay shouting and making violent gestures, spear anyone who dared come ashore, slaughter the sheep and cattle left behind, roll rocks over the edges of cliffs in an attempt to kill intruders, raid the cargo of ships at every opportunity, and refuse to allow any foreign invader entry to their territory.[22]

In October 1815, Aboriginal men and sealers clashed at Green Cape, to the south of Twofold Bay. After being 'invited' ashore, the sealers were approached by three or four hundred 'Aborigines'. According to the report in the *Sydney Gazette*, the sealers were attacked and immediately decided to 'oppose force to force'. To assert their authority, they fired at random into the crowd of Aboriginal men, killing several and wounding many others, before retreating under a 'hail of spears'.[23]

Six years later, on an early June morning in 1821, a fearful group of passengers and crew from the *Mary* lay adrift in a longboat offshore, waiting in vain for a wind that would push them back to the safety of their ship. On the beach at Twofold Bay, Kudingal men stood wearing the clothes they had stolen during their raid on the ship the night before. Dressed in the clothes of their enemies, they held up their spears and waddies in defiance — proud possessors of their land.[24] Within ten years, many of these men, together with their wives and children, would be 'carrying bark' for the Imlays, sons of a Scottish surgeon and the first squatters to 'take up' land at Twofold Bay in 1832.

Until the late 1820s and early 1830s, the traditional life of Aboriginal people living in the hinterland of the far south coast, particularly in the Bega and Towamba valleys, had been subject to far less disruption than the Kudingal at Twofold Bay. Although all Aboriginal people had been affected by the spread of disease, those on the coast had long borne the brunt of initial contact with sealers and whalers. As a result, the Aboriginal population had been in steady decline, from several hundred in the early nineteenth century to a mere seventy or eighty in the 1830s. By 1832, despite three decades of resistance, they were clearly unable or unwilling to carry on the fight, at least at Twofold Bay.

The traditional life of the remaining Kudingal was altered further in the 1830s. Their movement patterns and liaisons, and those of their neighbours to the north, south and west, were changed by whaling and pastoral activities. They had long suffered deaths from smallpox, venereal disease and influenza. By 1832, there is no doubt that diseases had severely depleted the population, as had the sealers' theft of Aboriginal women and the shooting of Aboriginal men. When the first squatters were beginning to infiltrate the hinterland in the 1830s, on the coast the Kudingal had already 'come in'. They had learnt to speak English, carried guns, and assisted in the harvesting of whales and seals. As increasing numbers of Aboriginal people were displaced from their traditional lands over the next twenty years, John Lambie, Commissioner for Crown Lands, would do little more than complain that their constant migration made it difficult for him to obtain an accurate census.[25]

The frontier on the far south coast and the Monaro plains was constantly shifting. Between 1788 and the 1850s there was rarely a consistent or uniform pattern of contact throughout the region. The traditional life of Aboriginal people probably survived for longer in the hinterland than on the coast or the plains, but even by the time the Imlays had arrived at Twofold Bay in 1832, traditional life had already been undermined. [26]

Whaling attracted hundreds of Aboriginal people from up and down the coast and the Monaro to Twofold Bay. Some came for the first time, some stayed when they would not have done previously, some came for different reasons, but nearly all were relating to one another in ways that differed from traditional arrangements. Their diet changed, they lived more often in a multi-lingual environment, their sexual relations became more unpredictable, they wore European clothes, borrowed from the Europeans hunting and fishing techniques, and their laws and customs struggled to survive under the weight of the coloniser's institutions and values. As distinct linguistic and cultural groups, the Aboriginal people of Eden–Monaro were under severe threat well before the early 1830s. Yet well into the 1840s and 1850s, aspects of their traditional life continued — now described in a melancholy tone by British settlers in their diaries and journals, as if recording the last vestiges of Aboriginal culture was a necessary prelude to the triumph of British civilisation in the Australian colonies.

In *Discovering Monaro*, the renowned Australian historian WK Hancock attempted to explain the fate of the Aboriginal people of the Monaro:

> In Monaro, no evidence at all of physical conflict can be found, either in the diaries and letters of pioneers, or in official records. There, as everywhere else, the white men took the land, and some white men took the women; but there, as almost nowhere else, resistance and retaliation did not ensue. Quietly, the Aborigines submitted ... We could read tens of thousands of pages of newspaper print without tracking down a dozen references to the last agonies of the black people.[27]

Several years later, Geoffrey Blainey repeated Hancock's assertion that 'the wide Monaro district of New South Wales seems to have been occupied peacefully'. Hancock and Blainey were either turning away from the truth or unwilling to spend the time reading the primary sources. On the Monaro, and on the far south coast, the evidence suggests that in the first three decades of contact with squatters and their labour force Aboriginal people fought tenaciously against the invasion of their land. The diaries, letters and newspaper records indicate a state of sporadic warfare.

In their descriptions of the frontier and their memoirs, pioneers employed familiar phrases to refer to Aboriginal people. They were usually described as 'troublesome', 'wild', 'dangerous', 'hostile', 'aggressive', 'ferocious', or with thinly disguised euphemisms such as 'not altogether peaceably disposed'. On other occasions, the degree of violence lies in between the lines. Alexander Weatherhead, one of the first squatters to enter the Eden–Monaro area, claimed that it was after the 'Aborigines' became more acquainted with the whites that they were to be feared.[28]

There is overwhelming evidence of a familiar pattern of resistance by Aboriginal people: trailing intruders for observation, spearing cattle and sheep, ambushing settler camps. Contrary to Hancock's claim, the language of the frontier in Eden–Monaro is indeed 'like everywhere else'. Relations are described as 'acrimonious', the whites are 'forced to settle in the open' or 'go about in mutual protection'. The words used to describe the movement of the first wave of squatters suggest a state of warfare. The progress of English civilisation is described as having 'disarmed this part of the coast', squatters are 'forced to withdraw' from Aboriginal territory and 'abandon' or 'leave' their camps and huts. One description of an early squatters' hut near Mallacoota gives a reasonable indication of the state of relations during the first period of contact in the 1830s and 1840s:

> [Devlin's] house was quite a fortress. The walls were loopholed to sight and shoot at intruders. It was built of stout timbers and there were metal bars across the chimney to prevent the natives from gaining entry this way. The door was a massive great thing with a great bar inside. Devlin had occasion to shelter from the natives.[29]

In June 1839, a chilling letter appeared in the *Sydney Morning Herald*. It was signed simply 'from the south', and it reveals much about the mentality of squatters after Aboriginal people had attacked them:

> Your town is making a great fuss about the Aborigines. Here is a slap for your mistaken hypocritical philanthropists. Last Monday, a party of Maneroo and Snowy River blacks armed with many firearms. [They] surprised a party of Beeka blacks, close to one of Messrs Imlay's dairy stations and killed three men and one woman … Is it right that they should be allowed firearms? … Already a sufficient number of white men have been slain by them … The Aborigines Protection Society [should realise the Aborigines can] protect themselves. As for these Protectors, I would have them whipped at the cart's tail for accepting a situation the duties of which they could not know, much less fulfil, just for the sake of pocketing public money for doing nought. I wish I had one here now, if he had any shame, I would make him feel it … Have I not just had 50 or 60 of my cattle killed by them — and have I not had sufficient experience of their character to know that it is fear and only fear that will make them quiet?[30]

In 1841, a man who had lived and worked on the Monaro throughout the 1830s wrote to the *Sydney Gazette* recalling his experience as a bushman. His letter is another reminder of the quiet extermination of Aboriginal people. In a settler culture in which the killing of Aboriginal people was forbidden by law, it was wise not to publicise the brutality of the frontier, especially after the Myall Creek Massacre in 1838.

> The Aborigines have been accused of murder and the destruction of the property of the settlers; this is [true] to a very limited extent … but ten blacks are [then] murdered for one white … [a fact] studiously kept from the knowledge of the authorities … If space permitted me I could … instance where the blacks have been shot and slaughtered wholesale — and by whom do you suppose? By the felons of NSW? No … but by those in a far different grade — persons who should have known better. Is the slaughter of a few head of cattle a sufficient reason for massacring and poisoning whole herds of fellow men? … That the blacks from sheer necessity are driven to spear some of the settlers' cattle is true; yet … the savage considers the white man as the wrongful possessor of his country.[31]

Despite the fact that over the last three decades Australian historians have exposed the extent of violence on the frontier, it is still possible to find regions in Australia where the evidence of frontier violence has not been researched thoroughly or acknowledged sufficiently. If the above story is sounding familiar, it is important to remember that it does not form part of the fabric of community history in Eden–Monaro today.

In Eden, the positive contribution of Aboriginal people to the whaling industry dominates the representation of Aboriginal people in local history. As the local historian Harry Wellings wrote in 1931, 'Today there are no Twofold Bay blacks, but there are memories, and these memories are mainly centred in whaling incidents'.[32] The spirit of cooperation between Aboriginal people and Europeans in the whaling industry is understandably presented as a unique story, but it also tends to disguise the truth of the earlier history. There is a danger in writing the history of Aboriginal involvement in whaling as a positive tale of 'Aboriginal people contributing to mainstream Australian history'. A too rosy view glosses over the fact that the Aboriginal whalers were admired primarily because they were an efficient and reliable labour force — they were performing on the coloniser's terms. In addition, despite local mythology, they were not always treated equally, especially in the 1830s and 1840s.

Aboriginal cooperation in whaling on the far south coast has received far more focus than the 30-year period of contact with sealers before whaling began. It has also tended to hide what was happening 'beyond the bay' as the whaling industry began in the 1830s.[33] At Twofold Bay between 1788 and 1832, and in the coastal hinterland extending up to the Monaro until the 1840s, a violent struggle took place for the possession of Aboriginal land.

The spirit of the first 'pioneers' of the Eden area, the Imlay brothers, pervades the area today. Eden's main street is Imlay Street. The mountain that sits just to the south of the township, which the Kudingal had for thousands of years called 'Ballun', is now Mount Imlay — bearing the name of a squatting family which resided for little more than ten years in the district in the 1830s. Little is known of the Imlays' relations with Aboriginal people. Although stressing the brothers' personal kindness to the Aboriginal people at Twofold Bay, Harry Wellings appeared to be slightly uneasy in the 1930s when he wrote:

> On the whole, the Imlays dealt with the Aborigines in a more or less friendly manner and they were regarded as safe people by the Aborigines … Aboriginals also made him probably the best of friends and though raids were made by them they never assaulted or molested the Doctor … the Imlays also undertook long distance, overland droving of large herds of cattle and flocks of sheep, through what was then a wild and undeveloped terrain where they braved perils from the occasional bushranger or hostile tribesman whose territory they were unwittingly invading.[34]

If there were 'safe' people there were 'unsafe' people. Relations were 'less friendly', no doubt after 'raids' were made on the Imlay stations, or when confronting 'hostile Aborigines'. Like many other squatters, the Imlays often left one or two inexperienced stockmen or shepherds as custodians of their vast holdings. These men, armed, bored, fearful of attack and lonely, were the front line of European contact with Aboriginal people on the far south coast and the Monaro.

In the late 1830s, Dr George Imlay sailed to New Zealand. There he met up with his old shipmate and friend EJ Wakefield. Together they sailed from Nelson to Wellington and swapped stories of frontier life, accompanied by two Kudingal men dressed in European clothes. Wakefield recorded his on-board conversation with Imlay:

> I acquired from Dr. Imlay many interesting descriptions of the pastoral and semi-Tartar life of the Australian cattle holder … [and] he added some exciting details of the savage and merciless predatory warfare which is constantly going on between the stockmen and the unreclaimed tribes which hover on the outskirts of the pastoral tracts.[35]

Words such as 'savage and merciless predatory warfare' suggest that the Imlays' contact with Aboriginal people beyond the immediate vicinity of Twofold Bay frequently involved violent conflict and loss of life. Wakefield's conversation with Imlay also reveals how squatters told stories but were always careful not to record names, places and details. There was a culture of 'quietly we tread'. Over the years, as the first generation of settlers reached a venerable age, they began to reminisce about their experiences, usually in local newspapers. From the mid to late nineteenth century, when the pioneer legend first began to take hold, stories of the first pioneers' contact with the 'wild natives' featured frequently in the colonial press. Eden–Monaro was no exception.

In the *Bega Gazette* in December 1872, a historical article referred to one of Imlay's old station hands — 'Nelson by name' — who had worked at Kameruka near Bega, 'and of whom it is said that he used to hunt down the blacks with bloodhounds'.[36]

In the obituary of William Bartley, published in the *Bega Standard* in March 1920, there is a detailed recollection of the killing of a man named Dunn by Aboriginal men, another of the early station hands at Bega in the 1830s. William Bartley's father, Joseph, had found Dunn's body, his makeshift stockmen's hut splashed with blood and ransacked. That same night, alone in the hut,

> Bartley had to sit up all night in dread of his life … All along the river … were the blacks camps, and the glare from the fires made it look like a township at night … When day broke he saw 20 blacks crossing the river and heading for his hut … Bartley fled with his dog, a mastiff, they chased him for a long time … The dog kept pulling back so Mr. Bartley let him go at the blacks and sat down for a rest. The dog sprang onto one black and killed him … [Bartley] then kept on to the nearest white settler at Wandella near Cobargo but of course he didn't know whether this man would be dead or alive, as the bush was full of blacks … [Then they went back to Bega with 4 armed men and] … the blacks did not come near … them. [Bartley was left with a musket which] put terror into the hearts of the blacks, [eventually] the blacks gave him a young boy who learnt English and proved most useful … The blacks in time became quite friendly and could understand English. They were in thousands about Bega then.

Another account of the same incident, published in the recollections of Joshua Higgs in the *Bega Gazette* in 1883, told of how the 'Bega Aborigines' hunted the first squatters in the area away:

> Captain Rain[e]'s of Bathurst were the first cattle sent to Bega … [His men] came to Brogo made yards and put up a hut but the blacks hunted them and the cattle away … [When I was in the Bega area as a stockman in 1830s] fellow workers on other runs were in the habit of coming to our camp and we went out together for mutual protection … [After Dunn's death] we caught two black boys and made them tell us where he was. They took us to a waterhole, where we found his body and we took it out and buried it.[37]

Stories of the killing of Aboriginal people pervade pioneer memories in the Eden–Monaro. They have been passed down from one generation to the next, 'adjusting here and there at the edges', but remaining essentially the same. Memories of 'massacres', 'shootings', 'reprisals' and the poisoning of milk and flour by squatters are commonplace. At times these stories are horrifying: blunt admissions that squatters 'shot the lot', or that 'it was nothing to see a head on a stump as you walked through the bush'.[38]

When I conducted interviews with several non-Aboriginal residents in the area, I found that stories of shootings and poisoning still live today in the oral history of non-Aboriginal society. In my interview with Jack Burgess, a long-time resident of Bega, in May 1999, I was told how Alexander Weatherhead, one of the first men to own Nungatta Station in the 1840s, had killed many Aboriginal people. Part of the milk-making process was to put the milk pans out to let the cream settle on top. Attracted by the offering, Aboriginal men and women would skim the cream off. Weatherhead was apparently so annoyed that he laced the milk with strychnine and later, when the poison had done its work, disposed of the bodies. Burgess claimed he had heard this story from the manager of Nungatta Station in the 1960s. More than 120 years after Weatherhead had allegedly poisoned a large number of Aboriginal people, the story lived on, passed down from one manager of the station to the next.

From other residents, similar stories emerged of the poisoning of Aboriginal people at Pambula, north of Eden, in the mid-nineteenth century. Jim Collins, manager of the Bega 'Grevillea' winery, told me he was nursed as a child by an Aboriginal woman of the Bega tribe. She told him of the poisoning of flour and milk at Pambula in the 'early days' that resulted in the deaths of many of her people.

Interviewing another local resident, Sue Norman, from Kiah, just south of Eden, I was told how a man by the name of Whalan, the first settler to own the property on which she now lives, erected fences and placed guards to 'fight off the Aborigines'. Whalan's property contained a corroboree tree and an Aboriginal burial ground. Sometime later, reading the journals of Oswald Brierly, I found that Brierly had described Whalan as a 'perfect ruffian'.[39]

In 1932, the Eden journalist and historian Harry Wellings interviewed 'Old Bill', then 80 years of age. Bill was allegedly one of the few remaining examples of 'the hardy men of the Snowy'. Born in 1850, he told Wellings the story of old Tongihi, 'the last of the Monaro blacks'. Bill claimed that every member of Tongihi's tribe had been shot by settlers 'down the mountain towards the Cann Valley'. Bill's uncle, Sandy, was a 'stockman on the Monaro in the early days'. And 'my word', said Bill, 'he could tell some tales of the things some of the early settlers did to the blacks in those days'. Uncle Sandy told him that they must have killed thirty or forty 'Aborigines', leaving Tongihi, at 8 years, the sole survivor. Wellings' article was published in the *Bombala Times*. The editor added that a Mr C Cootes had written in to say that indeed Tongihi was well known in the district, although he too had heard that Tongihi's father and possibly his tribe were shot 'down Nungatta way'.[40]

On other occasions there are stories in the oral history of non-Aboriginal society which, although different in place and detail, contain similar images:

Aboriginal people being pushed over cliff faces or their bodies being loaded in carts and thrown off coastal headlands into the sea. In these stories there is an element of dramatic execution, a suggestion of total extermination that conveniently condenses the explanation for the disappearance of Aboriginal people into one apocalyptic event.

About 30 kilometres north-west of Eden, close to Towamba, there is a sheer granite rock face that juts its way out into the bush, known as 'Jingera Rock.' Some local residents today claim that Jingera Rock is the sight of a mass shooting of Aboriginal people. No date. No names. No details. Just a story that lives. But interestingly, in 1938, a traveller who passed through the area told a similar story with one important difference.

Jingera Rock, from Towamba–Wyndham Road. [Mark McKenna]

the road … for some distance [passes] through forest country and the rocky side of the Jingera mountain makes a striking landmark, especially with the western sun shining on it. Although this mountain is known as Jingera, the correct name is Jingo, which in aboriginal language means 'place of death', the aboriginals believing that in the far distant past there had been a big land-slip which buried many of the blacks, and left the mountain in its present state as if a slice had been cut off.[41]

Here, Jingera Rock is still a place of Aboriginal death, but on this occasion death is the result of natural catastrophe. In Aboriginal culture as represented by Europeans, and in settler culture generally, striking landmarks can sometimes be used to explain the disappearance of Aboriginal people. Such stories may reveal more about the struggle to come to terms with dispossession than they do about real events — as if stories of falling and being pushed or thrown over cliff faces have become rural myths for the whole history of dispossession.

Few of these stories of frontier brutality can be verified, but there are too many embedded deep in the oral culture of the far south coast for them all to be fabrications.

To tell the story of the dispossession of the Kudingal people of the far south coast and their neighbours on the Monaro, from the first contact with sealers in the early eighteenth century to the initial confrontation with squatters in the 1830s, does not mean that wanton violence was the only form of interaction. There were many opportunities for misunderstanding with tragic consequences. There were some settlers who tried to understand the feelings and rights of Aboriginal people. And there were examples of individual Aboriginal men and women and colonists being capable of both wanton violence and extreme kindness in different contexts.

But the early period of frontier contact from 1788 to 1850 contains irrefutable evidence that an ongoing state of warfare existed in Eden–Monaro. The front line of this war shifted constantly, yet there is an undeniable truth underlying the history of land settlement in this area. The sealers with their dogs and guns, and the squatters who came with their sheep and cattle, together with their motley crew of armed stockmen and shepherds, killed hundreds of Aboriginal people in retaliation for Aboriginal attempts to defend their land. They were intent on making one thing abundantly clear: the land would be won for the invaders who would settle there.

Current research suggests there were 4000–5000 Aboriginal people living on the Monaro and the far south coast in the late eighteenth century. These estimates are both conservative and speculative. Population density on the coast was almost twice that of the Monaro. After the first settlers arrived in the area in the 1830s, census records and blanket distribution records indicated an Aboriginal population on the coast of just over 500, and 120 on the Monaro. By the 1890s, this figure had dropped to approximately forty-three on the coast and forty on the Monaro. As unreliable as these figures are, it is clear that between 1788 and 1850, the Aboriginal population in Eden–Monaro declined rapidly — from 4000–5000 in 1788 to less than 700 by 1850.

We will never know exactly how many Aboriginal people lost their lives in violent conflict with those who invaded their lands. Many died from smallpox, influenza and venereal disease, and many died on the fringes of the fledgling settler encampments after they were displaced from their homelands. But it is also true that significant numbers died in sporadic warfare, on rare occasions in massacres, and sometimes from poisoning. Eden–Monaro was not settled 'peace-fully'. Like many other areas of Australia, violent conflict was part of the story of 'settlement'.[42]

Reading the recollections of the pioneers, and the existing oral history inter-views with long-time residents that have been recorded by several local histori-ans in Eden–Monaro, it is possible to understand how history is much more than something that can be reduced to facts and numbers. The weight of the past can sometimes be felt, revealing itself as an underlying truth which successive gen-erations have kept alive. This 'geology of fable' carries a profound moral truth. The stories in settler and Aboriginal cultures concerning frontier violence have 'taken root' because they tell the stories that have been frequently denied in the formal historical record of Australia's public culture — subversive stories that time has preserved.

2

DID THE NSW GOVERNMENT AND THE COLONIAL OFFICE INTEND THAT THE RIGHTS OF ABORIGINAL PEOPLE IN SOUTH-EASTERN NEW SOUTH WALES BE PROTECTED?

After Geoffrey Blainey, Henry Reynolds is probably Australia's best known living historian. While the current focus of conservative commentators in Australia centres on Henry Reynolds' interpretation of frontier violence, the most interesting aspect of Reynolds' work is often overlooked.[1]

In 1976, still in his thirties and already living in Townsville, Reynolds delivered a paper at an ANZAAS conference in Hobart in which he outlined what would eventually become the major preoccupations of his scholarship. The paper is revealing because it possesses the confidence and certainty of youth and is typical Reynolds: didactic, searching, blunt, and full of the promise of change.

> Discussion of Aboriginal resistance brings home to us the close relationship between history and the political and moral issues involved in the cause of Aboriginal advancement and the struggle against racism in Australian society … [The work of the historian] cannot be sealed off from the community … history should not only be relevant but politically utilitarian … it should aim to right old injustices, to discriminate in favour of the oppressed, to actively rally to the cause of liberation … [Other, more traditional voices insist that the historian's goal] is not to condemn or to praise but to understand … Future debate on the historiography of race relations will be conducted from these two moorings. Those lacking the anchor of complete moral certainty will find themselves uneasily adrift between the two.[2]

Reynolds' article would eventually be published in the *Journal of Australian Studies* in 1978.[3] As he 'dug' for evidence through the 1970s, Reynolds maintained the framework of absolute 'moral certainty' that had initially guided him in 1973.

By choosing to focus on the history of the frontier, Reynolds knew there was no arbitrary line dividing contemporary politics from historical scholarship. To expose the true history of the frontier was itself a political act. As Reynolds said in his introduction to *The Other Side of the Frontier* in 1981, the purpose of the book was not to provide a model of 'detached scholarship' but to be provocative and 'inescapably political'. Presenting history as a rolling queue of binary opposites — a succession of stark moral choices — soon became one of Reynolds' trademarks.

In 1989 he published *Dispossession*, a collection of documents relating to frontier history. Belying the diversity of the documents within, Reynolds' chapter titles frame history as a succession of moral polarities: White Australia: Guilty or Not?, The Frontier: Peaceful Settlement or Brutal Conquest?, The Land Question: Are We a Community of Thieves? A similar tendency is evident in the first pages of *Frontier*, published in 1987, where Reynolds asks whether Australia 'was settled or invaded? pioneered or conquered? won by sweat or won by blood?'[4]

This way of packaging history, as if it were a legal contest to be settled in a court of law, implied that the nation awaited sentence if it were found guilty. In lending itself naturally to the media, it also created a framework for the public discussion of frontier history which would later be adopted in a much cruder fashion by conservative commentators who would attempt to prove Australia 'not guilty'.

With the publication of *Law of the Land* in 1987, Reynolds focused on the legal history of land settlement in the Australian colonies. Whereas his first books had contextualised frontier history, *Law of the Land* was an attempt to prove that the conventional view of Australian settlement was both legally and historically incorrect.

At the heart of Henry Reynolds' reading of colonial history was a particular view about the choices that were perceived by Australian colonists in the early nineteenth century. In *Law of the Land* and elsewhere, Reynolds argued that Aboriginal native title, and the right of that title to coexist on pastoral leases granted by the Crown, was never extinguished in the common law. This was the view which, as Reynolds has claimed recently, was ultimately endorsed in the majority judgment of the High Court in the *Wik* case in 1996.[5]

Reynolds argues that the legally binding instructions of the Colonial Office despatched to the governors of the Australian colonies clearly instructed colonial officials to ensure that Aboriginal native title was recognised and respected, especially by the late 1840s. On this basis, he believes a clear line of justice can be drawn from the despatches of the 1840s to the four judges who formed the majority in the *Wik* case in 1996.[6]

Reynolds was pursuing a particular line of historical reasoning that could be sustained within the confines of the law. His focus was necessarily on official policy, not on the wider and more complex history of the frontier — a history that he knows intimately.[7] But Reynolds did step over this line in one crucial respect:

he suggested that the history of Aboriginal dispossession in Australia could and should have been different. In his 1992 postscript to the new edition of *Law of the Land*, he claimed that the colonists had a clear choice: to recognise native title as the law demanded, or to dismiss native title and take the land illegally. He also passed moral judgment on the choice that the colonists made: 'The Colonial Office officials who recognised native title were right. The settlers who didn't were wrong'.[8]

Reynolds was not only suggesting that, in retrospect, the settlers were wrong. He was also claiming they were wrong because they refused the possibility of creating a different history. For the settlers 'not' to recognise Aboriginal native title, they must have made a choice — they must have been aware of their obligations to recognise native title and then decided to ignore them. This would be different, for example, from claiming that the settlers 'failed' to recognise native title, which would imply that they were ignorant or, for various reasons, unable to do so.

In an article written with Jamie Dalziel, which formed part of the plaintiffs' argument in the *Wik* case, Reynolds implied that the force of law carried considerable weight in colonial society, and that the squatters were aware of their legal obligations to Aboriginal people: 'At no time during the period leading up to the enactment of the 1846 [Imperial Wastelands] Act could the squatters claim that they had been led to expect that they would be able to exclude the Aborigines from their runs'.[9] In this sense, Reynolds claims that the Crown's ministers had no intention of denying Aboriginal people access to their traditional lands, and that they communicated this intention to the squatters. Yet on the Australian frontier, the squatters excluded Aboriginal people as they pleased.

By looking closely at the way in which colonial governments oversaw the dispossession of Aboriginal Australians in the south-eastern corner of New South Wales, I want to explain how Aboriginal people lost their land. But I also want to ask if Henry Reynolds' interpretation of the colonial administration of the frontier holds true.

I have been inspired by the political and legal impact of Reynolds' work. But to me, its most interesting aspect is the tension between the 'inescapable' politics of Reynolds' history, and the method of his scholarship. By exploring the history of one area in Australia, I hope to show that Reynolds has uncovered what Australia's history 'might have been' — a history of 'perpetual possibility' — rather than a history of what was.

What might have been is an abstraction
Remaining a perpetual possibility
Only in a world of speculation.
What might have been and what has been
Point to one end, which is always present.
Footfalls echo in the memory
Down the passage which we did not take
Towards the door we never opened
Into the rose garden.

TS ELIOT,
The Four Quartets[10]

What is law? Is it what is on the books,
or what is actually enacted and obeyed in a society?

BERNHARD SCHLINK,
The Reader 1997[11]

Between the early 1820s, when squatters first entered the Monaro, and 1837, when the limits of the colony were finally extended beyond Bateman's Bay, the squatters, together with their cattle and sheep, illegally occupied Aboriginal lands which lay beyond the formal limits of the colony. For the first fifty years of European settlement in Eden–Monaro, the colonial government struggled to adjust the legal and political administration of land distribution to the reality of the frontier. In every respect, the 'strong arm' of the squatters led the way. By and large, they were a law unto themselves, and the government trailed behind, sometimes not even pretending it was in control.

In Eden–Monaro, the acquisition of Aboriginal land took place at the whim of the squatter; conflict was common and almost impossible to police. Squatting runs were rarely surveyed, and their boundaries were unclear. As one historian of the region, Marion Diamond, has claimed, squatters collected runs 'like so many postage stamps on a map', both before and after the limits of the colony had been extended to Twofold Bay. In the 1830s, there were at least thirty stations on the southern Monaro, and the region was already being described as 'crowded'.[12] Both the Imlay Brothers and Ben Boyd, the squatters who held the largest runs in Eden–Monaro until the 1840s, were assisted by the colonial government in their speedy possession of Aboriginal land. Within a decade of their arrival at Twofold Bay in 1832, the Imlay brothers held nearly a million acres.[13] Like Boyd, they chose Eden–Monaro because they could more easily monopolise the economy. Their only concern with Aboriginal people was to assess their suitability as a compliant labour force. In the prevailing culture, men such as Boyd and the Imlays were treated as heroes, and this was not for ensuring the access of Aboriginal people to their land. They often ignored their rents and sought to evade the terms of pastoral leases.

Settlers wrote frequently of the land being occupied '*only* by Aborigines', comments that indicated they made little effort to respect Aboriginal rights to land. In 1856, the obligations of the colonist were explained by the *Illawarra Mercury*, at that time the only paper on the south coast of New South Wales:

> [So far as colonisation is concerned there is] an important moral principle; a social and moral responsibility; an obligation to promote the welfare of others. It is upon such … [a] principle that the British Government justifies the aggressive policy of establishing colonies and taking possession of territories formerly occupied by native tribes. It is to promote the welfare of our countrymen, and to advance the progress of civilisation, that this country is now under the British dominion, and occupied by the Anglo Saxon race. If [a] native chief should collect an Aboriginal force and take possession of the thousands of acres of wasteland in this district, and claim them as their own domain, in which to breed wallabies and snakes for their recreation and sustenance … an appeal would be made for the purposes of driving such … useless invaders from the soil … Many … acknowledge the hand of Providence in transferring such land, from the original inhabitants into their own possession. And was it not the object of government, in making grants and disposing of the land to advance the colony, by bringing such under cultivation and the settlement of population. There was a moral obligation implied in the transaction, but how little do many of the proprietors practically recognise it.[14]

This editorial makes several things clear. Long after despatches had been sent from the Colonial Office insisting that the colonists respect Aboriginal rights to land, there is little evidence that the spirit of these instructions was assimilated into the practice of everyday life on the frontier on the south coast of New South Wales. The 'moral obligation' perceived by the editor of the *Illawarra*

Mercury is quite the opposite. It is to supplant what he believes to be the primitive and 'useless invaders' with the 'civilised' occupation of British colonists. Consistent with the belief in the superiority of European civilisation, colonisation is understood as the aggressive occupation and conquest of Aboriginal territory, a God-given right, its major obligation being to protect the welfare of British citizens. There is no evidence of a frontier culture even minutely concerned with its obligations to Aboriginal rights, only one convinced of its right to dispossess Aboriginal people.

This is one reason why many of the journals and letters that related frontier experience to a British audience spoke bluntly and unashamedly of enticing others to emigrate and 'occupy the lands of the Aborigines'. Having occupied the land, the settler became a proprietor of something which he believed could 'never be taken away', or restricted in its use, least of all by Aboriginal Australians. This was the culture of colonisation in Eden–Monaro.[15] In November 1850, Charles Darwin wrote to his friend Syms Covington. Covington had journeyed with Darwin on the *Beagle* in the early 1830s, and now lived at Pambula. Darwin offered a glimpse of the true priorities of those seeking to acquire land in Australia:

> You have an immense, incalculable advantage in living in a country in which your children are sure to get on if industrious. I assure you that, though I am a rich man, when I think of the future I very often ardently wish I was settled in one of our colonies …Whenever you write again tell me how far you think a gentleman with capital would get on in NSW. I have heard that gentlemen generally get on badly …What interest can you get for money in a safe investment? How dear is food? How much land have you? I was pleased to see the other day that you have a railway commenced, and before they have one in any part of Italy or Turkey. The English certainly are a noble race, and a grand thing it is that we have got securely hold of Australia and New Zealand.[16]

Darwin's emphasis on capital was typical. The political culture of colonial governance may have demanded that respect for Aboriginal rights was an essential component of the public record of colonial administration. But the economic culture of colonisation demanded that colonists had 'secure hold' of the land and were unencumbered in their ability to profit handsomely, regardless of whether they were resident in London or Twofold Bay.

Years later, when the descendants of the first wave of colonists came to write about the way in which their forebears had won the land, they spoke of the 'practically unknown and free land of the far south coast'. They boasted of the way in which Governor Richard Bourke had, in 1832, 'given to his friends, the Imlay brothers, the pastoral district of the far south coast'.

In 1928, in an article headed 'Occupation of Land and Far South Coast Settlement before 1830', one newspaper editor explained the method of colonisation in New South Wales. Since the days of the Roman Empire, he said, there had been two kinds of colonisation. One via the 'creation of government and settlement', the second via the drive of young 'adventurous and independent' settlers 'who were prepared to push out into the unknown bush and form outposts of settlements'. Much of Australia was 'colonised' by the second method.

Looking back on the history of land settlement in south-eastern New South Wales, the image of a hardy race of settlers pushing into virgin bush to take up 'free land' became a means of erasing the memory of frontier conflict. Yet it was also a creation story founded partly on the reality of the frontier. The land could be remembered as 'free' because the settlers had taken it without any respect for the rights of its original owners.[17] The myth of 'free land' emerged naturally from the actions of the 'first' generation of settlers: despite government 'policy', they had been 'free' to disregard Aboriginal rights to land. And just as they came to see the past as a land free of an Aboriginal presence, they imagined the future in similar terms. Thus the editor of the *Bega Standard* wrote in 1875: 'In the future all seems bright for this colony; millions of acres of land are yet available, unbounded mineral wealth only requires development. Pastoral and agricultural pursuits are never more profitable'.[18]

Looking closely at the period between 1830 and 1850, much of the communication between the colonial government in Sydney and settlers in Eden–Monaro reveals that the settlers were either unclear or uninterested about their obligations towards Aboriginal people.

In 1830, complaining of Aboriginal 'outrages', some squatters near Batemans Bay wrote to Governor Darling, explaining their desire to make 'Aborigines' aware of their 'superiority of power'. One pleaded with the Governor to 'let me know what steps I am to take to punish them'. The question at issue was not how to allow Aboriginal people access to their land, but how severely to punish them. Governor Darling suggested that offending 'Aborigines' be brought to Sydney and, seemingly oblivious to the tone of the letters he had received, tentatively advised that the squatters withdraw from the area. He also admitted he had not heard of any attempt 'to soothe the natives' feeling'. Throughout the next two decades, this pattern of communication would be repeated frequently. When squatters asked for government protection or advice it was to make their control of the land more secure.[19]

The years between 1835 and 1838 were particularly crucial in south-eastern New South Wales. Squatters had already trespassed on land beyond the boundaries, and Governor Bourke was under pressure to extend the colony as far south as Twofold Bay. In early 1835, in an effort to gain an appreciation of the issues involved, he inspected the area himself. At the same time, the Colonial Office was deciding on its response to John Batman's treaty with Aboriginal people at Port Phillip. By 1838, with George Gipps as the new Governor, officials in Sydney and London were also dealing with political pressure from almost a hundred squatters between Yass and Port Phillip. They had signed a petition requesting the opening up of the country and military protection for themselves, their flocks and their herds. If there was a time to make the government's policy in relation to Aboriginal people clear, it was now.

When Governor Bourke returned to Sydney after his journey to Twofold Bay, he wrote to Lord Glenelg, the Colonial Secretary in London, explaining that the area between Batemans Bay and Twofold Bay was already 'depastured by flocks and herds' and 'attended by shepherds and stockmen'. Given that the squatters were present in considerable numbers, Bourke understood the challenge for his administration: 'how may this government turn to the best advantage a state of things which it cannot wholly interdict? ... to refrain from settlement at Twofold Bay through the fear of dispersion is ... a fallacious policy. The dispersion will go on, notwithstanding the discouragement, but accompanied by much evil'. In supporting the extension of the colony to Twofold Bay, Bourke was admitting that his government was virtually powerless to stop the squatters extending the frontier. To avoid the 'evil' warfare that had already begun, it was best to establish a 'civilised' township at Twofold Bay.[20]

Writing in reply to Bourke on 13 April 1836, Glenelg agreed that Batman's treaty could not be sanctioned by the Crown, and explained the policy to be adopted towards Aboriginal people in 'the unauthorised settlements at Port Phillip and Twofold Bay'. His response is a perfect example of the duplicity of much of the British Government's policy. Although claiming he was 'anxious' that the rights of Aboriginal people be defended, Glenelg refused to curtail the advance of squatters beyond the boundaries of the colony. He claimed that 'the sanguine ardour of private speculation [will always] anticipate the more cautious movements of governments'.

In a later despatch, Glenelg made it clear that Aboriginal people could not sign treaties with settlers because the Crown was sovereign. They were to be considered as 'subjects of the Queen', not as aliens 'with whom a war can exist'. Oddly, this was supposed to be their source of protection. If Aboriginal people would have been informed of this strange logic they would surely have laughed. The argument went as follows. By relinquishing sovereignty of 'the whole of their ancient possessions' to the Crown, they were afforded the protection of Her Majesty's government and the common law. Native title existed within the sovereignty of the Crown; it could never be external to that sovereignty. The Crown would define and protect Aboriginal native title through the administration of government and the common law.[21] Aboriginal people merely had to wait until 1992 for this policy to be put into practice.

Glenelg was satisfied for the squatters to run ahead of government in their rush for wealth — the Crown would not protect Aboriginal people from this invasion. Yet at the same time he insisted on their right to be afforded protection under the law. This was a politically expedient position for Glenelg to adopt. It assuaged the concerns of the humanitarians in London, left a written and legally binding record of the government's determination to defend Aboriginal rights, all the while fully aware that the squatters would ride roughshod over those that Glenelg had called 'that helpless and unfortunate race'.

In early 1838, George Gipps, the new Governor of New South Wales, wrote to Glenelg admitting his government's difficulty in stopping the frequent outrages on the frontier. Repeating Glenelg's instructions in his Order in Council later that year, with all its empty promises of 'justice and humanity', he continued to receive letters from squatters in southern New South Wales threatening to 'levy war' against Aboriginal people. Some of the squatters' remarks were chilling. As one stated, 'it is only when [the Aboriginal people] have become acquainted with our power and determination to punish their aggressions that they have become orderly, peaceable, and brought within the reach of civilisation'.

On 23 June 1838, Edward Deas Thomson, the Colonial Secretary of New South Wales, replied to the squatters' petition on behalf of Gipps' government. He first followed conventional practice, reminding the squatters of their duty to protect 'Aborigines' and the opinion of the 'British public'. He then explained that the government would do what it could to protect the squatters: 'after having taken entire possession of the country, *without any reference to the rights of the Aborigines*, it is now too late for the government to refuse protection to persons, who [have] brought with them their flocks and their herds ... but every wanderer in search of pasturage cannot be attended by a military force' (my italics).

Thomson's response is fascinating for several reasons. Although it demonstrates that some squatters were informed of their duty to protect Aboriginal people, it also shows how the language of colonial politics was intentionally ambiguous, mainly because of the political context in which it was formulated — attempting to appease the distant humanitarians in London on the one hand and the rapacious squatters on the other. As the Australian historian AGL Shaw wrote in 1968, the Colonial Office often spoke with 'two voices'. So too did the colonial administration in the colonies.[22]

Even more important is the inherent contradiction in Thomson's reply, showing how difficult it is to ascertain definitively the intent of colonial communications. If, as Thomson says, the colonial government and the squatters had taken 'entire possession of the country, without any reference to the rights of the Aborigines', his noble preface about justice and humanity is nothing more than the necessary lies of a political bureaucrat. If this was Thomson's understanding of what happened on the Australian frontier, it is impossible to argue that the intention of all colonial officials was to ensure the continued right of Aboriginal people to access their lands, or that they understood the instructions from their superiors in London in a consistent manner.

Both the despatches from the Colonial Office, and the Orders in Council which emanated from these despatches in Sydney, had the force of law. But that law was a product of the political environment in London. It was born partly of political expedience, and existed on paper only, not in the realm of colonial government or in the daily life of the Australian frontier, where a completely different type of law was in operation. This law was not written down or filed meticulously for the use of future historians, but it was 'obeyed'.[23] As always, the gap between government policy and frontier practice was vast, even more so when the policy emanated from offices in Whitehall thousands of miles away and communication was hindered by the length of sea voyages.

This was nowhere more evident than in 1839, when the colonial administration decided to appoint Aboriginal 'protectors' in the Port Phillip region, and new Commissioners of Crown Lands in other areas of New South Wales. The decision was made largely in response to political pressure exerted by humanitarians in London. After the end of slavery in British colonies in 1833, this was a time when the issue of indigenous rights in New Zealand and Canada was also prominent in London. In language clearly calculated to appease the humanitarians, Glenelg stated that the task of the Protector was to 'watch over the rights and interests of the natives, protect them … from any encroachments on their property and from acts of cruelty, oppression or injustice, and faithfully represent their wants, wishes or grievances … to the government of the colony'.[24] By the early 1840s, humanitarian activists were condemning the scheme as an abject failure.[25]

John Lambie was reappointed Commissioner of Crown Lands for the Monaro in 1839, partly in an attempt to restrain the unauthorised occupation of Crown land. In 1841, Gipps had provided Lambie with a small mounted police force known as the border police. Later Lambie moved with his police from Queanbeyan to Cooma, and his patrols took him over the present New South Wales–Victoria border into Gippsland. Governor Gipps described Lambie's duties as follows: 'to exercise a control over the very numerous grazing establishments which have been formed in these districts under licences from the government, and to prevent collisions between the men in charge of such establishments and the Aborigines of the country'.[26]

From 1839, John Lambie was responsible for an area which stretched from Moruya on the south coast of New South Wales to the northern coast of Victoria and up to the Monaro, including all the Snowy River catchment. The vastness of his domain meant that he would have had great difficulty in protecting anyone other than himself. He knew little about the diverse range of Aboriginal language groups in the area, and understood almost nothing of their culture. In practice, his job was to measure and record their decline, and to write predictable reports, as he did in May 1848. The 'Aborigines', he said, were 'harmless' and 'fast decreasing in numbers' — 'there have been no collisions with the whites that I have heard of'. Politically, it was in Lambie's interest to hear nothing, otherwise he would need to explain his efforts to 'prevent' such collisions. Measured either by the standards of Lord Glenelg's original instruction to protectors in the Port Phillip region, or Governor Gipps' instructions to Commissioners of Crown lands in New South Wales, the colonial administration in Eden–Monaro was a sham.[27]

It is unlikely that Henry Reynolds would disagree with much of the above interpretation of frontier history in Eden–Monaro. But his generous reading of colonial despatches, and their legal status, is contentious for three reasons. First, it is possible to interpret these despatches and the law differently, as David Ritter and Jonathan Fulcher have done.[28] While there is no doubt that the Colonial Office officials showed concern for Aboriginal rights, this concern cannot be read at face value. Second, there is insufficient evidence to suggest that the Australian colonists saw a choice between two alternatives: to obey the instructions of the colonial administration and protect the rights of Aboriginal people, or to ignore them. The history of the Australian frontier was far more complex than a choice between two

The opening of the post office at Eden, watercolour by Frederick Garling, 1848. Typically, Aboriginal people are positioned on the 'fringe' of the new settlement. [R11448, by permission of National Library of Australia]

moral polarities. Finally, in his effort to render history useful in politics and the law, and to achieve justice for Aboriginal Australians, Reynolds has overlooked aspects of the history of the colonial administration of the frontier which do not suit his conclusions.

Leaving the latter charge aside for the moment, the first two criticisms can be dealt with simultaneously. Henry Reynolds has claimed that it was the Colonial Office and the Imperial Government's assessment in the 1840s that 'it was both necessary and possible for Aboriginal people and pastoralists to share the same land'.[29] This argument, and Reynolds' suggestion that there was a clear choice presented to colonists in New South Wales, may be sustainable if the focus remains solely within the prism of the law, interpreting the historical intent of colonial despatches as legally binding documents. But it is problematic as 'history' because of its limited focus.

Writing in 1996, the legal scholar David Ritter pointed out that 'it was the discourses of power that accompanied the colonisation of Australia that actually caused Aboriginal people's interests in land to be formally ignored'. In practical terms, Aboriginal people stood outside the protection of the law. Far from hovering over the frontier as an angel of justice which the settlers failed to heed, the law, as it functioned in colonial society, was actually complicit in the dispossession of Aboriginal people. In practice, the law reflected the colonists' dismissal of Aboriginal rights. Ritter makes the point well: 'in a society in which the dominant discourse defined Aboriginal people as "wandering tribes living without certain habitation and without laws", the absence of Aboriginal land rights was not a matter for judicial decisions, it was a truth that was self evident, and the law was predicated upon that truth'.

It is Reynolds' retrospective reading of colonial despatches, and his desire to reverse the historical injustice of dispossession, which leads him to read the despatches expressing concern for the protection of Aboriginal rights as the clear intention of the law in the 1840s. In a similar fashion, it is the changing political and social values that have allowed the courts to interpret the legal history of land settlement in Australia in a new light and which, particularly through the *Mabo* decision in 1992, ensure that contemporary values are reflected in the common law. In other words, it is not, as Reynolds suggests, that history was 'wrong' in not heeding the law, but rather that the history of the frontier, and the way in which the law operated on the frontier, was consistent with the ethos that prevailed at the time.[30]

Reynolds' reading of the despatches also places too little emphasis on the political context in which they were written and the distance of this context from the Australian frontier. The political culture that prevailed in London in the 1830s and 1840s, and the bureaucratic culture of empire, were acutely aware of the importance of maintaining a politically sensitive and humane legacy on the public record. It was required that colonial despatches express concern for the rights of Aboriginal people. Politically, this was the necessary rhetoric of colonial rule at the time. The officials who drafted these dawdling despatches also read the despatches that arrived from Australia which explained that the government was powerless to stop the squatters from doing as they pleased. At the same time, the British Government and many investors were content to reap vast profits from the squatters' theft of Aboriginal land. As Charles von Hugel remarked in 1834, referring to England's treatment of indigenous people as its 'brand of shame': 'Very rigorous views on popular rights are held in England, but a study of history compels one to admit that this sentiment does not go beyond words and is neither more nor less than a mask of hypocrisy'.[31]

Von Hugel's criticisms may have been excessive, but Louis De Freycinet, who first journeyed to Australia with Nicolas Baudin in 1802 before returning in 1819, came to a similar conclusion when writing up his journal many years later in France:

> The very fact that Europeans landed and established themselves at Port Jackson was, as far as the Aborigines were concerned, and according to the laws under which they lived, a hostile action … This invasion of their soil immediately destroyed a most essential part of [their] means of livelihood … and it could even be said that the fundamental principles of human rights, that in other parts of the world are so vigorously invoked and respected, were, in this place, completely ignored and unscrupulously violated. The resistance of some of the more valorous amongst them was treated as rebellion, and the Aboriginals' reprisals as criminal onslaughts. Finally the Europeans … waged murderous war against them.[32]

The neglect of the 'fundamental principles of human rights' continued in Eden–Monaro. The history of the frontier in south-eastern Australia demonstrates that there was very little possibility of Aboriginal people continuing their traditional use of the land. The attitudes of the squatters towards Aboriginal people and the protection of Aboriginal rights were rarely compatible. The creation of Aboriginal reserves from the late 1840s actually hindered their right to continue their traditional use of land. The squatters disregarded the terms of pastoral leases and mostly ignored requests to protect Aboriginal rights, forcing Aboriginal people off their land and asking for government assistance if Aboriginal people resisted.

Reynolds has framed his interpretation of history as choice between two alternatives: 'the Colonial officials who recognised native title were right and the settlers who didn't were wrong'. But the context in which these 'right' and 'wrong' decisions were made was radically different. The dominant culture of the frontier was, as Don Watson has claimed, one in which Aboriginal people were seen as oppressed because 'they were not agrarian' and 'no settler questioned his right to take the land and farm it'. Most settlers in Eden–Monaro were untroubled by any sense of obligation to Aboriginal people. They may have chosen to drive them from their land, but the issue of whether the squatters saw this choice as simply as Reynolds suggests — a choice between right and wrong — is unclear. On the one hand, the colonial administration instructed squatters to respect Aboriginal rights to land, while on the other it did little to stop them trampling on indigenous rights.[33]

Because of the controversy surrounding Henry Reynolds' work, it is important to clarify his role as a historian. In the last fifteen years especially, Reynolds has endeavoured to make his history 'politically utilitarian' and to 'rally to the cause of liberation' — the liberation of Aboriginal Australians and the 'struggle against racism in Australian society'. His passion for change explains why he is able to focus his history so sharply and with such conviction.

Since 1987, with the publication of *Law of the Land*, Reynolds has focused his attention on the history of the law. The use of history in a court of law demands that one line of reasoning is pursued and a particular conclusion proved. The law has great difficulty in accommodating history as equivocation, doubt or exploration.[34] Reynolds has shown Australians what their history 'might have been' if the law, as he perceives it, had been understood and enforced. In this sense, he has given us a history of endless speculation and 'perpetual possibility', a history of the 'door we never opened'.

PART TWO

forgetting

3

'A CULT OF DISREMEMBERING'?

The land was bare,
they were never there,
shadows of the
small clouds only.
Stretched beneath
the midday sun
the country was a
kind of parchment
waiting for the quill.

GEOFF PAGE,
from 'Justice Blackburn sails with Cook' in *The Great Forgetting*[1]

One of the most influential critiques of Australian history, WEH Stanner's 1968 Boyer Lecture series *After the Dreaming*, inspired a generation of historians in their efforts to break what Stanner called the 'Great Australian Silence'.

I remember reading Stanner's lectures in the late 1970s as an undergraduate, and the powerful effect they had on me. They were part of the core reading for my first-year course in anthropology, but they spoke more directly to my interest in Australian history. Unlike much of the reading I encountered in my first year at university, Stanner's prose was clear and concise, his voice personal and passionate.

Stanner admitted he was 'no historian', instead preferring to describe his reflections as an 'anthropologist's view' of black–white relations in Australia. But after Stanner's 'partial survey' of published works on Australian history, in his second lecture he concluded that the absence of Aboriginal people in Australian history could not be explained by 'absent-mindedness'. It was, he said, on 'such a scale' that it constituted a national 'cult of disremembering'.[2] Reading Stanner, I had the feeling that a profound truth awaited discovery, as if a veil were about to be pulled back.

The theme of Stanner's second lecture was continued when the cultural historian Bernard Smith delivered his 1980 Boyer Lectures, *The Spectre of Truganini*. Smith's language evoked images of psychological repression, nightmares and guilt. He argued that Australian writers and artists had thrown a 'white blanket of forgetfulness' over the 'central tragedy of Australian settlement'.

> White Australians have tried to forget. Indeed at times it would seem as if all the culture of old Europe were being brought to bear upon our writers and artists in order to blot from their memories the crimes perpetrated upon Australia's first inhabitants. In recent years however both sides, black and white alike, have become aware increasingly of the continuing colonial crime, the locked cupboard of our history.[3]

Between Stanner's Boyer Lectures in 1968, and Smith's in 1980, the research Stanner called for had begun. Emerging also was a better understanding of the chronology of the 'Great Australian Silence'. As Henry Reynolds claimed in 1981, Stanner's 'cult of disremembering' was a fairly recent phenomenon, beginning in the early twentieth century, at the time of Federation, and lasting until the 1960s.[4]

Once the colonies federated on 1 January 1901 and the framework for the writing of national history was in place, the desire to forget the violence of the frontier, or to at least dismiss it as an inevitable by-product of a far greater good, became stronger. The history required to build the nation was to be different from the history that accompanied colonisation. The nation-state and the historical profession often walked hand in hand, with every political act and gesture conscious of its place in history. Many historians sought to set Australia apart and define its identity. As white Australia and the British connection, the central ideas that sustained the nation between Federation and the 1960s, began to unravel in the late twentieth century, so too did the history of forgetting.

As I carried out my research on the south-eastern corner of New South Wales, I began to understand how the settlers had come to forget Aboriginal Australians, both in the practice of everyday life and in the making of their history. I realised that I had to try and explain how and why they forgot. I needed to ask how Stanner's 'cult of disremembering' had come to be.

As I did so, I also saw that the history of the settlers' forgetting of Aboriginal Australians was far more complex and subtle than the simple locking of a cupboard or the obscuring of a window. There was never one point in time when it clearly began, never one moment when it came to an abrupt end. Narratives that acknowledged frontier violence, for example, coexisted with historical narratives that erased the frontier from settler memory. This is true especially in the nineteenth century, and the period between 1970 and the present day. Equally, the self-conscious manner in which the settlers created their history explained much of their desire to forget their relations with Aboriginal people on the frontier.

Ultimately, thinking about the way in which settlers sought to explain the dispossession of Aboriginal Australians and invent their past gave me a better appreciation of the gulf that separated the historical memory of one culture from another.

'THIS WONDERFUL INVASION'

[The British have] invented all sorts of ridiculous
tales concerning [Aboriginal people], in order that
they may be furnished with an excuse for taking away
their lives.

LIEUTENANT HW BRETON,
1833[5]

E very community needs a creation story, a story which explains the genesis and
growth of a people and their culture. In Eden–Monaro, as in many other areas
of Australia, explanations for the presence of settler culture have always included
reference to the bald fact of prior Aboriginal occupation. Since colonisation began
in south-eastern New South Wales, the story of one culture's progress has been set
against another culture's decline. Creating local history has meant finding an
explanation for local dispossession.

In *Hunters and Collectors*, Tom Griffiths wrote of the 'unconscious reflex' of
silence regarding the history of dispossession that has pervaded much of Australia's
settler culture.[6] On the far south coast and the Monaro, these silences have sometimes been so deafening that they reveal a deep sense of unease in relation to the
history of settlement. In southern Eden–Monaro, there has rarely been a rational
or comfortable creation story. Almost always, in the region's press and in local histories, there has been a struggle to explain, to forget, or to come to terms with
unpleasant memories. But the struggle of settler culture to explain the presence of
Aboriginal culture, and the way in which this has changed over time, tells us much
about the making of history in Australia.

Creation stories often represent comfortable beliefs rather than events that we
can verify through historical evidence. In Eden, for example, some people prefer
to believe that their town was named after the biblical Garden of Eden rather than
learn that it was named after the man who was Secretary for the Colonies in
London when the town was first surveyed in 1843 — Baron Auckland.[7] If Eden
is paradise found, it is probably found more easily in the Book of Genesis.

In a similar way, there have been many preferred beliefs about the dispossession of Aboriginal people in Eden–Monaro. Chief among them is the belief that

Aboriginal people 'died away' after 'contact with whites' — passive and primitive victims of disease who bowed to the inevitable; extinction in the face of a superior civilisation.[8] Many towns in the region had their own Truganini story. In Cooma, 'Biggenhook' died in 1916 — 'the last Aboriginal'. Other newspaper reports in the region referred to the 'last remaining Aborigines', usually as Aboriginal people were being forcibly removed from settler towns to coastal reserves at Wallaga Lake to the north or Lake Tyers to the south.[9]

From the 1830s, imagining the 'last Aborigine' became a way of imagining the triumph of 'civilisation'. It was also a useful means of denying the frontier wars of the early nineteenth century and believing that the few Aboriginal people who lived with settlers from the 1830s in Eden had been brought to the brink of extinction by natural causes alone. But there were many variations on these themes. Sometimes settlers predicted the inevitable decline of Aboriginal culture while at the same time stating their desire to preserve an ethnographic record of traditional society, as in this letter to a Bombala paper in 1875:

> There are residents in this district who can remember the time when the blackfellows with their gins and piccaninnies were accustomed to collect together in hundreds for the purpose of keeping up their periodical celebrations, of holding their sports, and of settling their differences … All that remain now are just some half-dozen, two or three of whom are but occasionally seen in the streets of Bombala … In the course of the next 50 years no individual of the race will be left … but if we have by our presence been the means of their destruction, we ought at least to make [the] best amends we can by preserving the recollection of what they were.[10]

Recalling 'what they were' meant gathering a 'genuine … ethnological collection' to 'bestow on future generations'.[11] This 'scientific' interest expressed the belief that Aboriginal culture was best preserved in the glass cases and filing cabinets of museums. But the settlers' insistence in the late nineteenth century that 'Aborigines' would soon 'cease to exist' often hinted at a distinction that would come to determine government policy towards Aboriginal people in the twentieth century. Those who made the claim that 'Aborigines' were destined to die out often emphasised that 'full-blood Aborigines' were disappearing, implying that Aboriginal people of mixed ancestry did not qualify as 'Aborigines'. This distinction was sometimes combined with another belief, that 'local' or 'original Aborigines' were the only authentic 'Aborigines', while those who had 'moved in' from 'somewhere else' were illegitimate. Therefore Aboriginal people could be said to be 'dying out' when settlers believed there were 'none left from round here'. In September 1856, the Cooma correspondent for the *Sydney Morning Herald* reported that there were not more than four or five 'Aborigines' left in Cooma, most in the town emanating from Gippsland. The 'real natives of the Maneroo', he said, were no longer living; they had been killed by disease caused either 'by their friendliness with the sea coast blacks … or their vicious intercourse with unprincipled whites'. The result was their 'almost entire extinction'.[12]

Once they had been displaced from their traditional lands by squatters and settlers, Aboriginal people moved to other areas where settler culture often denied their status as indigenous people. From the moment the settlers invaded Aboriginal lands in the 1830s until the present day, non-Aboriginal Australians have employed a familiar strategy to deny Aboriginal people their right to land. They have argued that those with the only legitimate claim to land are descendants of 'traditional' Aboriginal societies. This strategy is unjust because of the way in which Aboriginal people were removed from their lands, and because it ignores the various ways in which they have belonged to 'country' — through mother, father, conception, birth, death, burial, totemic connection, succession and conquest.[13] Aboriginal people in Eden–Monaro in the mid-nineteenth century lost their land to the squatters, and many lost their indigeneity as well, at least in the eyes of settler culture. In 1903, the only newspaper in Eden explained the disappearance of Aboriginal people from Twofold Bay:

> [Long ago] a strong race of Aboriginals lived and fought and hunted along and around the shores of Twofold Bay. They exist no longer, not one of them; for with the exception of a few of a newer race who visit Eden during the whaling season, all are dead and gone. The last buried here was poor old Brierly, called, probably after Mr. Brierly the painter; and it is quite pathetic to hear of the old man's last request to be placed alongside of his father in the Aboriginal burial ground at East Boyd.[14]

Despite the fact that Aboriginal people were in 1903 living and working around Eden, they were now described as a 'newer race' who had forfeited any claim to being indigenous. Instead, 'old Brierly' became Eden's Truganini, the last of his 'race', and the presence of Aboriginal people could be erased.

Perhaps the most common way of explaining the sudden decline in the Aboriginal population in Eden–Monaro, well into the late nineteenth century, was to blame Aboriginal people for killing one another in 'black massacres'. To emphasise the violent nature of indigenous societies, newspapers also carried repeated stories of 'Aboriginal cannibalism'.[15] In pioneer recollections, stories of black-on-black violence survive far more frequently than white-on-black violence. Europeans who found themselves in a situation in which they needed to explain the decline in Aboriginal populations without incriminating their fellow colonists often seized on evidence of Aboriginal warfare as a convenient explanation. Even the language of those men who had a relatively deeper understanding of

Aboriginal culture, such as George Robinson, could betray this tendency. When Robinson passed through Bega in 1844, he remarked that 'an *exterminating* warfare by the Twofold Bay natives and their allies has nearly depopulated the country; happily their feuds have ceased, and *the few that remain* live in peace' (my italics).

Harping on tribal warfare was sometimes used as a way of accounting for population decline before Europeans arrived, thereby absolving settlers of complicity in the killing of Aboriginal people.

In the Bega Valley area, the story of a battle between the Monaro and Bega tribes, witnessed by one of the first British settlers to enter the Bega Valley, WD Tarlinton, quickly became a myth of Aboriginal self-destruction. In pioneer recollections published in local newspapers and in early local histories, the story of this battle that allegedly left scores of Aboriginal men dead was conveniently positioned after Tarlinton's 'valuable discovery' of the Bega Valley. The white man discovered the land and the 'Aborigines' dutifully destroyed one another the very next day. Like the 'empty land' myths in the Afrikaner histories of South Africa, the first wave of pioneer histories of European settlement on the south coast of New South Wales told the story of a land left for the taking.

In 1882, WD Tarlinton, then in his seventies, was seen as one of 'founding fathers' of 'civilisation' in the Bega Valley. Early that year he officiated at the opening of the Cobargo Bridge. After leading a small crowd in a walk over the bridge, the pioneer hero broke the mandatory bottle of champagne against the bridge and named it 'the Cobargo'. He then turned to address the crowd, explaining how he had been led to the valley by 'three blacks' who fortunately understood the language of the twenty-three 'Cobargo blacks' he encountered. He told them that his party had explained things 'as best they could' to the 'Aborigines', and 'friendly relations were soon established between them'. Tarlinton then 'looked well around and saw that he had made a valuable discovery'. According to newspaper reports of Tarlinton's speech, Aboriginal people had no objections to Tarlinton's occupation of their land — 'as the white settlers treated the natives with prudence and consideration, there was never any trouble with them'. Finally, Tarlinton reminded his audience what had happened to the 'Aborigines'. 'When I came down … Aborigines roamed the district and blacks from the tablelands frequently journeyed down to make war on the Cobargo blacks.' Tarlinton's story of the Aboriginal war at Cobargo was recounted in the first history of the Bega Valley written by AB Jauncey in 1916.

> About the beginning of the last century the Monaro tribes had encroached on the land of the coast tribes, and the savages' way of settling disputes was by war. As was usual, the chiefs met beforehand to decide all particulars, and the spot chosen for the combat was where the Cobargo Showground now is. This was about 1830, and the actual fight was witnessed by the late W.D.

Tarlinton. The battle lasted all day, being won in the end by the Monaro tribes, and the next morning there were 60 dead blacks on the field.[16]

At this point, Aboriginal people disappeared from Jauncey's narrative. After several pages detailing the history of settler institutions, Jauncey mentions the Tarlinton episode in order to wipe Aboriginal people from the historical narrative, or more precisely, to allow them to wipe themselves out — conveniently on the very ground that would later become one of settler culture's most sacred sites, the showground.

In the twentieth century, Tarlinton's story of Aboriginal self-destruction became part of the fabric of settler history in the Bega Valley. In 1941, the Bega branch of the Rural Bank of New South Wales presented a dramatised history of Bega. In the opening scene of the play, an Aboriginal tribe from the Monaro plains descends into the Bega Valley exclaiming 'Bega! Bega! the beautiful!' Soon after they are seen in fierce battle with the Bega tribe. After the carnage, the story of settlement begins.[17]

Tarlinton's story reinforced the settler stereotypes of Aboriginal communities as warring savages. But it also revealed the way in which the common references to 'hostile' or 'dangerous Aborigines' were dropped when the pioneer concerned was not anonymous.[18] Conveniently, it was a genesis story which saw settler history begin not with the sealers or squatters who passed through fleetingly, often leaving a trail of devastation in their wake, but with the farmer who came to build a home for his family. History was settler history. Any form of transience, Aboriginal or European, was frequently cast outside history.[19]

By the mid-nineteenth century, the acquisition of firearms by Aboriginal people allowed colonists to accuse Aboriginal men of the reckless slaughter of their own people. In July 1886, two months after the anthropologist AW Howitt had visited Bega to attend an Aboriginal initiation ceremony he had himself instigated, the editor of the *Bega Gazette*, WH Braine, published a letter from John E Kelly, a man who had probably worked on Aboriginal missions. Braine made a point of endorsing Kelly's letter, remarking that there was 'too much truth in the following':

I have experience with the blackfellow … and I say of the blackfellow if you wish him to live on this earth happily … leave him alone. I have seen some hundreds of blacks who never saw a white man before they saw me … What became of them? the white man killed but very few of them … nor did grog have much to do with their destruction … [After the blackfellow is] taught the use of the gun off he goes to a missionary camp to shoot his next door neighbour butcher his piccaninnies plunder his camp and bring home his gin … I knew one [blackfellow] who had hundreds of notches in the stock of his musket, and each notch told of the departure of a human soul from the body.

Nor was this a solitary instance, the man who could show most nicks was most honoured by his own tribe and indeed we must have hundreds of such examples in North Australia and Queensland this very day … Is it untrue that we cannot muster 1 per cent of the number we are known to have had eighty years ago? … [The white man has not murdered] one tenth of the number he has received credit for. No. Culture is the criminal, culture of the few, who, when thus armed, preyed upon their ignorant brethren.[20]

In this extraordinary letter, the responsibility for the death of Aboriginal people is laid entirely at the feet of gun-happy Aboriginal men. We are meant to believe that from Bega to Queensland, Aboriginal people were honouring men for shooting their own people. So powerful was the myth of Aboriginal self-destruction that it was sometimes used to explained the disappearance of 'authentic Aborigines'. In the recollections of Celia Rose, a social worker from the Moruya area, Rose was reported as claiming that 'when the blacks got drunk they would fight and kill each other, and now there is not one full blooded black left in this district'.[21]

On other occasions, settlers placed the blame for the shooting of Aboriginal people on Aboriginal stockmen. According to one pastoralist, HT Fleming, one of the early stations near Bombala was 'Ashton', taken up by a man named Atkinson who left 'Black Tom' in charge of the sheep. Fleming claimed that 'a lot of blacks were killed at Ashton by Black Tom in self defence and the bodies were burnt'. He also alleged that 'Murdering Range', not far from Bombala, was named after the murder of a white hutkeeper by a 'blackfellow'. In this case, the Aboriginal act of murder is etched onto the settlers' map of the landscape. Aboriginal people allegedly kill one another, burn the bodies of their brothers and sisters, and these acts of cruelty become core myths in settler oral history.[22]

Tribal warfare and black-on-black violence did occur, and this certainly affected Aboriginal population levels, but such conflict was also exacerbated by the disruption to traditional Aboriginal lifestyle caused by colonisation. The invading settlers forced Aboriginal people to alter their traditional movements and boundaries, often resulting in changes to power structures and the cultivation of a feeling of impotence in the face of enormous change. But perhaps the most interesting aspect of the surviving accounts of black-on-black violence is the way in which settlers in southern Eden–Monaro managed to transform these stories into myths which absolved colonists of any wrongdoing in the dispossession of Aboriginal people. The land was a battlefield which simply had to be mopped up before it was won; conquest was a matter of moving in to Aboriginal lands left vacant by warring tribes. As one local historian wrote as recently as 1999, 'fortunately for the settlers, few of their number were killed in interracial disputes with the Aborigines who appear to have largely confined hostilities to inter-tribal warfare'.[23]

In 1885, a journalist visiting Pambula noted the existence of a sacred gum tree 'on the near margin of the highway … across from Doherty's store'. It was locally known as the 'woman tree' because it represented a 'perfectly formed' female body. Locals and visitors stopped regularly to view the tree and saw it as an evocative and powerful symbol. The author suggested that it might be possible to see the tree differently, perhaps as 'the figure of a warrior bold, such as one of those who disputed sovereignty of the colony in the days before the advent of the white man, when the most degraded characters of the human race held possession of our island continent and engaged in their pristine form of warfare'.[24]

Local historians relied frequently on stories of natural disasters to explain the decline of the Aboriginal population. In the 1930s, Harry Wellings, the first historian to research the history of Eden, presented evidence of tribal warfare together with stories which had probably survived from the oral history of Aboriginal people in Eden, telling of the drowning of a whole tribe of Aboriginal people in caves to the south of Eden. Wellings wrote that 'the numbers of the Aborigines [had] dwindled very sadly towards the period at which white men came into contact with this section of Australia'.[25]

Emphasising natural disasters and tribal warfare also allowed another myth to flourish in settler culture: that there were few Aboriginal people left by the time the whites arrived. This belief created yet another escape hatch in explaining how the land was won. If there were few Aboriginal people remaining on the far south coast by the 1830s, how could there have been a frontier war? Thus the *Bega Gazette* claimed in 1872 that the Imlays, the first squatters to enter the area in the 1830s, had found themselves in 'undisputed possession of the soil'.[26]

As always, there were glaring contradictions in the accounts of the early colonial period that appeared in the local press after the 1860s. Only one week before the above claim appeared in the *Bega Gazette*, another historical feature on the early history of the area claimed that at the time the Imlays came there was 'a goodly number of tribes' around Bega who previously had been undisturbed in their 'original possession of the soil'.[27] If so, on what grounds are we to believe that Aboriginal people relinquished possession of this soil?

Well before the 1870s, it was common for settlers in southern Eden–Monaro to acknowledge Aboriginal people as the 'original possessors of the soil'. But references to Aboriginal people as 'owners', or as people who had the distinction of being the 'first into the district', afforded them no rights to land.[28] Their possession of the soil was 'original' only, a primeval ownership that lasted until such time as it was supplanted by British civilisation, a possession in waiting for dispossession. There was therefore no contradiction in George Haydon's advice to British emigrants in the 1840s that his book would be of interest 'to those who intend emigration [to Australia] and are about occupying the lands of the Aborigines'. Once occupied by colonists, the land no longer belonged to the 'original possessors of the soil'.[29]

Shield tree, photographed near Bega, c. 1950.
[By permission of Bega Family History Museum]

When WD Tarlinton helped to organise the first Cobargo Show in 1889, the *Bega Standard* claimed that the Showground, where Tarlinton had first camped fifty years earlier, was then unknown, 'except for the blacks'. The Aboriginal meeting place had become the site for the pageant of the settlers' agricultural show. The indigenous presence on the land was displaced swiftly not because Aboriginal people and settlers chose different places, but because they often chose the same place.[30] Yet despite the settlers' conquest of Aboriginal places, the public silence over the prior occupation of Australia was not always matched by a personal or inner silence.

From the moment the settlers arrived in south-eastern New South Wales, they encountered physical evidence of Aboriginal culture. When king tides lashed the coast and eroded the sand dunes, the settlers found the bodies of Aboriginal people in the sand, 'doubled over in the fashion of burial'. When they searched for oysters at Wapengo Lake, north of Bega, they found their bodies in layers in the banks of the tidal lake. When they walked the land they saw the corroboree rings, the canoe and shield trees, the middens and the burial grounds. On the coast they came across the caves that Aboriginal people had used for shelter. When they ploughed the land they found Aboriginal bones, teeth, axes and tools. With every layer of the surface removed, the land 'without a past' revealed an antiquity the settlers failed to comprehend.

In the early twentieth century, Aboriginal women around Bega continued to make their baskets as they had always done from the rushes near the lagoon. As the settlers moved backwards and forwards on the old punt crossing the Bega River, the women would sell their baskets. Just as the first settlers in Sydney took the shells from the middens around the harbour foreshore and crushed them to make the lime for their sandstone cottages and public buildings, on the far south coast builders 'carted dray loads of shells and bones' from middens at Moon Bay and used them in the building of the old Bank which still stands in Bega's main street today. The material history of indigenous culture was recycled into the temples of settler history, into homes, banks, post offices and police stations.

Sometimes the settlers collected Aboriginal artefacts as trophies or odd items of interest. On other occasions they simply destroyed them or threw them away. In Bega, one Aboriginal elder is said to have given an early settler a large stone marked with the traditional boundaries of indigenous societies on the far south coast. The settler's grandsons destroyed the stone. In the words of Sister Bernice Smith in the 1960s, one of Bega's first historians, when settlers did show any of the objects they had collected to Aboriginal people, 'they would never speak, they would just look away ... some of their sacred stones, simple little things that we wouldn't think of, would be part of their life, part of their treasures. The spirit world is very very important to them still'. The settlers' contact with the material evidence of Aboriginal culture was a constant reminder that *they* were not the original possessors of the soil. Perhaps this is one reason why they struggled with the knowledge of how the land was won.[31]

At Bombala, on the Southern Monaro, an area where historian Keith Hancock claimed that Aboriginal people 'quietly submitted' to the squatters, the evidence available in some of the earliest local newspapers suggests that the settlers were fully aware of the manner in which the land had been made their own. In an editorial in one Bombala paper in 1863, little more than thirty years after the first squatters reached the Monaro, the editor described the fate of Aboriginal people on the Monaro in graphic and candid language:

> People generally look upon the savages of our country as a race to whom it is folly to show mercy. On the outward stations they are almost invariably treated with reckless barbarity. A gun is levelled at them as soon as they make their appearance on the run … The blacks entertain the greatest dread of the whites. This terror has been inspired in them by a long course of barbarous actions.

Although the editor was keen to point out the callousness of the squatters 'in the North' of Australia, his comments were not specific to one geographical area. Nor did he make any attempt to dissociate the Monaro from what he described on several occasions as the general pattern of 'reckless barbarity'.[32] Little wonder that he later summarised Australian history with a deliberately understated and wry aside: 'romantic events are not common in this country'.

In 1875, on the eve of the centenary of American Independence, the Colonial Secretary requested copies of newspapers from across Australia which were to be sent to the United States to an international exhibition at Philadelphia, in an attempt to give Americans some picture of life in Australia. Many papers in New South Wales devoted one issue to the event and almost all set out to explain the genesis of their community. Sometimes the Aboriginal presence was invisible, sometimes it was hinted at, and sometimes it was presented as tragic decline. After offering the predictable spiel that told of those 'daring and dashing young Australians' who had 'opened up' the Monaro in the late 1820s and 1830s, the editor of the *Bombala Times* attempted to explain how the indigenous presence had been dealt with on the Monaro:

> We must not think that the lands taken up and acquired by these early settlers were done so without meeting opposition from the native lords of the soil. The native chiefs and their dusky retainers of both sexes were seized with terror at the first sight of the white man, and cautiously hid themselves, sending messengers to their different tribes to 'pialla' the news of this wonderful invasion of their territory; but soon their timidity was removed.[33]

Here was blunt acknowledgment of Aboriginal resistance on the Monaro and the eventual victory of the colonists. The colonial project began as an invasion, and in a culture convinced of its own racial superiority it was entirely appropriate for the editor of the *Bombala Times* to use the adjective 'wonderful'. There was nothing to hide: those Aboriginal people remaining after the victory were deemed to be 'proud to be the guest of the pale faced invader'.[34]

Running side by side with these frank and patronising accounts of dispossession were equally frank admissions of the brutality of the frontier wars, yet with one important difference: the triumphant tone of 'this wonderful invasion' was accompanied by disquiet, sympathy and regret, occasionally bordering on guilt. This way of responding to the reality of the frontier began with the first years of settlement in Eden–Monaro and survived even during the height of Social Darwinism in the late nineteenth century.

Exposing the true nature of British colonisation was always easier for those who were not British. When the Austrian John Lhotsky passed through the Monaro in the 1830s he condemned the English approach to 'Aborigines' as 'a cheap and easy philanthropy'. 'I consider this extinction of an entire race … as one of the greatest blames of all the different governments … in these colonies [, more often] … owing to the whites and not to the blacks'.[35] Lhotsky's fellow countryman, Baron Charles Von Hugel, was no less scathing shortly after he visited Twofold Bay in 1834: 'With very few exceptions, the Englishmen living [in the colony of New South Wales] show no sympathy whatever for the New Hollanders, about whom they know only that they are black, live in the woods and are useless as labour'.[36]

When George Augustus Robinson travelled through the far south coast in 1844, he reflected in his journal on the impact of colonisation on Aboriginal people. After listing the vices and diseases which Aboriginal men and women had 'contracted [through] European barbarity and cruelty', Robinson asked forlornly, 'What have we Europeans to say to these wrongs?'[37]

Many men like Lhotsky, Von Hugel and Robinson, who moved widely through the frontier, witnessed the suffering of Aboriginal people at close hand. The tradition these men represent, of lamenting the effects of colonisation on indigenous people and castigating British settlers for their unjust treatment of Aboriginal people, probably has its origins in the raw emotional power of the stories told by the men and women who confronted the human tragedy of dispossession. This legacy could be denied or transferred to others, or even legitimised as the collateral damage of colonisation, but it could not be extinguished.

One of the most moving reflections on the history of dispossession came in the editorial of the *Moruya Examiner* on 26 January 1888, the day of New South Wales' founding. If, as TS Eliot wrote, 'human kind can only bear so much reality', this editorial, written by Reginald Herbert Barlow, a man who had the confidence of Aboriginal people on the south coast, goes close to explaining why.

Whatever we have to boast of having done in the past 100 years, it certainly is not in having done our duty to the aboriginals ... We came amongst them for our own advantage, there was not a shadow of pretence that we intended to improve them religiously or morally, [or] physically ... It was [only] just and natural that they should resent our coming, especially as they saw as time advanced what our real object was, namely, taking from them the land which the All Wise had given them for a home. And at the present time when we are thanking and praising that same All Wise Being for having done so much for us during the last century, might we not also ask him to pardon the tremendous sins we have committed, not only in having taken from the aboriginals their lands without one iota of compensation, but also having debased them in every manner conceivable. Depend upon it ... the time will come when we in Australia at large shall pay heavily for our shameful treatment of a race which we have supplanted ... the subject is painful and very humiliating to think upon.[38]

The fact that editorials such as this were written at the same time as the pioneer legend was being created is evidence of the diverse nature of settler responses to the history of dispossession in Eden–Monaro. Throughout the twentieth century, the laments would continue, in newspapers and local histories. As early as 1931, Harry Wellings, a local historian writing in the local press in Eden, admitted that the 'Europeans had much to be blamed for' in their treatment of Aboriginal people. 'Truly', he said, 'the Aboriginal population of Australia ... has little to thank European invasion for ... In the march of so called progress little consideration is given to original inhabitants when the white race sets out to possess a land'.[39] Statements such as these were never the most frequent response, and they were sometimes patronising, pleading or guilt-ridden. But they did acknowledge the killing, the shootings in retaliation for spearing stock, the taking of land, the ignorance of Aboriginal culture, the poisoning of food or milk and the driving away — though the perpetrators almost always remained anonymous.

In many of the pioneer recollections published in the 1880s and 1890s, it was often felt necessary to explain what happened to Aboriginal people. Explaining what happened sometimes involved one person denying that they were responsible for Aboriginal deaths but implying that others were. In 1898, the obituary of the Bega pioneer William Bassingthwaighte provided one example:

Good old Bassingthwaite! He is one of the last race of pioneers unhappily extinct. He told me he never had any collision with the blacks and never shot one in all his life ... He said I do not remember any humane man with ... the just sympathies of a gentleman who ever had any serious trouble with the Australian Aboriginal.[40]

From the moment the pioneer legend was created in the mid to late nineteenth century, pioneers were revered as pipe-smoking grandfathers reclining on vine-clad verandahs. They were the 'old hands', the bearers of stories from 'olden times' imbued with a special wisdom.[41] And so another means of distancing Australians from the frontier wars was found — pushing the past back. From the early 1870s, historical features in the local press were already referring to the 1830s as a decade that was almost 'primeval'. By the 1880s and well into the 1920s, journalists were making clear that the present generation was far removed from those who had opened up the land only a few years earlier. This had apparently been done 'years ago' by their 'ancient departed fathers'. As early as the passing of the Free Selection Act in 1861, the animosity towards the squatters provided an opportunity for settlers to wash their hands of any responsibility for the inhumane treatment of Aboriginal people. In 1865, the editor of the *Monaro Mercury* condemned the squatters for exploiting labour and encouraging shepherds to drink their wages before finally taunting them with the following rhetorical question: 'has there been no cruel extirpation of the degraded and unfortunate Aborigines of the country, or is it a worse crime to swindle a white man than to murder a black one?'[42]

When it suited those involved in the politics of land settlement to identify with Aboriginal Australians they did so. And the anti-egalitarian ethos of the squatters only provided further incentive for the next generation of settlers to distance themselves from the 'olden times' of the frontier. It was also easier to moralise about the actions of past generations than those of the present. In 1893, one newspaper correspondent claimed that the Australians who journeyed to Paraguay had more courage than those who recently 'felt it their duty to go and chop up poor blackfellows in Africa, after their fathers had Christianised the blacks of Australia with poison and bullet and then in later days [spent their time] kidnapping in the South Seas to replenish the blacks slaughtered by our dear departed fathers'.[43] Frontier violence could be blamed on the 'elitist' squatters, their ignorant convict workforce, or nondescript 'exiles', anyone except the 'pioneer'.[44]

The desire of many Australians today to distance the present generation from those who fought on the frontier or removed Aboriginal children from their families is another example of pushing back the past, partly in order to wash our hands of responsibility for dispossession. Of course Australians have always been selective. They are frequently prepared to reach back to the early colonial period in an effort to trace the origins of national and cultural uniqueness. Yet when dealing with responsibility for Aboriginal dispossession, they prefer to distance themselves, naming the British or the 'previous generations' as the perpetrators — as if the frontier wars occurred in some pre-Australian time.

The process of distancing the past in settler culture contrasts sharply with Aboriginal culture where, as historians Bain Attwood and Andrew Markus have rightly pointed out, oral history tends to produce accounts of the past that empha- sise its continuity with the present rather than its difference from the past.[45] In this sense, Australians are still not reconciled. One culture pushes away from the past as the other moves forward, the past inseparable from the people's everyday life.

The main street of Narooma, on the south coast of New South Wales, photograph by William Corkhill, 1901. [TT292, by permission of National Library of Australia]

4

EMILY'S
STORY

In May 1870, Emily Wintle sat in Sydney's Central Criminal Court, the primary witness in a quite extraordinary case. Barely 20 years of age, she was there to explain events that had taken place six years earlier, late on the evening of Sunday, 9 April 1864. For most of her childhood, Emily had lived at 'Bredbatoura', the Tarlinton family homestead near Cobargo, 40 kilometres north of Bega.

Emily had been 'taken in' by the Tarlintons at 6 years of age, after her parents' relationship had descended into endless quarrelling and violence and her mother had decided she could no longer look after her. Like many young women at the time, Emily assisted her foster family with domestic chores in exchange for her board and lodging. On this particular evening in 1864, Mr and Mrs Tarlinton were away in Sydney and would not return for several weeks. Emily, then 14, was at home alone, together with her sister, the Tarlintons' daughters Elizabeth and Margaret, and the Tarlintons' sons Alexander, James and Thomas.

On Saturday evening, 8 April, Emily had gone to bed around 9 pm. In the room next to her, as always when their mother was away, slept the Tarlinton sisters, Margaret and Elizabeth. Shortly after going to bed, Emily was woken by the sound of the sisters moving to an upstairs bedroom. They were forced to pass through Emily's room to reach the stairs. Emily immediately got out of bed and stood at the foot of the stairs, listening to the sound of Elizabeth and Margaret moving about upstairs. They had never slept upstairs before. She waited for around ten minutes and went back to bed.

The next day, Margaret Tarlinton was ill and remained in bed. Emily visited Margaret in her room, and tried in vain to comfort her as she 'roared out with pain'. Later that same evening, Sunday, 9 April, Emily and her sister again slept in the parlour where they had slept the night before. After a few hours, she was woken by the sound of a baby crying in the upstairs room. Again, Emily got out of bed and stood at the foot of the stairs. She listened to the baby's cries until she heard Margaret Tarlinton call out, 'You little wretch, you have caused me all this pain'. It was midnight. Emily went back to bed but was unable to sleep, kept awake by the Margaret's constant moaning and the cries of the child.

'Just before daylight', Emily heard Elizabeth come downstairs. She lay awake, her eyes closed, her body perfectly still, as Elizabeth stood for a moment over her

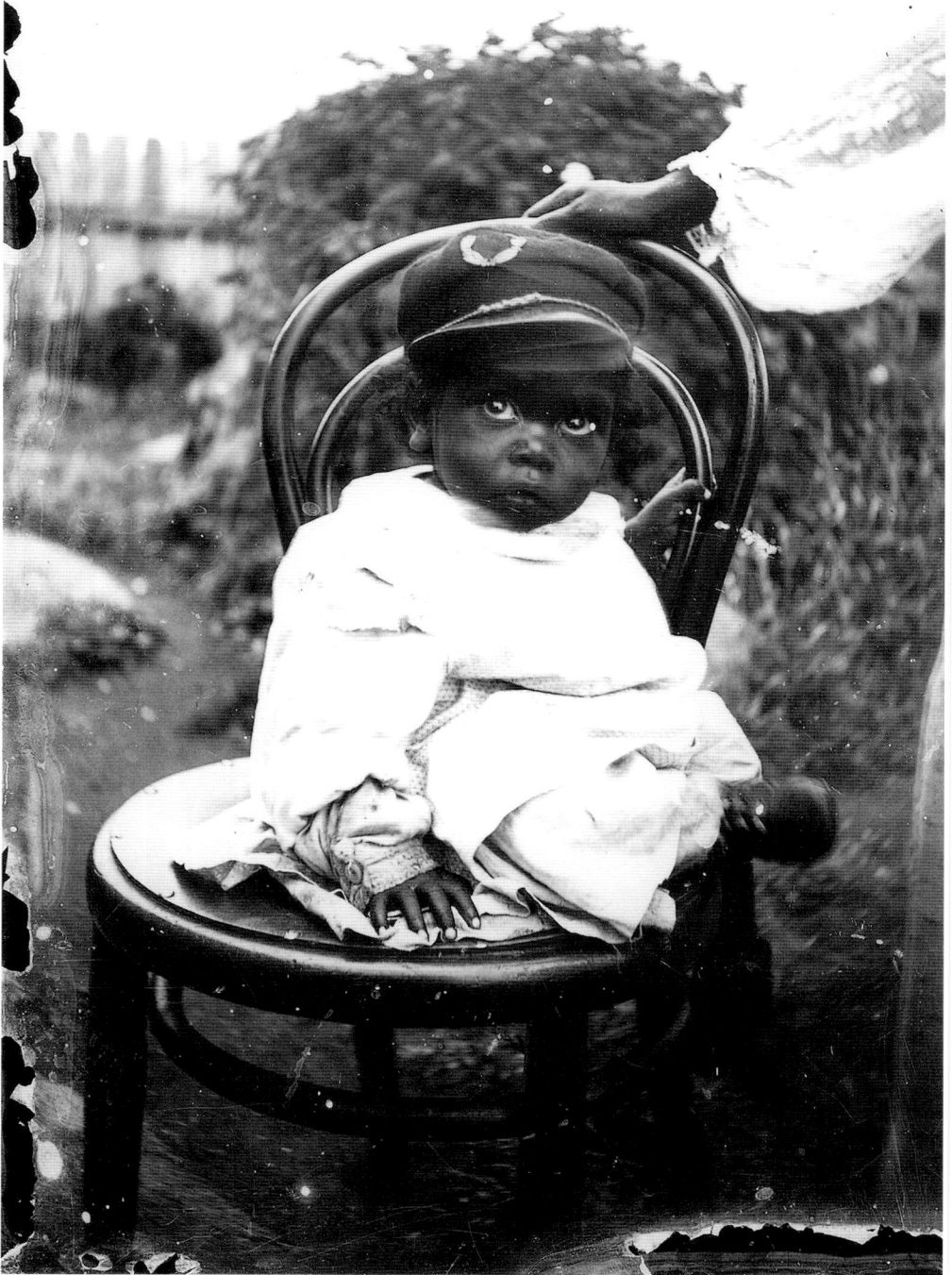

Young Aboriginal boy on a chair, south coast of New South Wales, photograph by William Corkhill, 1905. [TT380, by permission of National Library of Australia]

bed. Certain that Emily was asleep, Elizabeth hurried back upstairs before coming down again, but on this occasion Emily could see she was carrying a 'black bundle'. When Elizabeth had passed through her room and out the front door of the house, Emily got out of bed and looked through the parlour window. She watched as Elizabeth took a spade hidden in the raspberry bushes, walked through the garden and down into the orchard. Alarmed, Emily hurried back to her room, put on her clothes, and walked round the back of the house. As she approached the water closet, she saw Elizabeth Tarlinton digging a hole near the fence. She waited quietly, being careful not to be heard. When Elizabeth had finished digging, Emily saw her place the 'black bundle' in the hole and lay a wooden board on top, before filling the hole with earth.

After Elizabeth had gone back upstairs, Emily scratched away the earth with her bare hands. It was now daylight and she was worried that 'the blacks' would see her and think that it was her child. Removing the soil, she found the body of a female infant with black curly hair, its skin dark and yellow. Wrapped in a black silk petticoat, the child had a piece of white calico tied around its neck. Emily washed the child's head with water, wrapped it in the petticoat and reburied it. The next morning, she saw bloodstains on the floor of the upstairs room where Margaret had given birth to the child. They appeared to be smeared, as if someone had tried to wash them away with soap and water.

She told the court how two 'darkies', Dick Bolloway and 'Briney', who had been hands on the station for three or four years, were often seen 'skylarking' with the Tarlinton sisters. Mrs Tarlinton had apparently once found Dick's trousers under Margaret's mattress. William Tarlinton, the man who 'discovered' the Bega Valley, had also one day found his daughter Margaret and the 'half-caste' Bolloway 'skylarking'. He threatened to break Margaret's legs if he saw them at it again.

One month after the birth of the child, Mr and Mrs Tarlinton had returned from Sydney, and Margaret had recovered from the birth. Her conscience racked with guilt, Emily told Margaret what she had witnessed that Sunday evening. She felt she should reveal the information to others. Margaret warned her that 'she would fetch her into it' if Emily dared to tell anyone. Sometime later, when Emily was about to make her first confession, she asked Margaret what she should say to the priest. She was worried that if she didn't confess what she had seen, she would remain in a state of sin. Margaret told her it was not Emily's sin to confess. She told Emily she would confess to the priest herself, and again warned her not to tell anyone. Emily tried to do as she was told. But she would eventually tell Margaret's mother what had happened. Foolishly, she also told her father, the person who had beaten her as a small child, and who now threatened to 'punish her' if she revealed the matter to anyone.

Emily stayed on at the Tarlinton homestead until she was 18, and remained silent. One year later, she married, immediately telling her husband what she had seen five years earlier. In October 1869, her husband supplied the information to local police. Four weeks later, a Bega police officer, Senior Constable Cleary, visited the Tarlinton homestead. He informed the Tarlinton family of the allegations, and why he had come, although by this time they were no doubt well aware of the purpose of his visit. Digging in several places, Cleary uncovered the bones of an 'infant' close to where Emily had told him the child had been buried.

In court, Emily's evidence was cast in doubt by the counsel for defence. He alleged that her husband, a man who had selected land close to Tarlinton's property, was known to be in dispute with Tarlinton. He also cast aspersions on Emily's character, exposing her violent family history and her uncertainty about the child's date of birth. The witness who Emily claimed had told her Margaret was pregnant when she visited the Tarlinton homestead six years earlier, now denied she had made the remark. Finally, doctors called in by the court to comment on the bones found by the police stated that while they were probably that of a newborn child, they were in such an advanced state of decay that little could be proved by examining the few that remained. Remarkably, at the end of the case, the foreman of the jury stated that he did not wish to hear the judge sum up, and found the prisoner not guilty. She could leave the court, he said, 'without a stain on her character'.

Reporting the judgment, the editor of the *Bega Gazette* expressed relief, claiming Emily's allegations had been little more than a vindictive conspiracy against a 'most respectable resident in the district'. But reading the transcript of the proceedings, it is difficult to believe that Emily's allegations had been fabricated merely for the benefit of scoring points in a petty squabble. The detail is too precise, and the evidence, though not conclusive in a court of law, certainly suggests a high probability of truth. Emily's recollection of events, driven in part by her desire as a recently confirmed Catholic to be truthful, appeared convincing. She was not wealthy, she was uneducated, and she had little to gain by going through the ordeal of telling her story in a Sydney court, 500 kilometres from her home. It would have been much easier if she had remained silent. Instead, she left the court with her reputation tarnished, while that of the founding squatter's family, and his daughters Margaret and Elizabeth, remained intact. Emily's sister, still living at the Tarlinton homestead, had refused to speak to her from the moment she went to the police with the information.[1]

At the time I came across this story in the local papers, I was writing the following section on the making of settler history in south-eastern New South Wales. The more I thought about the case, the more I came to see how much Emily's story revealed. The veracity of the story was still important to me, but I would never be able to know or prove it to be true. I could only come to a conclusion based on my retrospective interpretation of events. Yet in her story, the story of an illegitimate child, born of an Aboriginal father and a white mother, there are many implicit meanings. The midnight burial of an Aboriginal child, strangled at birth, was emblematic of the settlers' desire to erase the history of sexual relations between black and white, especially those between European women and Aboriginal men, and ultimately, Aboriginality itself. But it also erased a history of frivolity and sexual pleasure, a history of shared humanity that did not fit comfortably in the prevailing ethos of settler culture.

When I thought of the earth being shovelled hastily over the child's body, I came slowly to see it as a metaphor for the repression of the memory of indigenous Australia. But in Emily's story, I saw a different metaphor, one that would eventually break the cycle of repression, and help to create a different history.

MAKING
SETTLER
HISTORY

The squatters, lyrically, from Sydney
are fanning out to *make the nation*;
their sheep and drays, their hapless shepherds,
are vanishing in westward haze,
the smoke fires of the myall blacks
a distant colouration.

GEOFF PAGE,
from 'A Classic Text'[2]

It is true Bega has no antiquated past
[but] … if Bega has no past, it has a delightful present.

VISITOR TO BEGA,
1885[3]

In a land deemed for so long to be without a past, the urgent need to create history in Australia encouraged settlers to distance themselves quickly from the early colonial period. It might also explain why there often appears to be a race to become 'historic' in Australia, as if every park stump is a historical treasure. Because the time before Cook has been seen as a time before history, this has tended to generate an even greater urgency to create a colonial antiquity — 'olden times' — a period in between darkness and the coming of civilisation when the land was won.

The frequent references in pioneer recollections to the 'first white man' — or 'the first white child to be born' — are an attempt to create a history of founding moments. The pioneer history of Eden–Monaro overflows with stories of the first white man:

- the 'first white man who trod foot on Pambula flat'
- the 'first white man to travel through the district in that direction'
- the 'first white woman to cross the river … in a log canoe'
- 'almost the first white woman to come to Bega'
- 'the first to drive a bullock team to dry river'
- the 'first man to put bells on cattle and horses'

- the 'first white born on the southern side of Bega river'
- the 'first to drink the water of Slacks' creek'
- the first to 'kill fresh beef'.

With each step of the 'first white man', the 'darkness' of thousands of years of Aboriginal occupation was replaced with a new creation story.[4]

When the pioneer WD Tarlinton opened the Cobargo Bridge in 1882, he reminded his audience that he was the 'first white man who had set foot on the ground where Cobargo now stands'. Although Tarlinton's use of the adjective 'white' implicitly acknowledged a prior Aboriginal presence, it also served to deny its legitimacy. The Aboriginal presence was obliterated by the 'white' creation story.[5]

On occasions, the kudos to be had in settler culture from being seen as the 'first white' resulted in farcical arguments between settlers in the local press as to who had been the first white to be born 'on the northern side of the river'. At other times it encouraged some amusing hyperbole. One pioneer obituary in 1874 was devoted to 'Big Jack' (John Hayden). 'Big Jack' was alleged to have carried several sacks of wheat on his back from Pambula to Bega in a day, the seeds from these sacks resulting in the first planting of wheat in the valley. After delivering the seeds of civilisation, he then carried 100 pounds of flour on his back for 17 miles. Yet despite his talent for long-distance sack-carrying, 'Big Jack' was reported to be so 'fleet of foot' he could 'run in the wildest bullock on foot'.[6]

One of the most interesting aspects of the 'first white stories' in south-eastern New South Wales is the manner in which they focus on the farmer-settler. In 1980 one resident of Bega, Jack Burgess, described how he had descended from the 'first white child to survive in the Bega Valley'. His tale echoed a biblical creation story — the role of the nameless Aboriginal woman being merely to act as a prop for the coming of God's chosen people.

> In the year 1844 Fred Moon who married Jane Duff, set out from Camden Park and reached Braidwood. From there they decided to move with the first sheep for the Bega Valley [Kameruka], and settle in the valley. They travelled overland from Braidwood to Broulee, south of Bateman's Bay, with their sheep. From Broulee they had to take the sheep in small numbers by boat, to Moon Bay en route for Kameruka. Arriving at Moon Bay, Mrs Moon gave birth to a daughter, with assistance from an Aboriginal woman. The daughter was named Caroline, and the birth took place by the spring which is still at Moon Bay. Then, still in the year 1844, Fred Moon set off on foot to seek assistance for his wife and infant daughter, left at Moon Bay. The clothes were pinned to his own clothes on his back for safety. Caroline Moon was the first white child to survive, who was born in the Bega Valley. Time passed, and Caroline married George Burgess ...[7]

This first white story is truly a 'creation story', unlike the first white story which tells of the survivors from the wreck of the *Sydney Cove*, who walked from near the present New South Wales–Victorian border to Sydney in the summer of 1797. These men are often described in local histories as 'the first white men to traverse the coast', walking a distance of 965 kilometres, men 'with fair hair and blue eyes dressed in rags', left to the mercy of the 'natives'. Their story is a pilgrim myth, but it is not a myth of pilgrim settlers, merely of pilgrim white skin. The men are seen as forlorn figures, desperate castaways who are lost and alone. They walk not to create history but to escape an alien land, their solitary hope being to find Sydney. Only the first white babe wrapped in the settler's shawl is able to make history.[8]

Historian Graeme Davison has written of the way in which 'local history links our aspirations for community to a sense of place, and our fragile present to a seemingly more stable past'. Local historians are often born and live in the area about which they write. Even today, much pioneer history in Eden–Monaro is written from the perspective of settler culture, frequently on bended knee — no doubt out of respect for the harsh conditions endured by those who 'blazed the trail' or the institution which has funded the project. The role and duty of the local historian is to build and defend the heritage of the community, and it is not hard to understand why many find it hard to write critically of the history of their community.[9]

In the postwar period, more than 250 historical societies have been formed in New South Wales, most of them since the 1970s.[10] In south-eastern New South Wales the majority of historical societies were formed in the 1960s. As Davison suggests, many were focused on family history or 'ancestor worship'. When a historical society was formed in Bega in 1967, the editor of the *Bega District News* exclaimed: 'the present generation of historians must uncover this history before it is too late … [and secure information] on the settlement by the white races of this district'.[11]

At a time when settler culture was seeking to deepen its understanding of 'white' history and family connections, many Aboriginal Australians were still being separated from their families by state and territory governments. Initially, the renewed interest in local and regional history was motivated by a desire to save the built environment and to preserve the relics of the colonial past. On the far south coast, Australian historians such as RM Crawford, Professor of History at Melbourne University, and Manning Clark, Professor of History at the Australian National University, personally assisted the efforts of local historians to stimulate interest in Australian history. Both had strong links to the area, Crawford near Merimbula and Clark with his 400-acre property at Wapengo, north of Bega. In 1968, Crawford wrote to local papers in an attempt to save the old schoolhouse at Merimbula: 'This is an area rich in history and rich in historical documents and relics. Their collection and preservation is a matter of extreme urgency … The Merimbula schoolhouse is more than a local building; it is part of our past as a nation, and its preservation, intact and uncluttered, is a matter of national interest'.[12]

Like many historical societies across Australia, Crawford's plan was to find a home for history. The old schoolhouse, like the old post offices, courthouses, police stations and banks in other towns, would become the historical museum, most probably planted out with a 'native garden' — the perfect setting for the preservation of 'native history'. The belief that settler history needed to be sheltered and housed, to be made visible and given a physical presence, suggested that a people without a history were a people without a soul, a community without a shared memory. But it also indicated a sense of fragility.

At the time of the Bicentenary in 1988, interest in family history was deepening. The Bega Valley Genealogy Society was formed in 1987, its aim being to 'preserve the history of pioneer families in the Bega Valley'. Between 1987 and 1990, the society's members transcribed inscriptions from every gravestone in the shire. In their eyes, each gravestone was a 'historic site'. They claimed they wanted to save history from 'the ravages of time'. The bush reclaimed so many pioneer graves so quickly that the society's members saw maintaining settler history as a race against time. The society's search for the unmarked graves of early settlers called to mind the reverence for the Unknown Soldier. Special importance was placed on children's graves which, with their small leaning wooden crosses, bore the image of innocence and suffering so crucial to pioneer history. They were also nostalgic, like the ruins of homesteads that can be seen today from the highway, or the rows of old pines that lead to a stand of trees on a hillside where a homestead once stood.[13]

The local histories written in the 1970s and 1980s in Bega, Eden and Bombala emphasised the themes of pioneer hardship that had already formed the basis of the first pioneer stories told in the 1890s. Repeated tales of hardship were used to stress the indebtedness of the present generation to past generations, and to whip the 'lazy' citizens of the day into a frenzy of 'progressive' activity. On occasion, searching through the early newspapers of the area, I would come across stories that seemed to capture the spirit of the legend the settlers later came to remember and commemorate. Some of the events reported in the press which had never been given a life by local historians seemed more evocative than the more common tales of pioneers marching through the wilderness.

In late July 1914, on an isolated homestead not far from Delegate near Bombala, Ethel Roberts, 'three years and three months' of age, was playing together with other children in the paddock of her parents' farm. It was mid-afternoon, and her mother was inside the house, still within earshot of the children. Ethel's father was away at work. In the paddock, one of the children spotted a smouldering log and encouraged the others to gather sticks and debris to make a bonfire.

As the children piled on more and more wood, Ethel's clothes caught fire. Screaming, she ran towards the house. Hearing her daughter's cries, her mother rushed out of the house towards her. She tried desperately to put out the flames with her bare hands, burning them badly. Finally she managed to extinguish the flames with her own clothes. But by then Ethel's skin had been burned severely; only her legs had escaped the flames. A doctor was called, but came too late. All he could do was to dress the wounds and ease her pain. She died at 6 pm that night surrounded by her family. The funeral took place on Wednesday, 29 July and her body was buried in Delegate cemetery. Another wooden cross to mark the loss of a child's life.[14]

'Please Fence Me In.' A family photographed in front of their cottage at Tilba Tilba on the south coast of New South Wales by William Corkhill, c. 1900. [TT132, by permission of National Library of Australia]

The image of a child running, her clothes on fire, her mother rushing desperately towards her, arms outstretched, was one which affected me deeply. Perhaps it was because I also have a daughter of the same age, but it was also because this story seemed to encapsulate so powerfully the difficulties faced by many early settlers, especially women. Yet while the settlers identified with the story of Ethel Roberts and the many settlers who had lost their lives in bushfires or floods, or had struggled to get by at times of drought, they did not identify with the suffering of Aboriginal men, women and children on the frontier. In most of the local histories published after the 1970s, there was little attempt to address the true nature of the settlers' relations with Aboriginal people in south-east New South Wales, despite the emergence of a new version of frontier history in universities and sections of the media.

Instead, the renewed interest in settler history retained its focus on the history of the 'white race'. In Bega, history continued as a tale of settler attachment to the land, a history which had its origins in the 'first' settlers to come to the valley in the 1830s and was later consolidated with the Free Selection Act of 1861. Once the yeoman farmers 'covered the valley', the past could be imagined in agricultural terms, primarily through the vehicle of the agricultural show, which began in the early 1870s.[15]

In 1922, on the occasion of the fiftieth anniversary of the Bega Show, the 'Back to Bega movement' gathered the remaining pioneers in the district. Similar 'back to' movements would be formed in other rural towns in Australia between the wars. At Bega, crowds watched as the old men marched out onto Bega Showground like returning soldiers. 'Badges with the words Bega Pioneer, printed in gold', were pinned on their chests. Speeches were given eulogising the Anzacs of the frontier — 'they had made it possible for those who came after to live in comfort' and they had given Bega 'a sense of security'. Watching the pioneers lined up in military fashion, the medals shining on their lapels, the crowd stood with the same sense of solemn occasion displayed at the unveiling of memorial stones for those who had lost their life in the First World War. In the 1920s, the decade that schoolchildren, clergy, and townspeople first gathered at local showgrounds to pay tribute to the fallen diggers, investing the memory of war with a profound religiosity, they employed similar rituals of remembrance with the pioneers.[16]

'The Back to Bega' movement assembled a select cast of history-makers who, in the words of one resident, would bring 'before [the people of Bega] the history of their early settlement'.[17] Speeches given by local VIPs harped on the theme of the pioneers' discovery of a chosen land, a 'Palestine' where God's children were left to freely populate verdant pastures, a myth that would by the 1970s work its way into Bega Cheese advertisements. Throughout the twentieth century, the agricultural show became the primary means of creating history in the image of the agrarian male. Esteemed members of the Agricultural Society would frequently have their names memorialised in local buildings such as the 'Herbert Marsh Memorial Poultry Pavilion.'

Public representations of the area's past rarely mentioned Aboriginal Australians. In 1969, following an initiative by Bega Council and Bega Historical Society, a 'Thanksgiving and Historical Observance' parade was organised in Bega. Behind Anglican and Catholic cross-bearers walked the Mayor and the council, followed by local schoolchildren and their teachers. In the words of the editor of the *Bega District News*, 'the Christian Cross, on Saturday afternoon, was borne through the streets of Bega, surrounded by countryside clothed in lush green pastures, bright and crisp under the warm spring sunshine'.[18] In this parade, the history of the Bega Valley was made holy. The settler past was revered, the Bega Valley transformed into a God-given gift. This innocent and precious past the settlers were creating made it more difficult for them to listen to those who attempted to view the same history from an Aboriginal perspective in the 1970s and 1980s.

Because making history meant recreating the valley in the settlers' terms, this raised a problem: how could settlers create their own history when the names of so many towns and places were Aboriginal names? In 1922, one resident wrote that he found it 'painful' to think of Bega as an Aboriginal name. He preferred to believe in 'old world' history, where Bega was an Irish princess who lived in the seventh century and was 'the first professional nun of Britain'. Three days later came the following response:

> Look at it in this light. Here we have a tract of country, roughly 80 miles by 80, and almost every name, whether of town, village, mountain or river is Aboriginal. The few exceptions are named after local celebrities. In the centre of this tract of country we find Bega, a name that looks and sounds Aboriginal. Is it not odds on that the name is akin to the others — Wolumla, Pambula, Tathra, Cooma, Bega?[19]

Try as they might, settlers could not erase Aboriginal names from their map of the landscape, but they could ignore them, trivialise them, or pretend that the land had simply fallen into their laps. This was certainly the way in which many local historians continued to explain the area's history well into the 1970s and 1980s. *Their* history was *their* attachment to *their* land, born of *their* suffering. On the coast, at Eden, history was the story of the settler's battle with the sea.[20]

Unlike Bega, the township of Eden always seemed to have a more tenuous hold on the land. The history the settlers craved on one level was undermined constantly by the nature of the colonial economy. The economic patterns of European colonialism often worked against the creation of history as permanence and 'civilisation'. People shifted constantly in search of short-term wealth, communities sprang up and disappeared overnight, roads were built then let be, townships were deserted when minerals dried up.

But the sea was constant in Eden's history. Throughout the area today there are memorials to the men and women who lost their lives in shipwrecks, and in Eden, a museum devoted exclusively to whaling. At Rotary Park in Eden is the Shiralee Memorial Wall, erected after 'the loss of the Shiralee with all hands on deck in August 1978'. The memorial reads:

> The people of Eden had this wall constructed to serve as a memorial to all seamen who have sailed from this port, were lost at sea and have never returned … Those who go down to the sea in ships And follow their trade on great waters, these men have seen the works of God, And his waters run deep. Psalm 107.

Like Anzac, this memorial commemorates loss of life, in part because commemorating the loss of life is one essential ingredient in creating community respect for the past, but also because the sea is the vast space traversed in order to settle, the site of the journey and the leaving, the first pilgrimage and the first sacrifice of the settler caste. These would-be settlers' graves cannot be marked; their final resting place will always remain unknown.

If shipwrecks gave Eden a tragic past, whaling provided the adventure. From the moment the first recollections of Eden in the 1830s and 1840s appeared, whaling dominated settler memory. At Eden Killer Whale Museum, the romance of this past is epitomised in the skeleton of 'Old Tom', the killer whale with personality. 'Old Tom', since memorialised as a kind of Phar Lap of the deep, was for many years the leader of the killers who herded the Southern Right whales into the bay. In 1930, he was found dead on the shores of the bay. His skeleton was preserved as a permanent reminder of the special relationship between the killers and the whalers.

The memory of whaling in Eden is dominated by the figure of Benjamin Boyd, despite the fact he was not the first to whale there. Unlike those who preceded him, Boyd had no desire to live in a bark hut. By building his own town, 'Boydtown', Boyd took the first step in creating history. From the beginning of the tourist industry in New South Wales in the early twentieth century, tourists were encouraged to come to Eden to visit Boyd's 'ruins'. By leaving behind a town as stage set, Boyd made Eden more 'historic' than it could ever have been without him. Together with tales of whaling, newspaper features on local history in the twentieth century carried repeated tales of Boyd's bold plans and sudden departure. Remembering Boyd was again remembering failure, but more importantly it was remembering the spirit of the entrepreneur who 'made things happen'. Journalists wrote in melancholic tone when they saw the inscriptions on the stone windowsills of Boyd's lighthouse: 'Sacred to the Memory of Peter Lia, who was killed by a whale September 22nd 1881', or 'sacred to the memory of Jimmy the Killer who was drowned in 1896'. Above the front door of Boyd's Seahorse Hotel is inscribed 'Boydtown commenced A.D. MDCCCXLIII'. Each inscription the beginning of a sacred memory. But Boyd had also gone out of his way to leave another mark, as one reporter noted in 1903:

> Midway between East Boyd and the old lighthouse is a cave, about 10 feet by 12 feet ... That it was at one time the camping or, judging by the great quantity of mutton fish shells about, feeding ground of some of our Aboriginal race, there appears little doubt. Shells are to be seen in all directions, each and every one of them having a hole in the upper part, as if made by a spear or some sharp instrument. The smoked appearance of the cave tells of many a fire having burned in the interior. Here again we find Mr. Boyd's imprint, for well chiselled and deeply in the rock are the words 'B. Boyd BOZ 1843'.

The awareness of an Aboriginal past, if only as a kind of feeding ground, is overwritten by the chiselled words 'B. Boyd', the year 1843 signifying a more 'authentic' history than a scattering of mutton fish shells.[21] Together with the stories of shipwrecks and whaling, the creating of Eden's history through sea stories was aided by the commemoration of the voyages of men such as George Bass and James Cook. In 1970 and 1997, the bicentenaries of the respective journeys, celebrations took the form of historical re-enactments and period costume parades, by then a common feature of public commemoration of the past.

Commemorated from the early twentieth century with varying degrees of enthusiasm, and sometimes used merely as an excuse to call for development, the first journey of George Bass and his entry into Twofold Bay was presented as a heroic tale of discovery. In 1903, one Eden journalist claimed that 'the people of Eden do not intend to forget the day it was discovered, nor the hero who discovered it'.[22] Forget they did not, but after Bass left the bay in 1797 the history of Eden, as it is commonly told, waits until 1832 when the Imlays settled at Twofold Bay to begin again. As the editor of the *Bega District News* wrote on the occasion of the Cook Bicentenary in 1970, 'It was here [at Point Hicks on 20 April 1770] that Captain James Cook and his crew first made sightings of the new continent ... [but] it was not until some 59 years later that the white man came back to settle on the far south coast'.[23]

In this way, the story of Cook and that of the discoverer Bass is seen as legitimate history, as is the story of the first settlers. But the 40-year period between the late eighteenth century and the coming of the settlers in the 1830s, the period of the sealers and the early squatters, the period during which Aboriginal societies fought for their land, is missing from Eden's history. Settler history in Eden begins with the arrival of George Bass, then waits until the Aboriginal people are largely dispossessed before starting again. By the time the Imlays arrive in the early 1830s, Aboriginal people are represented as compliant, living on the fringe of white settlement.

In April 1970, Manning Clark came to Bega to speak at the 'Bega Captain Cook seminar'. In the audience of a hundred were people like Doug Otton, a local bean farmer, who told Clark proudly that he had a portrait of Cook in his lounge room 'in a place of honour'. Clark explained how Cook was 'associated with the coming of civilisation to a weird barbaric land'. On board the *Endeavour*, said Clark, Cook would propose a toast once a week 'to all pretty women'. Whether these comments helped to stimulate local interest in Cook's voyage is difficult to ascertain. Clark had come to Bega to help create enthusiasm for the Cook celebrations. As one newspaper editor remarked, 'the Cook celebrations *should* have special significance on the far south coast'. Yet the Cook celebrations had little impact in Eden, Bega or Bombala. Unlike the major capital cities, there were no reports of settler enthusiasm, and nor was there any questioning of the celebrations. There were no reports of Aboriginal protest and no attempts to discuss an Aboriginal perspective on the meaning of the celebrations. Like Manning Clark in 1970, the people of south-eastern New South Wales were content to see Cook as the first sign of 'civilisation'. The Bega Family History Museum was opened on the day of Clark's visit.[24]

Because so much of settler history had been built on denuding the land of an indigenous presence, there was little chance of settlers viewing history from an indigenous perspective. In the obituary of one pioneer, written in 1937, the author explained that although 'blacks were numerous and at times troublesome', Patrick McNamara had 'lived to see them almost entirely disappear. He saw the district transformed from a wilderness into its present state'.[25] McNamara's life epitomised the duty of the settlers. To make their history was to live to see Aboriginal people 'disappear'. For settlers to empathise with the suffering they and their ancestors had inflicted on Aboriginal people would be to risk destroying this history. If history was *their* suffering and curtsying before the pioneers, to admit complicity in Aboriginal dispossession would be to bring the whole house of cards tumbling down. It would also be painful. This was a confrontation which, when it finally began in the late 1980s, would take decades to resolve.

Some local historians in the 1970s and 1980s admitted openly how the culture of forgetting in south-eastern New South Wales had begun: 'in many cases descendants [of the pioneers had burned] what was written ... some of the early settlers wished certain episodes in their life to be forgotten'.[26] Instead of facing the truth of the settlers' relationships with Aboriginal people on the frontier, local historians told stories of settler suffering that had been caused by Aboriginal men seeking vengeance or spearing stock.[27] Recollections of 'pioneering days', published in the 1980s, still preferred to cast the settlers as victims.

Like the pioneers they sought to eulogise, they relied on similar strategies to deal with the history of dispossession: denial, placing the blame for the killings on convicts or the lower classes, trivialising Aboriginal resistance as just another obstacle or 'problem' in the face of the intrepid pioneer, implying that the physical hardship endured by the pioneers in 'opening up the land' outweighed any consideration of the morality of their actions, or finally offering crude characterisations of every historical actor regardless of their ethnicity. There were also times historians just left things unsaid, admitting that relations between the settlers and Aboriginal people had not always been 'friendly' but keeping the details to themselves.[28]

In his 1968 Boyer Lectures *After the Dreaming*, WEH Stanner wrote that the inattention of Australian historians to Aboriginal people was on such a scale it could not be explained simply by 'absent-mindedness'. He insisted that historians had carefully placed a window 'to exclude a whole quadrant of the landscape'. Over time, he said, this simple forgetting turned into a 'cult of forgetfulness practised on a national scale'.[29] In Eden–Monaro, Stanner's 'cult of forgetfulness' was present in the making of settler history. But settler history was more than simple forgetting. Even settlers who acknowledged the brutal treatment of Aboriginal people attempted to evade responsibility for dispossession. Each generation of settlers who succeeded the first wave of colonists attempted to distance themselves further from the frontier. Looking back to 'olden times', they excluded Aboriginal people in their desire to create history in their own image. Invading the continent meant not only 'civilising' the land, it meant 'civilising' history. While there were always those who tried to tell the truth of the frontier, admonishing their fellow men for their treatment of Aboriginal people, they were a minority.

In 1968, Stanner was optimistic that the 'Great Australian Silence' would buckle under the weight of the historical research that was then just beginning to undermine the traditional view of European settlement in Australia. But Stanner underestimated the immensity of the task and the time that would be required. In Eden–Monaro, as in other areas of rural Australia, the struggle to end the silence is ongoing. Stanner could not foresee that acknowledging the true history of settlement in Australia could also become a means of keeping Aboriginal people outside history. Some local historians in south-eastern New South Wales who had clearly read or been influenced by the new histories of the 1970s admitted the settlers' callous treatment of Aborigines' in general terms only. Acknowledging that the settlers had poisoned or shot Aboriginal people also allowed historians to remove them from their historical narrative. Once the unpleasantness was out of the way, history could continue as a non-Aboriginal story, as in this example from one historian writing in Merimbula in 1975. The early settlers 'risked attack from the Aborigines whose traditional hunting grounds they had invaded … By 1845 there were few Aborigines left in the district … towards the end of the century they were almost extinct. The old tribal corroboree grounds ... were deserted. The white settler had displaced or killed them all'.[30]

The difficulty today for the local historian is to build a sense of pride in the community's past and at the same time acknowledge that their town was founded on the violent theft of Aboriginal land. But the historian also needs to go beyond acknowledgment and explain why such injustice demands a recasting of settler history. In other words, the historian must try to explain how *our* history and *their* history are not separate histories, but part of the continuing story of post-1788 Australia. The local dilemma is the national dilemma. As Laurie Neal, a local historian of the Cooma area, pleaded in 1978 after struggling to admit 'Cooma's dark days': 'The [European] people of Monaro were not cruel, they did not set out to hate the Aborigine, harm him, shoot him or trap him. Their culture was a different one ... The settlers' education and breadth of understanding was just too limited to enfold a people of such a different culture and such different heritage'.[31]

Between 1970 and 2000, the people of Eden–Monaro would continue to struggle in reconciling their history. In part, this struggle was explained by the way in which they had come to imagine their own past.

PART THREE

abandonment

5

THE ARCHITECTURE
OF GRACE

One of the first histories of Australia I can remember reading is Manning Clark's *A Shorter History of Australia*. From memory, it was my textbook in Year 9 History. We were instructed to read a chapter each week, before the 'test' on Friday afternoons. Looking back on reading Clark as a 14-year-old in the early 1970s, there were two things that seem to have made a deep impression on me. The first was the paperback's dark green cover, with its rough map of Australia seemingly holding out the promise of knowing all the Australian history one would ever need to know. The second was the gravitas of Clark's prose and the moral drama he was able to invest in his stories, as if God were watching Australians' every move.

Today, I find it difficult to read Clark. But in his portrayal of Australian history as an epic struggle between the forces of Protestantism, Catholicism and the Enlightenment he opened my eyes to the importance of religious belief in understanding the psychology of settler Australia.

Twenty years after the first squatters entered Eden–Monaro in the 1820s, there was still no resident minister of religion. There were no churches and few signs of the civilisation the settlers had left behind in Britain. When Bishop Broughton toured New South Wales in the 1840s, he saw the purpose of his visit as keeping the settlers' faith alive until the church could arrive. The efforts of his ministers in travelling the 'scattered' settlements of the colony was necessary if the establishment of what Broughton called 'the Dominion of Atheism' in New South Wales was to be resisted.

One of the men who attempted to take up Bishop Broughton's call was the Reverend EG Pryce, who toured Eden–Monaro in 1843. After months spent wandering the Monaro plains, ministering to 'a people who [had] been shut out for years from participation of the means of grace', Pryce wrote to Broughton in January 1844, near the point of 'spiritual' exhaustion. He pleaded with Broughton to allow him 'a home to return to' where, 'if only for a few days at a time', he could return to relax and 'study'. The word 'scattered' appears repeatedly in Pryce's letters, as if he longed for the concentrated settlements of the towns of the Old World. Living in the bush, he feared for his own faith and discipline.

Without a 'stated and regular congregation' to attend, and only constant wandering in search of the exiled shepherds with their flocks and herds, he described himself as being in a state of 'spiritual sloth'. 'Cut off from all intercourse and communion with his brethren in the ministry', he felt adrift and alone. On the Monaro, the presence of his God was harder to sense, harder to believe. The vast open plains must have made him feel insignificant. His civilisation, without 'a home to return to', a memory only.[1]

What I found most striking in the letters of Pryce and Broughton was their need for the physical structures of faith and civilisation — the architecture of grace. These ministers of God struggled to retain their culture in a new land where the material structures that had previously given their beliefs meaning were absent. As Broughton wrote during his visit to the Monaro in February 1845, only when there was a 'visible centre of religion' would it be possible for the settlers to behold some manifestation, 'however humble, of the beauty of holiness'.[2] As the cultural identity of Aboriginal people was inseparable from the land, the settlers' faith and civilisation was often inseparable from bricks and mortar.

To understand the history of European society in south-eastern Australia is not only to understand the progressive construction of institutions, towns, cities and homes. It is also to appreciate the settlers' longings, their insecurities, and the things they believed they lacked. Reading the journals and press from the nineteenth century, I had the feeling that settler society in south-eastern New South Wales has always been a society in waiting. Together with the usual stories of pioneer hardship and the sacrifice of the Anzacs, the settlers' history of suffering began with their banishment to a land where, without churches, schools, courthouses and homes, their identity and culture was always incomplete.

Many settlers could find no home and no sense of belonging until this incompleteness was conquered. Without the theatrical props of civilisation and religion, they could not 'own' the land to which they had come. Without the architecture of grace, they would remain settlers forever.

'WAITING FOR CIVILISATION — LONGING FOR HOME'

Browning and Shakespeare would have
committed suicide in this country.

FRANCIS WEBB,
'A Drum for Ben Boyd' 1973[3]

There is no home in Australia and if home is
blotted out of the map then the virtues
of home must disappear.

Letter from HUGH MCKAIL
of Shellharbour to the *Illawarra Mercury*, 7 July 1856

In the first week of June 1834, the Austrian Charles von Hugel sailed from Sydney on a 'pleasure cruise' to Twofold Bay. After twenty-four hours at sea, strong south-westerly winds left his frigate no more than a 'few miles south of the entrance to Botany Bay'. Thinking that the weather had set in, von Hugel's party decided to drop anchor in the southern part of the bay. When the rain had subsided the next morning, they went ashore. Later that afternoon, after a disappointing day's collecting, they came upon the only house on the southern side of Botany Bay, 'situated on a green rise within gunshot of the shore'. It was just before sunset, 'the clouds tinged with dark red'. Approaching the house from the rear, von Hugel was the first to walk around to the front to look at the view:

Here I found a blind old man sitting alone. His folded hands were holding the cap he had taken from his head, covered with sparse white hair. His lips were moving slowly and his whole posture showed clearly that he was praying. This man fitted so perfectly into the surrounding scene that, reflected and moved, I looked down at him for a long time: lonelier still through having lost his sight, rather than by reason of the great remoteness of this place from human habitation; the very picture of stormy days now past, of faith as life's one last ray of hope, long obscured by fervent passions but now lighting up the inner life of this old man, as the sun in the west was lighting up the scene before it was overtaken by night … He has reached the point where his past is a matter of indifference … and the faith expressed on his features is worth more than a happy past life. The man appeared to be poor, and I was holding a few shillings in my hand to give to him, but I could not bring myself to disturb him, and at length I simply followed the rest of the party who had gone ahead.[4]

Von Hugel's parable of the blind man sitting alone at the edge of the world, anchored only by his whispering faith, is one of the most powerful images in colonial literature. Full of pathos and hope, it expresses the depth of European longing for salvation, a longing felt acutely in a distant colony which remained in 'a state of nature' — a land then believed to be without the scaffold of civilisation.

Like many areas of Australia, the history of European presence in Eden–Monaro is a history of that which was absent from the land as much as a history of what was found. Discovering the land meant discovering absence — and waiting for the 'means of grace' to arrive. When the Reverend EG Pryce toured the region in the early 1840s, he commented on the 'deplorable' and 'ungodly' state of the frontier society his party encountered: a collection of ex-convicts, ticket-of-leave men and other immigrants 'who have been long in the bush without the means of grace'.[5]

John Lhotsky also remarked on the absence of 'the consolatory or admonishing voice of a minister of religion' as he passed through the Monaro in 1834. He saw shepherds at Lake George near the site of present-day Canberra who passed their time by making straw hats while others spent their days in 'brutal apathy' leading a 'wretched existence in rags and misery', many of them infected with syphilis. The parlous state of settler society on the Monaro was mirrored in the indigenous society that Lhotsky described memorably as 'not civilised but corrupted'. Once beyond the limits of the colony, Lhotsky painted the scene on the Monaro in biblical terms, writing of a land of 'banishment' and 'desolation'. Neither republic nor monarchy, the Monaro, he said, was a place 'surrounded by absolute anarchy'.

In the colony of New South Wales, God's people were a people in need of sacred ground. But the land could not be made sacred until the church bells pealed and God's ministers consecrated the earth.[6] Still, there were settlers who believed that not even the presence of the church could save them from the depravity of life in the bush. As one newspaper editor remarked wryly in 1864, 'to preach reading may do for cathedrals, but not for the bush'.[7]

In 1860, after a 30-year period without a resident minister had come to an end, it is possible to sense the relief in the words of one Eden resident when he exclaimed proudly, 'Let it never be said again by strangers who leave our shores …

Palm Sunday at the Holy Trinity Church, Tilba Tilba, c. 1900, photograph by William Corkhill.
[TT732, by permission of National Library of Australia]

that the district of Eden has no minister of religion'. Perhaps this is why the early colonists in Eden–Monaro had placed so much importance on the visit of Bishop Broughton in 1845. When Broughton christened a child or administered the sacraments to the sick or dying, he walked in Christ's shoes. With each sign of the cross he was planting God's seed, a seed that would eventually become a vine of faith and guidance for the whole community. In 1866, when John Dunmore Lang officiated at the opening of the Presbyterian Church in Eden, he told the congregation: 'We pray that [God's] blessings will continue to be poured upon us as we seek to fulfil His will in this place, not dissimilar to its name in the Old Testament, where man and woman in a beautiful place also struggled with God's will'.[8] The struggle with 'God's will' was also the struggle with the absence of 'civilisation'. But the settler struggle would always seem so much more poignant in Eden, the irony of failure so much greater. The biblical Eden was the place where God's people were created, a place of indescribable beauty, sullied only by the stain of original sin. But Eden, on the far south coast of New South Wales, was a garden without a founding ideal, a place in waiting, whether for God, civilisation or the next development scheme.

To compensate for the absence of a founding ideal, early settlers sometimes wrote of their first experiences in Eden–Monaro using the same literary devices they found in biblical parables. Thus John Jauncey, the father of the Bega historian AB Jauncey, described his journey to Moruya on the south coast in 1848 in a manner reminiscent of both the flight from Egypt and Christ's search for John the Baptist: 'I, my wife, and a black boy, in 1848, carried a child each, on horseback, across the tidal inlets, then all open to the sea, to Moruya for Baptism, by chance hearing that a visiting clergyman would be there'.[9]

In their effort to create sacred ground, other settlers named their properties after the Garden of Eden or imagined their land as the 'historical land of promise' — especially if they settled in the Bega or Towamba valley. By the late nineteenth century, 'the valley' was seen in pioneer memories as a virgin paradise, unique and closed off from the world, a place of shelter with the greatest potential for the realisation of British rural life, and a place reserved for the privileged use of God's white people. When a pioneer recalled in 1882 first seeing Candelo near Bega from Chapel Hill in 1858, he presented his story as an epiphany. Arriving at the top of the hill on horseback, he looked down into the promised land, surveyed the 'lovely view', and proceeded to assume his natural destiny by descending into the valley and taking possession of unoccupied land.[10]

Whether or not the settlers wrote these parables in a conscious attempt to draft the Book of Genesis in the making of their history of innocence is difficult to tell. Perhaps these stories of a divine power sanctioning the settlers' discovery of an 'empty' land were written in the same way that other aspects of the European cultural heritage were re-created in Australia. A cultural heritage exiled in a colonial world was expressed as much by habit as by design, somewhere between wakefulness and the half-light of memory.

For those few settlers who kept journals of record before pioneer botrytis addled their memory, there were various strategies for coping with the absence of European civilisation. In 1837, one of the first squatters at Nimmitabel, on the Monaro, Farquar Mackenzie, wrote enviously of the Aboriginal people's life of freedom: 'he can hunt without fear of game laws and is not pestered by tax gatherers. He is not annoyed by failures in his crops or flocks and herds and has no rents to pay or fear of ejection'. On the other hand, Mackenzie believed that the life of the Aborigine was 'sensual, cruel and vengeful,' deprived of the higher pleasures of the mind or the comforts of civilisation. Yet without the architecture of grace and civilisation around him, Mackenzie struggled to enjoy these pleasures himself. He admitted that he did 'not exactly feel at home' on the Monaro without 'having a house and books for amusement'.

His average day involved the following routine — rise at six o'clock, turn the sheep out, wash, breakfast, work till eleven, write in his tent till midday, lunch, write again till two or three, 'work or walk till sunset', then take supper, after which he passed the time as best he could till nine o'clock when he went to bed. With the onset of winter and fourteen hours of darkness a day, he was writing frequently of his loneliness. His only solace was to copy from the Bible into his journal. Like a missionary in exile, he wrote to remember his stories, to cling to his faith and the world he had left behind. At other moments, he writes honestly of his struggle to govern his 'mind and passions' and reject 'worldly thoughts', a struggle which paradoxically seemed all the more difficult on the plains of the Monaro, where the trappings of his 'world' were no longer visible.

Mackenzie's life as a squatter was an effort to fill in the empty spaces of his frontier.[11] His desire for monastic discipline, his battle with loneliness, and his determination to keep hold of his faith also go some way to explaining why von Hugel's story of the blind man praying at Botany Bay is indeed a parable. Unlike Mackenzie, whose faith is somehow dwarfed by the foreign nature of his new environment, the blind man's faith is so strong it transcends time and place. His means of grace is not the church or its ministers but personal prayer.

When Baron Charles von Hugel's 'pleasure cruise' finally arrived at Twofold Bay in early June 1834, he found no men praying on the shore. Instead, he was shocked at the state of the society he encountered, and seemed unable to see how it could be redeemed. The uncivilised conditions at the Bay appalled his cultured European sensibilities. One of the first things he did after coming ashore was to visit Dr George Imlay's hut.

> The bark hut somewhat astonished me. I found it difficult to understand how
> a man used to a life of comfort, such as that enjoyed by ships surgeons, could

bring himself to spend part of his life in such quarters, purely for the sake of getting rich quick. The large sheets of tree bark appeared to be merely [leaning against the frame], you could poke your hand into the interior wherever they met. The floor was the one created by nature. On a table in a corner stood the larder of provisions to be consumed over the next few weeks, on hanging shelves by the wall were about 100 books and in a corner stood the bed, which never needed to be remade.

Although von Hugel had no way of knowing at the time, it was in this hut that Imlay sat at night, surrounded by the 'darkness' of the forest and the roar of the surf, quill in hand, declining his French verbs, and writing out the history of the British monarchy in true catechist style: 'Question: 'For what purpose did Henry take his son over to Normandy? Answer: To receive the homage of the barons of that Duchy'.

Instead of reflecting on the environment around him, Imlay wrote of his distant home.[12] In 1847, George Imlay left his hut one morning and walked alone into the bush. His body was found by his brother Peter some days later. 'He had laid down, tied the trigger of his gun to his spurs and shot himself.' 'Melancholy suicide' was one way home.

Leaving Imlay's hut, von Hugel walked outside to find several young Aboriginal women dressed only in 'blue aprons as big as a hand' tied around their waist. As he well knew, these garments, which flapped about in the wind, 'denoted a consciousness of something that needed to be hidden' but that consciousness belonged to George Imlay, not the Aboriginal women. He walked on, past the slaughterhouse 'where a dozen slaughtered bullocks were hanging' outside. Nearby, a group of 200 Aboriginal people had gathered in waiting for the offal. After entering some of the Aboriginal huts, he was driven away by 'the stench and dirt of the camp'. Returning to the ship later that day, one image in particular stayed with him:

> This locality, which looks so beautiful from a distance, is not so in the least … we returned towards evening. The camp was even fuller than in the morning. The whale hunters' brightly beribboned belle had come back and was now sitting in front of the slaughterhouse, with a large raw marrowbone in her hands, from which she was sucking the contents.[13]

Von Hugel's description of Twofold Bay in 1834 reveals a fledgling outpost bent on the quick exploitation of natural resources. It comes as no surprise to learn that the Imlays lined the path from their huts to the shoreline with the vertebrae of the whales they had killed. There was no vision of community or 'civilisation', only the hope of 'getting rich quick' for the feudal baron Dr Imlay. Both indigenous and settler culture appear to be corrupted.[14] This image was replicated across Eden–Monaro between the early 1820s and the mid-1850s, when, as one newspaper editorial in Cooma later observed, 'a rough sort of civilisation had been established'.[15]

This 'rough' civilisation arose in part from the way in which the frontier expanded. Despite the fact that the formal limits of the colony extended no further south than Bateman's Bay until 1837, squatters had infiltrated Eden–Monaro as early as the 1820s, while whalers and sealers had been visiting Twofold Bay and its hinterland from the late eighteenth century. The ongoing war between settlers and Aboriginal people in what was then an extremely isolated area assisted in creating a particular type of frontier culture. The land was taken first by a largely anonymous group of men who constantly pushed out the boundaries of the frontier in search of more grazing land — women, government, education, police, the law, and churches came after the event. 'Roughness' went hand in hand with an isolated male culture.

John Lhotsky had made a point of noting the English translation for the Aboriginal word Monaro: 'like a woman's breast', a description that evoked perfectly the curved lines of the bare, rounded hills that rise on the Monaro plains. But when Lhotsky first rode out on the Monaro in 1834, his first comment was that the land looked 'extremely masculine'. Whereas the indigenous imagining of the land was nurturing and feminine, the settlers' image was often cast in terms of a depraved masculinity.[16]

In the 30-year period between 1820 and 1850, there is very little evidence of a 'community' taking shape in Eden–Monaro. Most of the surviving descriptions of the area during these years speak of a 'violent and crude society' racked by lawlessness and alcohol abuse.[17]

The physical hardships of frontier life, which were only exacerbated by the settlers' failure to understand the bush, seemed to push the settlers' dream of 'civilisation' further away. And because Aboriginal societies were considered to be primitive, the majority of colonists saw the presence of Aboriginal people near white towns as yet another threat to 'civilised' values. In Eden in 1856, townspeople complained when an Aboriginal woman gave birth to her child in the main street, her cries of pain attracting white children. A newspaper correspondent wrote that if this practice continued Eden would be 'minus of all morality'. Some days later, the 'public death' of a young Aboriginal man 'under a piece of bark' caused another outcry. Civilisation would only come to Eden when Aboriginal people had been 'moved on' and the reality of birth, death and interracial sex could be kept behind closed doors.[18]

The construction of Boydtown in the late 1840s eventually became a monument to the empty state of frontier culture in Eden–Monaro. The building of Boyd's inn, church, storehouse and lighthouse resulted in a stage set for the coming of civilisation. But almost no one came, and the few that did rarely stayed long. Boydtown collapsed as soon as Boyd's credit dried up in the late 1840s. His church was left without pews, its belfry without bells, his lighthouse lit rarely. This was Rome in a day, a city to let in waiting for civilisation, surrounded by forest and sea, 600 kilometres from Sydney or Melbourne — a constant reminder of unpaid debts. A visitor who stopped at Boydtown in 1899 wrote of the air of 'decay' and 'abandonment' that surrounded the buildings. He was moved by the 'melancholy

Oswald Brierly's watercolour of the 'Maneroo' plains, painted on Brierly's first visit to the Monaro in 1842. 'Sketches Made in Australia'.
[PXD81f.3, Mitchell Library, State Library of New South Wales]

survival' of Boyd's dream, remarking with some enthusiasm, 'even in a young country like Australia there is abundant material for moralising on the vanity of human wishes'. Boydtown was little more than an empty shell, but, as he observed wryly, 'once a town gets upon a map it has to stay there'.

Boyd, the man who had 'owned' 380 000 acres of Aboriginal land in Eden–Monaro and who was 'rich beyond the means of avarice', could not manage to bring civilisation in his wake. The inscription chiselled deeply into Boyd's lighthouse, which was built from Sydney sandstone, shipped to Twofold Bay, then dragged by bullock teams to the headland, probably captures Boyd's vision of civilisation. On the three sides of the tower facing the sea is one word — 'BOYD'.[19]

In 1847, two years before he left Twofold Bay and Australia for good, Boyd hit upon an ingenious scheme to solve his labour shortage. He had grown tired of shepherds and stockmen deserting their posts and complaining about their conditions. He wanted a cheap, reliable and compliant labour force and, with the consent of the NSW Government, he decided he would find his ideal labourers in the South Pacific Islands. In April 1847, sixty-five Melanesian men arrived at Twofold Bay on board the *Velocity*. They had been 'contracted' to work on Boyd's stations. Unable to read, write or speak English, they had allegedly agreed to leave their homeland in exchange for an annual wage of 26 shillings a year, a weekly ration of 10 pounds of meat, and two pairs of trousers, two shirts and a Kilmarnock cap. Boyd also promised to 'feed them plenty of potatoes'. Stolen from their tropical climate, they walked 70 kilometres from Twofold Bay straight into a Monaro winter. Astute judges of their future prospects under 'Massa Boyd', most bolted into the bush, some ending up in Sydney. Undeterred, Boyd arranged for what he called 'an additional quantity' of fifty-four men and three women to be taken from Vanuatu in October, only to be thwarted by the NSW Legislative Council, which by then had finally buckled under public criticism and put a stop to his scheme. Boyd's dreams of a slave labour force had come to an end, but in the process many of the men he had brought to Twofold Bay either died in Australia or were killed by their own people when they were sent back to their homeland.

Perhaps there was some poetic justice in the manner of Boyd's death. After leaving Australia in 1849, he attempted another land grab in the Solomon Islands in 1851. This he described as an effort to establish 'a Papuan republic', no doubt with himself as the self-appointed president. In October at Guadalcanal, a remote island in the Solomons, Boyd went ashore to shoot the morning's breakfast and never returned. Angered by what they believed to be Boyd's murder, eleven crew members responded by spending two days razing native villages to the ground.[20]

Fortunately, not every squatter in the south-east possessed Boyd's sense of vision, but the pattern of Boydtown's development certainly mirrored that of many enterprises established by squatters and opportunists in Eden–Monaro in the 1830s and beyond. Because their commitment was primarily to short-term profit rather than 'society', they quickly sold up their interests and moved on when the economic indicators turned against them. The Imlay brothers, for example, saw Twofold Bay merely as another asterisk of economic activity on their map of south-eastern Australia. Their interests stretched from South Australia to Tasmania and Wilsons Promontory. Others like the Walkers, who bought up many of the Imlays' properties after their departure, soon left defeated, eventually returning to Europe. Until 1861, when the Robertson Free Selection Act allowed for smaller landholdings and the break-up of the old squatting empires, vast areas of land changed hands frequently. The absentee landlords who owned the land were part of a global network of British colonial entrepreneurs and pastoralists who moved constantly in search of wealth; behind them, in the distance, trailed 'civilisation'.[21]

When stock prices became too low, frequently because of overproduction, the squatters simply boiled their animals down for the tallow and hides that would fetch a better price. Little wonder that visitors to Twofold Bay like Charles von Hugel found the place so unappealing in the 1830s. The man-made environment was a hastily built abattoir, every structure a cog in the wheel of the pastoral and whaling industries.

Aboriginal people must have marvelled at the stench of the colonists' export economy. Close to where Matthew Flinders had walked in 1798, and where much of the town of Eden stands today, the Imlays fenced in their cattle in large 'embarkation yards'. There the cattle were led into a crush, before being pulled by a line across the beach, swimming out to the waiting ships, and finally being winched aboard by sailors. Around the shoreline of the Bay, the carcasses of bullocks and whales hung on large hooks, the smell of their rotting and burning flesh filling the air. Such is the opening scene to the film of settler history in Eden.[22]

Yet despite this crude and naked exploitation, from the moment of first contact in the late eighteenth century, many colonists had the capacity to see their environment differently. While some wrote in a predictable fashion of the 'gloomy and impenetrable forest', others wrote of the 'majestic' forest. And just as most saw the patterns of Aboriginal land use as unproductive, there were always those who thought otherwise. When the Bega Valley was being opened up to free selectors in the 1860s, one selector wrote to the *Bega Gazette* pointing out that before the squatters selfishly claimed the land for themselves, Aboriginal people had supported several tribes on the land. Now it was kept as the private domain of one squatting family. 'Aborigines', he said, had put the land 'to better use' than the squatters. So would the small landholders. The following week an angry reply came back from an anonymous squatter: 'Why should squatters let lots of people on their lands? … Squatters are not philanthropists, they are each one for himself'.[23]

Settler concern for environmental degradation was also found occasionally in the whaling industry. Many of the men and women who were closely involved in whaling recorded their regret and sorrow at the suffering they inflicted on the whales. Some spoke of their anguish as they heard the whales moaning in the bay, especially when the females tried to protect their young. Alice Otton, who as a young girl had seen the last days of the whaling industry at Twofold Bay, recalled at the age of 15 rowing across the Bay in a dinghy and seeing a whale boat at work about three quarters of a mile away.

> It was a beautiful, calm morning … you could see the flukes glistening in the sun and I'll never forget hearing that whale moan. The killer whales were harrying it and the whalers endeavouring to spear it with the harpoons. They eventually got the whale, but it was the first time I realised that it was murder.[24]

Exploitation of the environment in Eden–Monaro was not always a one-dimensional tale of mindless greed. But the struggle of the colonists to civilise the land was in every way a struggle to create a home.

In 1842, Joseph Lingard travelled on horseback from the Monaro plains to Mallacoota on the north coast of present-day Victoria. Lingard's recollections of his journey and the time he spent in Australia are among the most prosaic yet strangely moving of any colonial diary. Lingard, who is no writer, manages to tell a poignant tale of the convict's search for home.

In the introduction to his diary he pleads with his readers that his story represents the truth as far as he can remember. In humble tone he begins: 'I was born at Chapel Milton, a small village in the Parish of Glossop, in the County of Derby, about the year 1789'. The son of the clerk and sexton of the local chapel, Lingard saw his parents and several of his brothers and sisters die of fever. He was one of five children left, 'now cast on the world to get our livelihood as best we could'. In December 1834, before he could learn cotton weaving, he was wrongly charged with stealing a drop latch 'valued at 6 and a half pence when new'.

He soon found himself standing in leg irons together with 600 other prisoners on a convict hulk at Portsmouth. After remaining on the hulk for one year in appalling conditions, Lingard was hospitalised with scurvy, before finally returning to the ship, only to be placed in solitary confinement — 'the black hole'. Fortunately, the ship's doctor and transportation 'beyond the seas for the term of 7 years' saved him from a fatal flogging. An orphan without any formal education, Lingard manages to tell the story of his transportation and his coming to the Monaro in 1836–37 as an assigned servant.

After the cesspit of a convict ship, Lingard worked in the kitchen of a pastoral station on the Monaro in New South Wales. Here, the would-be cotton weaver from County Derby found himself in constant contact with the Aboriginal people of the Monaro. He referred to them as 'the blacks'. Although his initial perceptions were negative, he was still able to appreciate the detailed choreography in Aboriginal corroborees, which he thought 'far more impressive than a ball, or play in London'. Close to the Towamba Valley, on his journey from the Monaro down to the coast in 1842, Lingard marvelled at the beauty of the eucalypt forests with trees '120 yards high' and '25 feet through the ball', the bush echoing with the calls of bellbirds and whip birds.

For his entire journey, Lingard was led by Aboriginal guides along ancient tracks. He followed the axe marks they left in the trees to show him the way. The first morning after arriving at squatter Captain John Stevenson's homestead at Mallacoota, Lingard went down to the beach, passing Aboriginal huts on his way.

> I got up early ... cleaned my gun and off I went to the beach ... the sea came foaming in against the shore like moving mountains ... I was loading my gun ... admiring the wonderful works of nature ... suddenly a black man popped his head up from one of [the] thickets, but on seeing me [he] instantly drew back. I felt much alarmed, my dog having left me; I thought there might be a whole tribe concealed here; to run was of no avail ... I beckoned to him to come near me; he advanced several steps then stood still staring at me, he had no weapons with him, he was quite naked, I beckoned him again, he then came forward and stood before me stroking my gun, talking to it in his own language. On casting my eye towards the thicket I saw another black man put his head out ... I beckoned to him, he came in like manner as the first. I began to draw back towards the bush, thinking to get out of spear shot, should there be any more concealed in the thicket.

After the Aboriginal men pointed to two crows in the trees, Lingard obliged by shooting them. The men ran to pick them up, went off and cooked them, and returned eating them. Lingard was then invited to their hut, which he found to be 'like a house inside; their implements of war were reared in one corner, the floor was strewed over with all kinds of shells and fishes bones, they had two fires of wood'.

A few days later, Lingard walked with Stephenson to the site of a ship wrecked two years earlier about 17 kilometres off Ninety Mile Beach. He described the scene of desolation. Like a battlefield after war, 'the ship was in thousands of pieces still on the beach, the shoes and bones lying among the rocks, some of which belonged to the crew and some to the blacks' who had fought with them.

On his way back to the Monaro, Lingard stayed on a station where the keeper and his wife were in such a 'drunken and debauched state' that he believed they might kill him. Terrified of the barbarity of his fellow colonists, he decided he would be safer with Aboriginal people and slept the night with them.

Lingard's recollections of his encounters in the frontier society of Eden–Monaro capture the fear, isolation and misunderstanding of Aboriginal culture which characterised so much settler experience in Australia. The man who loaded his gun also appreciated the beauty of nature. For Lingard there was no contradiction. By the time he was ready to return home to England, Lingard, himself a victim of inhumane treatment, found room in his heart to pity all who lived in the 'new land', black and white.

Arriving back in Sydney in early 1844, he remembered watching the British female emigrants disembarking from the ships at Sydney Cove.

> I saw them land on Camel's wharf, in a few days after I saw some of them crying at the ends of streets, neither a penny in their pockets, nor a mouthful of meat to eat, nor any friends to look at them, even begging of the bullock drivers who were going up the country, to take them, and do what they thought proper with them, for the sake of a morsel of meat.

All around him, on the frontier and in the towns, Lingard felt he could see 'nothing but distress'. But when he arrived back in London on 30 August 1844, his situation did not improve. At 2 am on 24 August, as his ship approached the English coast, Lingard caught first sight of 'dear old England'. He was so excited to see his 'native land' he ran up on deck wearing only his nightshirt. Lingard had longed for 'sweet home' since his departure in 1836. But weeks later when he returned to his home village in Derby, he found that his wife and children had vanished. The last line of the maudlin poem with which he concludes his journal reads, 'I found no home for me'.[25]

Lingard's story is one of displacement and exile, a reminder that colonisation claimed many victims. Initially, the struggle of all those who came to Australia from Britain in the early nineteenth century was to make a home in the mirror image of the home they had left behind. Making home meant explaining the culture and presence of Aboriginal people in terms that did not obstruct the process of colonisation. This meant developing a rationale for colonisation, and finding a way of living on the land and establishing a profitable economy.

The history of the colonial economy in Eden–Monaro and the south coast contains a long list of schemes that proved either momentarily or partially successful: sealing, whaling, abalone-fishing, gold-mining, the native animal fur trade — especially koalas — wattle bark, rabbit-canning and timber-harvesting.[26] The result was a capitalist economy that was as difficult to predict as the weather. There were periods of prosperity and periods of hardship; many industries that promised a long-term future ended abruptly, often leaving severe environmental degradation in their wake.

The way in which our colonial forebears attempted to create a home in Australia has much in common with the way in which non-Aboriginal Australians relate to the land today. When Henry Parkes visited Bega in 1888, he spoke at the Town Hall in front of a large audience. Like many local residents, Parkes saw the settlement of the Bega valley as an opportunity to build a community of law-abiding farmers — a land of rolling hills sprinkled with 'British homesteads'. Yet he also claimed more than this:

When driving out to Tathra today, I was struck as I went along the road with the fact that I saw no person who could be set down as an idler, or who had the slightest appearance of being a wanderer or a lost sheep ... The happiness of home life does not depend upon the amount of wealth which a man possesses, and there is no more honourable calling under heaven, no more honourable place in economy of society, than that filled by the man who cultivates the soil.[27]

The poetry of nineteenth-century liberal capitalism was the promise of individual wealth built on the honour and virtue of work. Parkes' words bear a striking similarity to Robert Menzies' forgotten people speech of 1942: 'homes spiritual and homes material'.

'Tilling the soil' was 'happiness', a therapy that held out the promise of self-improvement for convicts and all settlers who had come to Eden–Monaro. One of the most common demonstrations of the virtues of cultivating the soil in the early nineteenth century was the ploughing match. The land was marked into half-acre allotments, the teams drew lots to decide their patch of ground, 'gentlemen' were

Harold Cazneaux's 'The Toilers', photographed at Bega c. 1920, in a manner reminiscent of French impressionist evocations of the pastoral, exalts the humble nobility of the farmer ploughing the land. [CAZ.C30, by permission of National Library of Australia]

selected as umpires, and 'after a strict examination of the well turned furrows as to their depth and direct lines' cash prizes were awarded. One held in Braidwood, in the 1840s, provides a typical example:

> The popular choice for the winner was Abraham Clark who took one and a half hours to ride his bullock team over the half-acre ... [But soon after] one of the umpires noticed some of his last furrows appeared shallow and after measuring their depth he decided the prize should go to someone else ... [Dr Wilson addressed the crowd, many servants of convict background among them, and exhorted them] ... to receive the rewards of merit and good conduct rather than those which ... follow rapine and bloodshed.[28]

The ploughing match was an agent of civilisation — ploughing the furrows of order and marking the land as the settler's own. It also revealed the colonisers' obsession with measurement as a means of exerting ownership and control. Creating 'home' meant recording its dimensions, and feeling in control of the land meant traversing it as quickly as possible. From the moment the government surveyor, TS Townsend, cursed the Monaro 'Aborigines' in 1846 because the smoke on the horizon from their fires made it impossible for him to 'get any angles' on his 'distant points', the effort to understand the land by measuring it had begun. Creating home was drawing 'imaginary lines' on a map, naming the land, and establishing regions, parishes, counties, colonies and states. It was the pioneer William Rixon in 1882, driving his two horses, Donovan and Jack, 52 miles over Tantawangalo Mountain to Bombala in four and a half hours, and being half an hour under the specified time! It was a Balmain Brothers' car in 1919 taking only two hours and fifty minutes from Bega to Cooma, a distance of 130 kilometres![29]

The identity of local communities in Eden–Monaro today, such as the Bega Valley, is still connected intimately with the land. It is impossible to live in the area without encountering the usual expressions of belonging — 'the valley' is 'God's country', 'it's beautiful', 'it's peaceful', 'it beats Sydney any day'. Attachment to the aesthetics of place is woven into the fabric of settler culture. Explaining the presence of nearly all those who live in the area, 'the land' is their muse. And 'the man on the land' walks along the same paths as those who came before him.

In the 1880s, a visitor to Bega made some interesting observations on settler society, expressing his surprise that the democratic spirit that pervaded the rest of the colony was absent in Bega.

> the caste spirit was as fully manifest here as in any squire governed parish in England ... The local 'aristocracy' seemed to be founded on the possession of land, and 'society' consisted of landowners, and the professional classes ... It did not at all affect the rigidity of this social demarcation that the scholarly

attainments of some of the landowners were limited to their ability to write a name on a cheque.[30]

Although the 'possession of land' was a symbol of economic and social standing in settler culture, the relationship between the settler and the land was sometimes made more secure through the ridicule of indigenous culture. When Alfred Howitt, the renowned anthropologist, organised a corroboree in Bega in 1883, Aboriginal people walked to Bega from up and down the coast to attend. But Howitt was forced to abandon his first attempt to witness a 'grand corroboree' when a group of 'larrikins' from Bega harassed the 'Aborigines' and mocked their rituals. Writing in 1903, one man who remembered the occasion indicated that Aboriginal people had been the objects of derision: 'Mr. Howitt was up here then on some mission among the natives. And didn't we boys turn native too, with our boomerangs, spears, nullahs and woomerahs. I still remember their war cry. Old Horton was King and his lubra Beenva was Queen'.[31] For many settlers, every 'cry' of an Aboriginal person was a cry of war. The continued practice of traditional Aboriginal culture posed a threat to settler culture because it suggested another way of belonging to the land. It also reminded them that the valley's 'original possessors' had not politely gone away.

Slowly, the image of the Bega Valley projected in settler culture became one of quaint British homesteads nestled in a divinely sanctioned valley of industrious landholders. For the settler, possession of the land went to the very core of being, as Henry Parkes explained in 1872:

> And what is this land which we possess ? It is the element without which no human being could exist. It is as essential to human life as the air we breathe. Everything we possess comes from the soil ... When this land which we receive fresh from nature, passes under the seal of government and becomes private property, it assumes a condition and entails consequences that can never be undone. Once private property it remains so forever ... the soil cannot revert to its virgin condition.[32]

Only thirty years after the end of the frontier wars, the settler was given the land 'fresh from nature'. His duty was to ensure that it did not return to its virgin condition — private property and a permanent Aboriginal presence on the land were mutually exclusive.

So many of the colonists' perceptions and expectations of civilisation, the land and home inhibited their capacity to understand Aboriginal people and their culture. And it would take almost two centuries before settler culture began to question these assumptions and accept the common humanity of Aboriginal Australians. The time between rejection and acceptance was long, the obstacles many, and the gulf of understanding great. There was — and is — much to reconcile.

Journal

Of a visit to Twofold Bay; Maneroo, and Districts beyond the Snowy River.

Dec.r & Jan.y 1842–3

Writing for posterity. The front page of Oswald Brierly's Journal, 1842–43. [A535, Mitchell Library, State Library of New South Wales]

6

AGENT OF
CIVILISATION

Sometimes it is possible to gain an insight into what it must have been like to live in the frontier society of colonial Australia by reading the journal of one man or woman.

Early in 1998, I visited the Mitchell Library to read the journals of Oswald Brierly. I had known for some time that Brierly's journals and sketches, produced during the seven years he spent at Twofold Bay in the 1840s, contained one of the most detailed and extensive records of frontier life in south-eastern New South Wales. Like many colonial documents, these journals, scribbled in ink and pencil, are not easy to read. But Brierly was also an accomplished artist, and many sketches and drawings break his text. Of the eight or more of his journals in the Mitchell Library, one in particular fascinated me.

Shortly after Brierly arrived in Twofold Bay, late in December 1842, he travelled on horseback along the Towamba River, following the snake trail of the river from its mouth, south of Eden, to its source on the Monaro plains. It was Christmas 1842. Brierly travelled together with Ben Boyd and an Aboriginal guide, 'Budgenbro' or 'Toby'.

Shortly before Christmas Eve, they rode by Blackfellas' Point. Many times, standing on the verandah of my house in the early morning, and looking down-river, I have imagined Brierly and Boyd passing by in 1842. The clanging of the pots and pans hanging from Toby's horse would probably have been audible from where my house now stands. It would also have been possible to hear the sound of their voices and the horses' hooves on the sand. On this journey, Brierly kept a journal, reflecting on the beauty of the environment, expressing his curiosity with Aboriginal culture, sketching their camping places and Toby, as he cooked an 'explorer's breakfast'. This was the closest I could come to experiencing what it might have been like to encounter the country around me 150 years earlier.

Reading the journals, I was also struck by the way in which Brierly's ambition and drive seemed to reflect the settlers' unquestioned belief in their 'civilising mission'. Brierly was young, bright, talented, and 20 000 kilometres from home. There were many times when he wrote of his loneliness. But his extraordinary passion for knowledge and personal advancement made him determined to succeed as an agent of 'civilisation' in the colonial world. Never once did he doubt the mission of Empire.

The source of the Towamba River near Cathcart on the Monaro plains,
sketched by Brierly on his first journey up the river in December 1842.
The river was known then as 'the Kiah'. Ink sketch, Brierly Journal, 1842–43.
[A535, Mitchell Library, State Library of New South Wales]

The more time I spent reading the journals, the more I realised that Brierly's story was one worth telling. Unlike Benjamin Boyd, his role in the early history of settlement on the far south coast is relatively unknown. While Boyd's legacy is ingrained deeply in the area, Brierly has been largely forgotten. In contrast to Boyd, or the Imlay brothers, there are no monuments to his memory, and no mountains or towns have been named after him.[1]

I was also intrigued by Brierly's close friendship with Budgenbro, and what this friendship might reveal about the attitudes of both men regarding one another and the different worlds from which they came. It seemed to offer a rare chance to 'listen in' on a conversation between two cultures, one characterised not by suspicion and violence but by affection. Finally, I was interested in the fact that after seven years at Twofold Bay Brierly had come to see the far south coast of New South Wales as his 'home', a word he used himself on the day of his departure from the bay.

Brierly's reflections, as revealed in his journals, offered the best first-hand account of what it meant to be a colonist and to encounter Aboriginal culture on the far south coast in the early 1840s. This is Brierly's story.

'THIS
BLACK MOTHER
EARTH'

THE JOURNALS OF OSWALD BRIERLY

In December 1842, at 24 years of age, the artist Oswald Brierly entered Twofold Bay aboard Ben Boyd's steamship the *Sea Horse*. Brierly had been at sea for over a year, having already sailed with Boyd from England on the *Wanderer*, via Teneriffe, Capetown, Rio de Janeiro, the Indian Ocean Islands and Sydney. Twofold Bay was the last port of call.[2]

Benjamin Boyd, Scottish entrepreneur and opportunist, a pioneer of sorts, had chosen the south side of Twofold Bay as the site of his new Rome, an Elysium he would eventually name 'Boydtown'. Boyd had come to civilise the south-east with borrowed money, charm, champagne, and cheap labour. Brierly had come along for the ride and to make his mark in the world; he was committed primarily to using the colonial experience as an extended art workshop.

As a young painter immersed in the culture of romanticism that then pervaded the arts in northern Europe, Brierly didn't hesitate to join Boyd's colonial odyssey when the two men met for the first time in 1840. His idol was John Constable, the painter whose quaint images of rural England were set under vast softly lit skies; like many young painters in the 1840s, Brierly's work emerged under the shadow of the two most popular painters of the period, Constable and Turner.

While the British Empire represented an opportunity to amass vast personal wealth and fame for Benjamin Boyd, for the young Brierly the colonial venture held out the core promise of romanticism — the revelation of faith and self through communication with nature. Brierly would return with the glories of the distant 'colonial earth' rendered magnificent through his art. The first words in his journal after his arrival at Twofold Bay reveal a man enthused by the civilising mission of colonisation.

> Picture for yourself the place where we might have to remain for some weeks — a tent formed by a sail thrown over some poles — outside a fire of burning logs over which is a large cast iron pot — with mutton birds for dinner ... men from the steamer are sawing boughs to make a second tent ... [Underneath] a forest of gum and banksia ... the cattle are landing after swimming a mile from the ship ... there are no fences here once in the bush they are lost ... [I hear] the roar of the sea and the bellowing of oxen ...

[and] smell the tall gum trees. [I] imagine ourselves the founders of a new
Rome ... A blanket nailed to a post is the first ensign of the town of Boyd.[3]

Brierly watched as many of the crew walked up to the gum trees on the shore of
the Bay and carved images of their ship 'in full sail' on the trees, unaware that
Aboriginal people had been doing the same for years before them. He was swept
away by the grandeur of the scene: 'the trees lit up by the fires which now and
then blaze up ... then die away again ... the monotonous crash of the surf ... the
unceasing chirp of insects ... and the gins' incessant yabber yabber around the
fires'. In December 1842, Brierly's journal reveals a man still in the early stages of
fascination with the land and Aboriginal culture, keen to convey the epic nature
of the colonial adventure. On his first few nights at the bay he was unable to sleep.
Instead his curiosity forced him to steal out at night to observe Aboriginal people
sitting around their fires.[4] It is this curiosity, intelligence and drive which makes
Brierly's journals — the first serious attempt to give a picture of colonial life on
the far south coast — such a valuable and interesting source.

Brierly's waterclour sketch of 'Budginbro' (Toby's father), whom Brierly referred to as the
'chief' of the 'Twofold Bay Tribe', New South Wales. 'Sketches Made in Australia', 1843.
[Mitchell Library, State Library of New South Wales]

His stay broken only by trips to Sydney, Brierly would spend almost six years at Twofold Bay, during which time both the nature of European settlement and Aboriginal society would change significantly, as would his personal response to the Boydtown project. His journals and drawings reveal a sensitivity to the environment and Aboriginal culture unmatched by those around him. Romantic as he was, he was never afraid to expose the brutality of a frontier society that progressed under the euphemism of 'civilisation'.

Only days after he had written in epic vein of the colonial venture, he took his first trip across from the southern side of Twofold Bay to the site of the present town of Eden. As he walked up the hill overlooking Snug Cove, he could see the pegs which had been placed in the ground by TS Townsend, the government surveyor, only a few weeks earlier:

> posts and boards among the trees on the top of the hill marked the different directions in which the streets were to run, and near the beach were the sheds and huts of a whaling station; the bones of whales that had been taken at different times lay scattered on the beach. A few crows walked out amongst the deserted huts and the whole place looked as desolate and uninviting as any I had ever seen.[5]

During his first few weeks in Australia, Brierly's reaction to frontier society in Eden–Monaro swayed from one extreme to the other. He was drawn to the unusual beauty of the natural environment, yet he was equally repelled by the lack of social refinement in settler society. Initially, he spoke of his fears setting off into the bush. Like many 'new chums', Brierly's knowledge of previous British experience in the American colonies instilled a fear of Aboriginal people long before he encountered the Kudingal at Twofold Bay. He imagined that every acacia hid 'natives' waiting 'in ambush', like 'American Indians stealing up disguised in skins'.[6]

But these fears were short-lived. Brierly's natural curiosity, artistic sensibility and intuitive respect for Aboriginal culture soon found him sitting alone at his campsite in the early morning, immersed in his sketching. He would also develop a close friendship with Toby, who belonged to the Aboriginal people of Twofold Bay, the Mobullergunde.

Less than three weeks after his arrival at Twofold Bay, Brierly set off on a journey up to the Monaro. Benjamin Boyd wanted to cast his eye over the thousands of acres of Aboriginal land he had recently acquired. The land had now become Boyd's 'stations', at least on paper. On the morning of 21 December 1842, Brierly and Boyd, together with two of Boyd's 'staff' and their guide, Toby, set off for the Monaro, each person with their swag 'laid across the front of the saddle', Toby wearing a 'white jacket', 'pots and some pannikins suspended round his waist', not to mention the other bags 'of damper salt meat and sugar'.

The journal Brierly kept on this journey is one of the most magical in his collection. Infused with the enthusiasm of the recent arrival, open to every encounter, his starry-eyed prose is broken by extraordinary sketches in ink and pencil.[7]

The four men travelled from the Bay to the Monaro on horseback along a 'beautiful river winding between the hills with high trees growing along its banks' — the Towamba River. 'Shortly after sunset', they arrived at a 'very beautiful park like spot' with 'giant gum trees' and camped the night.

Over the next few weeks of the journey Brierly made frequent sketches of campsites, Aboriginal people and the natural environment. He wrote often of his astonishment at the beauty of the country through which he travelled, sometimes unwittingly revealing the seed of its future ruin: 'All round full of beauty and loveliness everything appeared so undisturbed … I have never seen a more beautiful country or one so well adapted for cattle'.

Brierly's affectionate sketch of Toby outside their tent on 28 December 1842.
Pencil sketch, Brierly Journal, 1842–43.
[A537, Mitchell Library, State Library of New South Wales]

On New Year's Day 1843, Brierly crept out of his tent 'in the grey of the morning', and sketched the 'sylvan' scene around him. 'Long shadows around the smoky embers, Toby and dogs fast asleep — rising sun gradually lighting up mountains — throwing long shadows — tufts of grass — black mother earth.'

The words 'black mother earth' suggested more than Brierly might have realised when he wrote them. Although he had come to view Ben Boyd's stations, as each day passed on his journey from the coast to the Monaro plains his understanding of the importance of the land to Aboriginal culture deepened. When the party camped at 'Murderer's range' near Bombala, named in memory of a white stockman who had been killed by a local Aborigine, Brierly was overcome by the 'haunting' atmosphere of the place — the 'mourning of the wind' and the 'mysterious sounds of [the] lone spot'.

The 'darkness' reminded him of a church graveyard he had passed through as a boy in England, and the fear he had felt as he walked past the graves. Now, half a world away on the Monaro, he looked out at the 'dawning sky, the wind

Camp at Murderer's Range, 'Maneroo' plains, New Year's morning, 1843.
Pencil and ink sketch, Brierly Journal.
[A535, Mitchell Library, State Library of New South Wales]

sweeping across with a melancholy sound which at times swell[ed] to a louder key and then [subsided]'. The next words in his journal are difficult to decipher:

> you might imagine the spirits of the
> wailing for the … … .
> the white man who was driving the
> before whom the few remaining tribes were melting away

Whether Brierly is imagining the wind mourning the death of one white stock-man or, as seems more likely, the Aboriginal people whom the white man was driving away, after only a few weeks in the area he is already confronting the truth of dispossession. There is a tension between the pro-active nature of the word 'driving' and the tragic inevitability of the word 'melting'. But Brierly clearly sens-es more than one murderer on the range.

Through his growing friendship with Toby, Brierly gradually came to learn more about Aboriginal culture. On the journey to the Monaro, he was impressed with Toby's ability to find food when the others had given up hope of surviving on anything but meagre rations. He watched in awe as Toby communicated with Aboriginal people from the Monaro 'in their language' and noted how every Aboriginal with whom they spoke was insistent on placing each member of the party by their name, 'which they never forget'.

Brierly was beginning to witness the way in which Aboriginal people attempt-ed to incorporate whites into their own kinship system. He also saw the enormous curiosity Aboriginal people displayed towards the white man, and marvelled at the way they 'crowded over each other's shoulders' just to gain a glimpse of the party as they sat in the 'gunyahs' Toby had taught Brierly and Boyd to erect for their shelter. Brierly was amused by Toby's antics in front of 'the Monaro and Pambula Aborigines', and describes affectionately the way in which Toby tried to impress them with his 'coat, straw hat and white trousers', placing one 'shot belt' around his waist and another around his shoulders.

As an artist, Brierly was sensitive to the more subtle aspects of the culture he encountered on the Monaro:

> Some of the men …walk with much grace. One of them … had two pieces
> of his hair tied up … like a turban, having a large white button, which had
> originally belonged to a great-coat, stuck on in front, his cheeks daubed with
> red ochre, his oily skin glistened as he walked about with a very well satisfied
> air, handling his wombra as a dandy would his cane.[8]

This image shows Brierly recognising the common humanity of Aboriginal people and Europeans, but it also reveals the particular point at which Brierly encounters indigenous societies in Eden–Monaro: a time when traditional society had long been accustomed to the presence of whites and already suffered severe dislocation, but also a time when the experience of contact was still novel enough to carry a sense of discovery and curiosity. This was nowhere more evident than after Brierly's return to Twofold Bay in January 1843.

Brierly saw Aboriginal people carrying tools, leading horses, rowing the Imlays' whaleboats, and wearing brass plates around their necks — the telltale signs of a servant class. He witnessed the sad and painful deaths of Aboriginal men and women infected with venereal disease, and he traded on a daily basis with Aboriginal people, often exchanging damper for 'fine bream'. He watched as Aboriginal people stayed close to his ship for protection when they were afraid of being attacked by other tribes. And he wondered at the many aspects of tradition-al life still practised at Twofold Bay — the dexterous manner in which the Aboriginal men ascended the gum trees with their tomahawks, the intricate ritu-

In his journal, Brierly sketched the bark shroud in which Aboriginal people at Twofold Bay, many of whom came originally from the Monaro, buried their dead. Pencil sketch, Brierly Journal, 1843. [A537, Mitchell Library, State Library of New South Wales]

als of the corroborees and burial services, the use of medicinal plants and springs, and the richness of Aboriginal spiritual beliefs. For the Aboriginal people of Twofold Bay, this was a time in between war and displacement, in between what had been and what would be, a momentary frontier of interdependence and partial cooperation.

Brierly made a point of recording the name of every visitor who came on board the *Wanderer* while the ship was moored in Twofold Bay. The Aboriginal names recorded reveal the diversity of their origins — Pambula, Bega, Twofold Bay, Monaro and Bemboka. The early impact of sealing, and the whaling activities which had resulted in more permanent settlement at the bay since the early 1830s, meant that by 1842 when Brierly arrived, the traditional movement patterns, territorial arrangements and customary laws of the Kudingal and their neighbours on the Monaro had probably been shattered.[9] Yet much of the knowledge of traditional culture survived, especially in the person of Toby, Brierly's friend.

From the moment he first met Toby, Brierly was impressed with his sharp intelligence and wit. He listened as Toby tried to teach him the correct pronunciation of important words in his language, Thawa, such as 'Ombarra' — blackfellow. By all accounts Toby was pedantic when it came to teaching his language or learning English. Near enough was not good enough. As Brierly described him,

> Toby wasn't satisfied with our pronunciation until we accented the word properly. He then went on to describe the various weapons and in one instance where he could not make himself sufficiently understood he took the pencil and drew the outline of the thing he wished to describe — the oval shield.[10]

Toby was the person who dictated several Thawa words to George Robinson in 1844 and, through his contact with Brierly and Robinson, is largely responsible for the few Thawa words that have been passed down to us.[11] Brierly was struck particularly by the kindness Toby displayed to his ailing father: 'not the least impressive trait in Toby's character is the care he takes of his father — one of the oldest men in the tribe — whenever anything is given to Toby — he first takes part of it to the old man who is almost helpless from the palsy'.[12]

Toby's father had told Brierly the story of how the first white men came to Twofold Bay, 'the Aborigines' fleeing in terror to the hills. Although one or two returned to approach the intruders, they were 'terrified' at the colour of the white men, whom they took to be spirits of their own departed ancestors who, as Toby put it, had 'jumped up again all white'.[13]

Brierly became so fond of Toby he tried to protect him from the vices which often destroyed Aboriginal people, particularly alcohol. He frequently entertained Toby and his gin, Bloomah, on board the *Wanderer*. And his affection for Toby was

Brierly's pencil and watercolour of Toby's gin, Bloomah,
wearing Brierly's shirt. Pencil and watercolour, 'Sketches 1842–44'.
[DGD19f.6, Dixson Galleries, State Library of New South Wales]

probably helped by the fact that he found Bloomah extremely attractive, especially when she came on board wrapped in an old shirt which Brierly had given Toby:

> she is by far the best looking gin I have seen. Her hair rather inclined to curl, is confined by a band passed around her forehead. For this we substituted one of the Wanderer's ribbons, with beads and tassels suspended over each ear. A string of large beads around her neck and some smaller ones around her wrists. She laughs in a musical tone.[14]

When Brierly tried to impress Bloomah by showing her one of his sketches of a black cockatoo, 'she burst out laughing'. Over the next few years, Brierly would present her with gifts of beads and clothing. Perhaps he envied Toby. He wrote in his journal of his inability to 'meet an interesting girl without falling desperately in love'. On his journey to the Monaro, he had indeed fallen in love with a teenage Aboriginal woman, writing of her coquettish manner and 'pensive downcast look' — her 'long shining hair hanging gracefully over her brilliant dark eyes'. Brierly confessed he felt 'deeply interested in the beautiful Aboriginal'. But he must also have felt disappointed when the first thing she asked him for was tobacco.[15]

Brierly travelled to Sydney several times during his five years or more at Twofold Bay, frequently in search of love. He would stay at Ben Boyd's harbourside residence at Mosman Bay, painting on the walls of his bedroom and attending balls at Government House.[16] But lonely as he was, he was too proud and reserved to find the love and affection he craved. After one ball in Sydney, he wrote in an aloof tone how unimpressed he was with the beauty of the Sydney women. There was 'scarcely a fine or commanding figure in the room', he said. But this harsh and critical eye did soften. As always, there was one woman who was different from all the rest. At one ball at Government House he was particularly taken by a 'Miss D', so much so that in an effort to win her attention he made a determined effort to improve his dancing, making copious notes and sketches in his journal — 'Gentleman extends his right hand to his lady … take your lady opposite you — retire advance again — bow and take your lady's hands'. Perhaps Brierly's desire to impress the mysterious 'Miss D' was behind this reminder note in his journal — 'If you remain in Sydney get into a regular line of exercise, get a horse if you can'.[17]

In Brierly's methodical approach to courtship there was more than a hint of the extraordinary drive and discipline that governed his daily life. Reading his journals, it is impossible not to be struck by his obsessive determination to make his stay at Twofold Bay of 'positive benefit' to himself. He wanted to secure his 'position' in life, but even more than this he wanted to increase his knowledge of his own cultural inheritance. Playing a role in the process of colonisation was a means to self-improvement. For Oswald Brierly, Twofold Bay was no leisure coast.

Shortly after taking up his position as manager at Boydtown, Brierly made one of the first of many entries in his journal, exhorting himself to work harder. Under the heading 'Plan' he wrote:

> You must now raise yourself, do not be content with this mere superinten-
> dence of a new town. You must fit yourself for a more solid benefit and you
> can only do this by improving and improving yourself. Conquer and bear
> down by industry and do not be continually seeing difficulties. Always see in
> the morning what you want to do and do it through thick and thin.[18]

In almost every one of Brierly's journals there are similar examples of self-flagellation. He would chastise himself for being 'sluggish and cowardly' and not rejecting
that 'miserable feeling of having done enough'. He would regularly list his faults, as
if writing them down would allow him to eliminate them more easily. He rose early
every morning to ensure something was achieved before breakfast, and took no
more than one glass of wine with his evening meal. Even his one recreation — the
game of chess — became a metaphor for his whole approach to life. 'Never despair',
he wrote, 'when you appear to be losing ground, persevere persevere!'[19]

Brierly's journal was itself a model of the scientific endeavour and craving for
progress that characterised colonial man. Not content with writing his journal on
first impressions alone, Brierly wrote only to rewrite. He observed in order to collect, collected in order to describe, described in order to classify, and classified in
order to understand. To do this and more, he sketched and painted, until his journal became not only a record of his experience in the colony of New South Wales
but a chronicle of his own self-advancement.

As an educated man of Empire, Brierly was steeped in classical culture, often
spending hours writing up abstracts of Pericles' speeches, Cicero's writings or
Plato's dialogues with Socrates. Familiarity with the weight of classical learning
went hand in hand with the acquisitive nature of colonial culture. Like Ancient
Greece and Rome, the British Empire became greater through expansion, spread-
ing virtuous and noble ideals to the far corners of the globe. In order to understand
difference, it was first necessary to possess it. As Brierly wrote in August 1843,
'Notes on black cockatoo — [I] made a drawing of [the] head from one shot during the day ... [On the next day] I examined [the] stomach of a Black Cockatoo,
[it] contained a mass of small flat oval seeds ... [I then returned on board and] wrote
out Pericles'.[20]

Brierly adopted the same scientific approach to whaling, devoting a whole journal — 'Cetacea' — to lengthy descriptions of the measurements, anatomy and economic utility of whales. This journal, more than any other, was the one he imagined would give him 'position'. Perhaps he pictured himself delivering long lectures
to the Royal Geographic Society in London and being feted by journalists.[21]

Brierly also wanted to capture the romance of whaling, and through his journal entries, sketches and oil paintings he was one of the first to represent whaling at Twofold Bay as an epic tale of colonial adventure, many of his descriptions later being copied or plagiarised by others. What was often forgotten, however, was that Brierly was also the first to expose the cruelty of whaling:

> Out on the whaling boat ... we first got sight of a whale — a large black one. There! it has struck one of the headsmen and knocked him out of his boat. In an instant he was hauled in and sends a lance deep into his side. The sight gave us redoubled energy ... in a few moments we were within a boats length of the huge mass ... now in his last agonies, blood pouring from gushes in its side and back discolouring the water around. What a scene — the shouts of the men, the splashing of the whale, the more languid motions when the fish becomes exhausted, the flukes flapping first one way and then another, sometimes a sudden rush to rid itself of its pursuers, the boat flying along with terrific rapidity, oars peaked, water boiling on each side. The hollow bursts when [the whale] is compelled to return to the surface to blow ... and now the [killer whales] are on him, surrounding and dashing at his tongue when the pain of his wounds causes him to open his mouth ... [The killers attack the whale in packs preventing his escape] tearing away portions of the lip and tongue ... then the whale rose for the last time ... he gave one tremendous shudder and was dead ... and in a few minutes the killers took him bodily down, large pieces of lip rising to the surface showed that a regular feast was going on below.[22]

Brierly later described how the whales were brought in and hoisted on blubber hooks and tackle, before their flesh was cut into strips. Eventually, the bones would lie along the foreshore of the Bay, cleaned by the crows and bleached by the sun. Brierly was attracted to the theatre of whaling and drawn to its visual drama. Like a photographer on assignment, he had come to Twofold Bay for different reasons. From the deck of the *Wanderer* in winter 1844, close to the point at where the Eden woodchip mill stands today, Brierly looked out at the scene around him:

> Immediately opposite the [*Wanderer*] is a beautiful sandy beach, beyond this a level green spot on which are some bark huts of whalers. The boats are out. A few gunyas of natives made of bark and bushes scattered around the beach ... Away to the West is the whole sweep of Twofold Bay, on a promontory running out into the centre of the Bay called Jorroroga is a beacon, the Wanderers tower, and beyond this rises Mt. Imlay, dark and blue. Long strips of dense white mist hang suspended in the valleys ... and around the shores of the bay sounds the crash of the tide ... the screams of black cockatoos ... the voices of men hoisting in the whale and the blacks calling to each other on the shore.[23]

Here Brierly describes the scene as if it were already on canvas — already one of the Queen's pictures. He is completely entranced by the poetry of the image before him. Yet for all his Kiplingesque worship of Empire, he was also capable of seeing things from the other side. Unlike many around him, he was not blind to the suffering Boyd's whaling operations inflicted on the whales. He wrote of his 'pity' for the whales that entered the bay, and movingly described their majesty in the water: 'At sea, with no land in sight, no bird or other living thing, in the cold monstrous grey of early morning, a lone whale steaming in solitary grandeur, his path marked at time by the cloud of his breath … [The scene] has something sublime in it'.[24]

Brierly spent more than five long years at Twofold Bay, from late 1842 to early 1848. Initially, in the early blush of enthusiasm, he was chuffed to be 'Governor of a town and entire commandant afloat' — the dependable face of Boyd's wild schemes for a quick pound.[25] But by 1847, though his desire to understand Aboriginal culture had not waned, he had come to see Boyd for what he was, a charlatan who was 'unfit' for the task he had set himself. By 1847, the Boydtown project was ailing and Brierly was bored and tired. He felt he had battled alone without support, all 'for the sake of [Boyd's name]'.[26] He had struggled with the harsh frontier created by his fellow countrymen, an alcohol-sodden outpost where 'a glass of grog' would make people 'say or assent to anything'. He even feared the opening of the inn at Boydtown he had helped to build because it would only bring the worst characters down from the Monaro, turning the bay into little more than a place of reckless pleasure for drunken shearers.[27]

In April 1848, Brierly needed little encouragement to take up Owen Stanley's offer to sail with him on the *Rattlesnake* to Cape York, the Torres Strait and the South Pacific. He would soon find himself sitting with Barbara Thompson, a Scottish woman who had survived a shipwreck in the Endeavour Strait and lived with the Kaurareg people in the Torres Strait Islands for five years before finally being rescued again by the *Rattlesnake* in October 1849. Over a period of several weeks, Brierly listened to Thompson as she tried in broken English to explain her understanding of Kaurareg culture, telling him of how she had sung her songs at night to remember her language. With the same ear he had displayed for the nuances of Aboriginal culture at Twofold Bay, Brierly painstakingly wrote, edited, and rewrote her recollections before time stole them away. The result of Thompson's testimony as recorded by Brierly is one of the most detailed and reliable sources of information on the traditional life and culture of the Kaurareg, the most southerly group in the western Torres Strait Islands.[28] Even by his own demanding standards, Brierly achieved a great deal in his six years in Australia.

On the day of his departure from Twofold Bay he wrote that his heart and feelings would always remain 'wedded to the place'.

[I] got up early … the moon shining very brilliantly [and] walked round onto the verandah. The Bay was quite still, the high land round the Bay, dark and distinct … the tall flag staff rising up in the moon light … the chill reality of moving when we are about to leave forever … So blue and still was this cloudless morning in the corner where I made my home.[29]

Brierly's 'home' was the shifting frontier of the British Empire. Yet he also formed deep attachments to people and place. On the morning he wrote these words he had been moved by the emotion of one whaler who was so upset at his departure he was 'unable to speak'. The 'whaler' may have been Toby. We will probably never know.[30]

The view across Twofold Bay from where Brierly stood on the morning of his departure in 1848. [Mark McKenna]

The cottage that Brierly had built and lived in at East Boyd, with its massive cedar doors and shaded verandah, looked out across the bay, surrounded by a garden of apple and mulberry trees. In the 1880s, at 'mulberry time', local schoolchildren would sail across from Eden every year to picnic and play. The cottage became one of Eden's tourist drawcards and a shrine for artists and writers. As Brierly had painted on the wall of Boyd's mansion at Mosman, they came in turn to write and paint on the walls of his cottage. Sometime in the early twentieth century the cottage was demolished and the trees cut down.[31]

Oswald Brierly's legacy is profound. Unlike the two 'pioneers' whose names are scattered so liberally throughout the area today, Imlay and Boyd, Brierly found a 'home' at Twofold Bay. He was a pioneer of understanding rather than a pioneer of industry. Together with George Robinson, in his journal and sketches, Brierly left the most detailed record of Aboriginal culture at Twofold Bay. He also wrote the most incisive, sensitive and interesting account of what it was like to live in the frontier society of Eden–Monaro in the 1840s. His contribution, and that of his friend Toby, is a history worth celebrating, worth sharing, and worth remembering.

One of the last photographs of Brierly's cottage before it was pulled down in the early years of the twentieth century.
[By permission of Rene Davidson, Eden]

7

'VICTIMS OF SINGULAR NEGLECT'

The goal of reconciliation between Aboriginal and non–Aboriginal Australians is both a political task and a social challenge. In every community throughout the nation, respect for the rights and culture of Aboriginal people is dependent upon establishing a dialogue, a conversation which is both local and national. Part of this conversation is understanding the perspective of others, particularly how each of us views our own past and the ways in which this past affects our identity today.

If reconciliation is to be achieved, it is necessary for non–Aboriginal Australians to accept the truth of the injustice that has been done to Aboriginal people. But equally it is necessary for Aboriginal Australians to understand the way in which non–Aboriginal Australians think of their history and identity.

Ann Curthoys has argued that reconciliation which rests on building a pluralist and more inclusive past remains 'unachievable' in Australia because of particular views non–Aboriginal Australians hold about their past and their identity:

> Many non-indigenous Australians have difficulty in seeing themselves as the beneficiaries of the colonisation process because they, like so many others, from the United States to Canada to Israel and elsewhere, see themselves as victims, not oppressors ... [For the victim], the legacy of the colonial past is a continuing fear of illegitimacy.[1]

The sense of victimhood that Curthoys describes is certainly present in south–eastern New South Wales. Indeed, it is not possible to understand the attitude of some non–Aboriginal people in the community towards reconciliation without first understanding one of the most powerful beliefs within their society.

Deeply ingrained in the ethos of settler culture in south–eastern New South Wales is the belief that the area has long been the 'victim of singular neglect'. In Eden, especially, it would be possible to write the history of the collapse of so many dreams of grandeur and development — not a black armband history, but a history that understands the insecurities of the settlers. Since the town was first established in the 1840s, the people of Eden have never managed to overcome their sense of physical isolation and economic insecurity. In many respects, the history of settler culture at Twofold Bay is one haunted by the melancholy of failure.[2]

Driving into Eden on 13 May 1999, one week after the town's fish cannery closed down, resulting in the loss of almost 150 jobs, I could see the evidence of one failure. Along the highway into town, signs cut hastily from cardboard had been pinned to wooden posts on the roadside — the words were simple but moving — 'Keep our cannery, save our town'.

The word 'save' seemed to conjure up much of the economic history of Eden. It carried the pathos and desperation that many settlers had felt since the mid-nineteenth century. As one journalist remarked flippantly in 1868, Eden was the 'poor man's Eldorado'. For most of its existence, Eden has been a town waiting to be 'saved' by the next major development, whether it is a railway, a cannery, a chip mill, a marina, or an armaments factory. The history of a town forever in waiting seemed all the more poignant because hopes and expectations always remained unfulfilled.

When Boydtown failed in the late 1840s, it left behind, in the words of one visitor from Sydney in 1856, 'a very early monument of decay in so new a country'.[3] The ruins of Boydtown stood as a permanent reminder of the difficulty in establishing Eden as anything more than a 'halfway house' between Sydney and Melbourne. The gold rush at Kiandra on the Monaro plains, which saw a period of 'mad infatuation' in the early 1860s, was over in two years. Subsequent dreams of a major port city, a national capital, or of Eden becoming the 'Manchester of Australia' were never realised.[4]

Visitors who recorded their impression of the far south coast in the early twentieth century repeated a common theme: in spite of its climate and 'unrivalled

'Keep our Cannery, Save our Town', Eden, 1999. [By permission of Magnet, Eden]

situation', the people of Eden had always felt that 'something was wanting to ful-fil [their] happiness'. Talk of the town becoming the national capital had for so long been 'the only topic of conversation, the only hope', that when it was final-ly put to rest in 1910, when the Fisher Labor Government announced Canberra as the site of Australia's capital, it left a feeling of despair. Physical isolation and a sense of bitterness at being constantly passed over in favour of larger centres only entrenched the belief that Eden was a victim of discrimination.[5]

As late as the 1920s Eden was still connected to towns to the north by dirt roads. The coastal railway that had been promised since the 1860s had not come to pass. Travellers crossed rivers by punts and if they wished to go to Sydney they could expect a journey of up to two days and one night, regardless of whether they journeyed by road or sea.[6] Traditionally linked more closely to the Monaro than the north coast, when the Snowy Mountains Hydroelectric Scheme began in the 1950s, it merely compounded the feeling that the far south coast was being left behind. In 1958, the Australian political scientist Don Rawson attempted to describe the vast electorate of Eden–Monaro:

> The South Coast of New South Wales is an area of many grievances, and alleges neglect by State and, to a lesser extent, Federal governments. This is more than the common belief in country districts that they are subordinated to the cities: the South Coast considers itself the victim of discrimination in favour not only of Sydney, but of practically all the rest of the State.[7]

For most of its existence, the metropolitan centres of New South Wales and Victoria had dictated Eden's fate. As early as 1902, the editor of Eden's only news-paper described the town as a 'remote province tacked to a far off governing cen-tre, the bond of union being brittle and loose'.[8] Residents believed that their administrators in Sydney were ignorant of the difficulties faced by the ordinary person in 'making a living' on the far south coast. This belief also underpinned much of the resentment felt by local timber workers in the late twentieth centu-ry. They saw their jobs threatened by urban 'greenies' and politicians in Sydney who paraded 'environment friendly politics' without any understanding of the timber industry. In this sense, Eden is still a frontier with an ethos at odds with the distant government that presides over it.[9]

In Chapter 5, I tried to understand the absences in settler culture in the nine-teenth century, absences that partly explain the grievances of some people on the south coast today. Now, I want to turn to the late twentieth century and try to understand the insecurities, fears and concerns of many people on the far south coast. Those who believe they have been asked to give repeatedly, find it difficult to give again. Immersed in their own grievances, they can find little space or reason to begin a conversation on reconciliation.

WAITING
FOR EDEN

I have seen Eden! ... it contained no theatres, no public
buildings, no newspaper, and ... no anything ... Boydtown is
as completely deserted as Nineveh, or the cities of Yucatan.

VISITOR TO EDEN,
1857

Eden, or as it has become the fashion in ridicule to
call it 'Paradise', languishes in a sort of dead and alive
style pitiable to witness.

THE FIRST WORDS OF A CORRESPONDENT
after the opening of telegraph communication
between Sydney and Eden, 1868

Bringing an economically sustainable 'civilisation' to the far south coast has always been a struggle. Long before the politics of the New Left in the 1960s and 1970s began to challenge traditional beliefs in non-Aboriginal society, the people of Eden perceived themselves as victims — victims of distant and uninterested state and federal governments and victims of fate. The story of Eden has not been a story of economic success and continuing prosperity. Until 1970, almost every scheme for major development had come to naught.

In late 1967, when the NSW Government announced that an agreement had been reached with the Japanese company Harris Daishowa to supply pulpwood from the forests around Twofold Bay for conversion to woodchips, community hopes were high. Newspaper editors claimed the mill would bring Eden and Twofold Bay a 'commercial boom' its population could never believe possible. Yet as they wrote naively of 'the most exciting development proposal in Australian history', they also noticed 'the growing ranks of conservationists' in their community.[10]

From the moment the chip mill was announced in 1967, it faced the opposition of conservationists, many of whom lived in the major cities. For every local media story on the woodchip *Wirtschaftswunder*, there was another on the worrying government proposals for national park 'land grabs'.[11] The mill had been established without community consultation. The State Government had provided no avenues for public discussion. Large tracts of land were simply handed over to Harris Daishowa. There was no attempt to assess the environmental impact of the mill. There was no management plan, no attempt to consult Aboriginal people, and there were no scientific studies of flora and fauna. In fact the decision was not based on any extensive knowledge of the forests around Eden.

Founded in 1916, the NSW Forestry Commission had not begun to supervise the Eden forests until the 1960s.[12] Before then the forests had been the domain of sleeper-cutters and local timber workers who did largely as they pleased. In the 1920s, thousands of sleepers were cut and shipped to Sydney for use by the NSW State Railways, while others were exported to India, China and Germany. Large trees were often felled without concern for wastage, with as little as 20 per cent of the log sometimes being used, the remainder being left to rot on the forest floor.[13]

Well into the 1960s, newspapers carried photographs of timber workers felling big trees. Like the photographs of anglers holding 'big fish' that often adorned the walls of hotels and clubs, lumberjacks were seen in the press standing proudly in front of trees with a girth of over 30 feet. Yet whereas the sleeper-cutters and timber workers had logged selectively for over a hundred years, Harris Daishowa planned to log the forests using a different technique, clear felling, or as it was termed euphemistically by NSW State Forests, 'integrated logging'.[14] Over the next three decades, as Harris Daishowa donated thousands of dollars to sporting clubs and the funding of community projects, providing regular injections of cash to the local economy, it cleverly cultivated an image of the company as the town's benevolent protector. In its first environmental impact statement for the NSW Government in 1977, the company claimed that the woodchip industry was 'totally integrated with other industries and operations in the town of Eden'. Apparently it was devoted to the 'general wellbeing of the people of the south coast and to the ongoing improvement of the forests of Eden'. Therefore any threat to the viability of the woodchip industry was a threat to the livelihood of the people of Eden. The Japanese pulpwood manufacturer was now the champion of the 'little Aussie battler' of Eden.

Throughout the 1980s, the company could do little to quell the growing opposition to woodchipping. Visual images revealing the cataclysmic results of clear felling had a significant impact on Australians living in the cities, many of whom saw the forests of Eden for the first time on *Four Corners* or *Sixty Minutes*. The woodchip industry came under attack largely for three reasons: the method of logging, the end product, and its ultimate destination, Japan. Measured against the majesty and beauty of the forests, the economics of woodchipping appeared brutal and short-sighted. In the 1970s, the campaign against woodchipping in south-eastern New South Wales was led predominantly by the Australian Conservation

Foundation and charismatic public figures from the cities. In 1977, for example, the plan to extend woodchipping into forests north of Bega such as Tanja and Bermagui brought the likes of historian Manning Clark into the debate.[15]

In January 1977, Manning Clark attended an anti woodchip meeting at Tathra. The meeting was called because of the fear that the surrounding forests were about to be intensively logged for woodchips. Clark had a personal interest in proceedings as a property owner in the area, and his status as the nation's most renowned historian ensured that he was the main speaker. As was his way, Clark spoke in a calm and hushed voice. Before him, the audience sat in adoring silence, as if listening to a funeral oration by a preacher.

> I don't know very much about the subject. But I am an Australian and I am worried about the future of our country … my nightmare is that we are about to hand our country over to the money changers. [Cook first saw the Aborigines of Australia] not far from here. The Aborigines could not have known that on board the Endeavour were the means of destroying large parts of Australia … an axe to cut the forest, a hoe to change the soil and a rifle and shot. [The Aborigines of New Holland had no axe; they hadn't perfected the soil of Australia.] At the moment we are confronted with the fact that man can destroy this country of Australia. [Therefore the question is simple:] do we keep what we have? … Those forests of gum trees along our southeastern coast are among the most beautiful and valuable things that we have … but thank God there are people who love Australia as it is … I still have that terrible nightmare that some people want to take [the forest] down and use it for what? For things like package industries, utterly useless things … I hope we shall preserve what we have and hand it on to posterity. The great and important thing for every generation is to take the flame from the past and hand it on undiminished, that's our task. Don't for God's sake hand our country over to the robbers or … to people with an unholy hunger. Keep it as it is so that a simple fellow like myself can go on catching huge salmon at Wapengo.

Clark ended his speech on a lighthearted note, seemingly unaware that Aboriginal people had been using stone axes on his property for thousands of years. But his support for the anti-woodchipping cause did help to halt logging in the forests. In 1977, the NSW Government extended the Mimosa Rocks National Park to include most of the forests around Tathra. The government also recommended the identification and protection of all Aboriginal sites, an issue that Clark did not raise, largely because his support for the conservation movement was then founded more on nineteenth-century European romanticism than the politics of Aboriginal rights. Yet Clark's address also contained the kernel of the new environmental politics that would come to be seen by many working-class Australians on the south coast as yet another attack on their way of life by 'city theorists'. Clark depicted Aboriginal culture and the 'virgin' forests as innocent, and painted European culture as avaricious and destructive. Ordinary Australians who worked for Harris Daishowa were only aiding and abetting the 'robbers' and 'money changers' whose 'unholy hunger' would destroy Australia.[16]

As the success of the conservation movement gathered pace throughout the 1980s and 1990s, and the pressure on forestry workers mounted, the people of Eden and Bombala would feel threatened from various quarters. They would have their values challenged by 'hippies' and alternative lifestyle advocates, environmentalists, and 'dole bludgers', although they often failed to distinguish between them. They would face indigenous claims to land they had always considered to be rightfully theirs. They would be told that only 'greenies' and Aboriginal people understood the spiritual nature of the land and the forests. They believed many of these philosophies to be the product of meddling outsiders and 'blow-ins' from the city, an impression that merely reinforced a long-standing historical grievance — that they were the victims of government policies formulated in Sydney or Canberra.

When logging on Mumbulla Mountain north of Bega was brought to a halt by Percy Mumbler, Guboo Ted Thomas and a broad coalition of protesters in December 1978, the reaction of residents in Bega and Eden provided an interesting insight into the thinking of many in the non-Aboriginal community. Before the protests over the logging of Mumbulla Mountain, they had not been accustomed to dealing with the objections of Aboriginal people when they wished to clear the land. Unlike the logging of the forests around Eden, which began in 1969, the logging of Mumbulla Mountain in 1978 confronted a highly politicised indigenous lobby group. As Guboo Ted Thomas said in 1980, 'no one bothered to speak to us until we started to kick up a fuss'.[17]

This 'fuss' was most in evidence between July and December 1978. Letters flooded the pages of the local press and public meetings were held to discuss 'the Aborigines'' claim that their sacred sites were being desecrated. To some, the term 'sacred site' suggested that the relationship of Aboriginal people with the land was more authentic and intimate than non-Aboriginal relationships. This suggestion seemed all the more threatening in a society that had struggled to achieve economic success in its own terms. Listening to protesters explain that Aboriginal sacred sites were akin to a church or house of worship also implied that non-Aboriginal Australians could find the sacred only in bricks and mortar. For them, the bush, the land, the sea, and the flora and fauna that inhabited the earth, apparently served only one purpose — to be subdued and exploited.

Reports on the Mumbulla dispute in the metropolitan press, particularly the *Canberra Times*, emphasised the difference between cultures and described two incompatible ways of seeing the land. Aboriginal leaders like Guboo Ted Thomas were presented as mystical figures bearing secret knowledge. One feature article on Thomas in the *Canberra Times*, written by Gary Raffaele and photographed by Geritt Fokkema, cast Thomas as the Australian version of the Hollywood American Indian, spinning hippie-like words of wisdom to his hapless western interrogators:

> For the Anglo-Saxon ... rocks are rocks and mountains are mountains ... [Visiting a logging coupe] an area half the size of a soccer field looked as though it had been through a massive explosion. Around its perimeter stripped tree trunks lay at crazy angles, bark curled to the sky, and the earth had all but disappeared, leaving stark sandy stuff in which it appeared nothing would grow. 'Woodchipping' said the Aborigine. He looked at the scene of war, then took a red headband from his pocket. 'Sign of respect for sacred site' — in spite of desolation. Still respect ... Thomas looked up at the mountain. Through the spindly eucalypts. There was a track. I fell many times. The black man looked back in sympathy but walked on ... fifty metres from where the woodchippers had done their latest work, the rock loomed; grey, almost a face, strong powerful, mystical ... [It] had a force, a strength, a presence ... The Sistine [chapel] is there, in Rome ... the Christian can find it on maps, in history books, and it is an edifice. Built by man for the greater glory of his God. Mumbulla Mountain is there, risen out of the ground. And the rock is there, similarly risen out of the mountain. There is no plaque, no history book, no official recognition.[18]

Accompanying the article was Fokkema's photograph of Thomas standing in the cathedral forest.

Reports such as these implied that non-material relationships with the land were specific to Aboriginal culture. Non-Aboriginal Australians could only stumble helplessly behind in ignorance, or push dismissively past in bulldozers. There were dangers in this stereotype for both sides of the debate. Aboriginal culture could only be made sacred through the bush, and non-Aboriginal culture was condemned to permanent alienation, being denied a spiritual connection to the land.

When residents attended public meetings in Bega in 1978 they were also forced to confront indigenous oral history. Many found it difficult to accept that Aboriginal people had any knowledge of the environment. Some tried to suggest that they knew the places that were sacred to Aboriginal people better than any Aboriginal person. Brian Egloff, the anthropologist the State Government had commissioned to report on the indigenous claims at Mumbulla, faced questions from locals who couldn't understand why they hadn't heard of the sacred sites before. The chief forester for Harris Daishowa, Rauol Dixon, claimed that as

Guboo Ted Thomas at Mumbulla Mountain, 1979.
[By permission of *Canberra Times*, 16 September 1979]

logging on the mountain had been carried out for a century or more there was no reason to stop now; 'after all', he said, woodchippping would not 'change the aesthetic value of the mountain'.

Fortunately for Egloff, Aboriginal oral history could be corroborated partly by the 'scientific' evidence of AW Howitt. But Howitt's work was still insufficient proof for many residents who attended the public meetings. They continued to insist that the Aboriginal people making the land claim were not the descendants of 'the traditional Aboriginal landowners'. Howitt, they said, had not provided the necessary 'genealogical evidence'. In a remarkable feat of rhetorical ingenuity, the local Labor MP, J Atkiser, quoted several statements from Howitt's indigenous informants. He pointed out that at no time did 'the Aborigines' suggest that whites be 'excluded' from land rights. They had spoken to Howitt of their place of birth as 'their country' and asserted that they 'always had the right to hunt over it', like 'all others born' in the Bega Valley. Therefore, said Atkiser, anyone 'born at Bega Hospital could lay claim to similar land rights'.[19]

The author of a letter published in the local newspaper in Eden also argued against the claim that Mumbulla Mountain was an Aboriginal sacred site on the grounds that the protesters were not the original descendants of the first Aboriginal people. Jean Draper asked, 'How many full-blooded Aborigines are there in the area today? ... The line has been broken'. Breaking the line was of course a euphemism for dispossession — Aboriginal people could no longer claim to be the 'original' possessors of the land because their line of ownership had been broken. On this basis, their claims to possess intimate knowledge of the traditional cultural significance of 'sacred sites' were bogus. Aboriginal people were the intruders.[20] So strong was the cult of the victim in non-Aboriginal society that many people came to believe they were now the victims of unfair and illegitimate land claims by Aboriginal activists. Press reports emphasised the plight of timber workers and the local economy. Honest working men and women, they said, would be left with 'nowhere to go'. The forest on Mumbulla Mountain contained 'the only good collection of sawlogs' in the area. If they were not logged the effects for the area would be 'catastrophic'.[21] At one meeting, Guboo Ted Thomas attempted to explain to local residents the importance of Mumbulla. '[Mumbulla is] important to us Aborigines, but we think it should also be important to white Australians as well. It is something that should be important to our Australian heritage'.[22]

When John Hatton, the Independent Member for the South Coast in the NSW Parliament, addressed another meeting, he asked the audience whether a white man whose family had been in the valley for a hundred years would want to have his lands desecrated.[23] But for many residents who had long seen themselves as victims, any suggestion that their land use patterns should be altered because of the spiritual significance of the land to Aboriginal people fell on deaf ears. Despite the pleas of Thomas for a shared heritage, for the vast majority of people in south-eastern New South Wales in 1978, non-Aboriginal heritage and Aboriginal heritage remained mutually exclusive.

In Sydney, the State Labor Government, under the leadership of Premier Neville Wran, was much more receptive to the indigenous campaign than the people of Bega and Eden. Percy Mumbler and other Aboriginal leaders from the south coast had addressed Labor Party conferences in the late 1970s and won over many party delegates. In 1980, after almost three years of intense debate and negotiation, Thomas and Mumbler succeeded in obtaining the NSW Government's agreement in declaring 7508 hectares of state forest an Aboriginal place. No logging was to be permitted in or around Aboriginal sacred sites. Although the decision was not an outright victory for indigenous claims, it still represented a watershed in the management of the forests in the south-east.

After Mumbulla, the NSW Forestry Commission supported archaeological surveys in other forests and consulted Aboriginal people more closely. The 1980s would become the first decade since European settlement when research into Aboriginal use of forest environments in the south-eastern New South Wales preceded logging.[24] But for forestry workers and many people in Eden–Monaro, the obligation to acknowledge and assess indigenous claims to land only added another burden to the shoulders of the 'working man', whose daily bread was allegedly being threatened by conservationists.

Releasing its second environmental impact statement on its future operations in the forests around Eden in 1986, Harris Daishowa claimed that the major environmental problems associated with woodchipping had been 'largely overcome'. This statement alone was sufficient to incite a broad coalition of protesters to blockade forests, chain themselves to trees, obstruct bulldozers and sabotage forestry machinery.[25]

The most intense period of conflict between conservationists and the forest industry came in the wake of Harris Daishowa's environmental impact statement. In the summer of 1986–87, more than a thousand people were arrested in the forests. So intense was the conflict that the NSW Government was forced to bring in its 'tactical response group' to support local police.[26] It was during this period that the social and political divide between local forestry workers and conservationists came to the fore. While forest workers cast conservationists as Reds in disguise, anarchists, dole bludgers and romantic tree-huggers, conservationists ridiculed the workers as buffoons bent on destroying the very environment that supported them. The local campaign for the conservationists, led by the South-East Forest Alliance, formed in 1985, mocked police in the tactical response group camp as fascists on parole from the Sydney Mardis Gras parade. The chorus of one of their campaign songs recited with much gusto in the forests in 1989 went as follows:

I wear jackboots, I shave my legs,
I put red lipstick on.
On weekends I chase Greenies.
And have me lots of fun.[27]

After the Australian Heritage Commission listed the Tantawangalo and Coolangubra forests on the register of the national estate in May 1986, and forest protests intensified, the State Labor Government halted logging in 90 per cent of the contested areas in the Eden woodchip area. The politics of the woodchipping industry in Eden was now playing an important role in stimulating the environmental consciousness of all Australians. But in Eden–Monaro, people cared little for the concerns of the wilderness calendar romantics in the cities.

When the NSW Labor Government under Premier Barry Unsworth declared Tantawangalo and Coolungubra national parks in early 1988, adding 80 000 hectares to the national estate, it reminded the electorate that Australia had 'lost two thirds of its trees in the last 200 years' and needed a 'new approach' in its 'third century as a European nation'. But in Eden and Bombala, the closure of local sawmills and the reduction in woodchip production was portrayed as an attempt to throw local workers on the scrap heap. Russell Smith, the Liberal Party candidate for Bega, referred to the 'socialist government' in Sydney, which he said was intent on forcing honest working Australians onto the dole. Lovers of freedom such as Mr Smith had also been irritated when the socialists introduced legislation restricting the sale of firearms. Stirred to anger, forestry workers demonstrated in Canberra and throughout the region. Signs were posted over the fire danger indicators on the side of major highways indicative of war: 'Greenies enter at your own risk! National Parks can't protect what they've got why give 'em more?' To most people in Eden–Monaro, every proposal for a new national park represented another 'land grab'. If nature was a free gift from the Lord above, it should not be 'locked up', least of all from the bulldozers of Harris Daishowa. Inspired perhaps by their opponents' talent for musical improvisation, forestry workers penned some songs of their own:

Australians all let us revolt
For we are no longer free
With Unsworth Hawke and tax for toil
We've lost our liberty
Our land once abound in nature's gifts
But they're no longer free
Instead we've got a monorail and taxes on our beer
So in joyful strains then let us sing
Unsworth must go this year.

And so the Premier did, though not only for the reasons listed above. Local papers in the area placed this 'new national anthem' on their front pages. Photographs below showed the distraught wives of timber workers clutching their children. As the propaganda war intensified, local support groups formed.[28] Those opposed to the 'greenies'' agenda began slowly to realise they needed their own 'forest protection' societies and 'timber support' groups. NSW State Forests positioned signs on the roadside informing passing tourists that the area of forest regrowth they could see through the tinted windows of their cars had been 'logged in 1974'. Like the front lawn, the forests 'grew back'. Leaflets produced by State Forests likened eucalypts to the pioneers: 'As soon as the forest is disturbed, eucalypt seeds spring to life … our eucalypts are aggressive colonisers'. Towns dependent on the timber industry such as Bombala had new signs planted on the highway proclaiming the town as a 'timber town'.[29] 'Timber' meant timber falling as opposed to timber standing. 'Greenies' who dared to enter the wrong social circles such as pro-logging meetings or certain local hotels in Bombala sometimes claimed to have been abused verbally, threatened with violence, or had the tyres of their vehicles slashed. By the late 1980s, a social and political divide had opened up in Eden–Monaro which is still present today — a divide between virtuous workers and parasite dole bludgers, between genuine locals and city blow-ins, between civilisation and feral gangs, and between 'common sense' utilisation of natural resources and romantic environmentalists who live under the illusion that 'wilderness' can remain unchanged.

Throughout the 1990s, one theme that surfaced continuously in the political campaign of the forest industry lobby groups was 'resource insecurity'. In 1998, a report prepared for the NSW Forest Products Association listed nineteen events and decisions that had imposed changes on the timber industry between 1989 and 1995. Most of those changes had resulted in job losses and had decreased hardwood sawlog volumes. In October 1990, the Hawke–Greiner Agreement, a joint agreement between the Commonwealth and NSW Governments, eventually ratified in 1993, created six new national parks in the south-east forests, together with two nature reserves. In total, the agreement transferred 45 000 hectares from state forests to conservation reserves.

In 1999, the Regional Forest Agreement (RFA), signed by the Commonwealth Government and the NSW Labor Premier, Bob Carr, attempted to end the uncertainty by guaranteeing a fixed quantity of sawlogs per annum for a period of fifteen years, while at the same time appeasing conservationists by securing the existence of the new national parks Carr had announced in 1998. The RFA was presented as the cure-all agreement, one that would satisfy the demands of both warring parties. It employed the catchphrases of both conservationists and the timber lobby. A national reserve system would allegedly promote the 'ecologically sustainable management' of forests and the 'long term stability of forest industries'. It insisted on the protection of 'old growth' forests, 'wilderness', 'endangered species', national estate and world heritage values, indigenous heritage values, and the 'economic and social values of forests', none of which were presented as competing interests. The RFA was the agreement for all seasons, but while the political conflict over woodchipping did subside it would not disappear.[30]

In the midst of the intense political battles that had preceded the RFA for more than a decade, another history was being created and remembered by forest workers and their supporters, a history that told of financial hardship and psychological stress, a history that told yet another tale of the victim's distress.

In 1997 and 1998, as part of the preparatory work on the RFA, the NSW Government commissioned private research on the social effects of structural adjustment in the timber industry. Workers living in Eden, Bega and Bombala were interviewed and their identities protected. Reading the statements published in these reports is a moving experience, regardless of one's political views. It is impossible not to feel for men who have lost perhaps the most important source of meaning in their life — work. Between December 1995 and June 1997, 130 workers in the native hardwoods timber industry lost their jobs.

One report in 1997 interviewed thirty-two workers and business owners who had been 'displaced' by recent changes in the forest industry. Nearly all had left school at 15 or 16, and most had worked within the timber industry all their working lives, some for as long as thirty years. Being made redundant was, for all men, their first experience of unemployment. Some stated proudly that they had lived within their communities 'all their lives' and envisaged remaining within them 'until death'. Their allegiance to place was strong, so strong that it deepened their sense of shame at being unemployed. Because communities were close-knit, almost everyone knew everyone else. Unemployment was a public and social embarrassment that that could not be hidden. There was no nearby suburb in which to seek work. All men felt they had been dealt a harsh blow by outside forces beyond their control. Their personal comments told a story of hurt and hardship:

> It's been hard on a lot of people — people with families paying cars and houses off. A lot of them must be feeling the pinch. The cannery put a lot of people off ... A lot of bushmen's wives worked there. When men and their wives both lost their jobs it was very hard, bloody awful.

> They said someone's gotta go and I was the one they told they didn't want any more. They said: 'We looked around at the people we wanted in the company and you're not one of them'.

> I feel the government put me out of work, tried to take me guns off me, took me job off me, and now [the CES] tell me, 'You're not trying hard enough for work' and we've worked all our lives.

We are the forgotten end of New South Wales, you feel as if you are unwanted.

I don't see no future — you haven't got no manual work so what are you going to do?

My life is gone, it hurts that much … people just can't relate to us being on the dole at all — especially when I've been working for such a long time.

I haven't been up the street for some time, I feel about this big — 'Look at him, he's a dole bludger'.

Interestingly, the men described their relationship with the forests as one of care and 'appreciation of the beauty and peace of their working environment'. They spoke of their love for the forests, especially the need to 'care about fauna' and to ensure the community's capacity to 'fight fires'. In fact a large part of their intellectual justification for logging rested on opening up the forest to fire fighters. This argument resonated in the town, because fear of fire was etched deeply into the psyche of the community. And because forest workers perceived themselves as 'carers of the forest' they claimed to be hurt by the 'greenies'' behaviour and attitude towards them. They claimed to have had excrement thrown at them, seen their machinery destroyed or sabotaged, and been frightened by the prospect that protesters lying in front of logging vehicles could be killed. The general climate of abuse and conflict surrounding the forest dispute had driven them to despair. Some men expressed 'suicidal tendencies', fearing for their health, personal relationships and future prospects. Others articulated their experience more broadly, linking it to the general feeling in the town of Eden, which they described as 'a sense of resignation' and a 'loss of hope'. The authors of the report agreed: 'Eden is a region under considerable stress, if not in crisis … There is a lot of anger in the community with a potentially explosive quality. People are taking things into their own hands and white community assaults on Aboriginals have increased'.

Although no evidence was cited in the report to support such an allegation, the connection between rural grievance and resentment of Aboriginal people in receipt of any form of positive discrimination is clear. Non-Aboriginal communities who see themselves as victims of unfair government decisions do not accept the same governments granting Aboriginal people what they perceive to be 'special treatment'. Every victim should be treated 'equally'.[31] The national appeal of Pauline Hanson's One Nation Party in the late 1990s is visible here on a local level, as is the appeal of the promises made by the major political parties in 2001 to defend Australia's borders from asylum seekers in leaky boats. If jobs have been lost or threatened, why should others be allowed into Australia until those jobs are made secure? The politics of grievance and protest, which the Australian political scientist Geoffrey Stokes has described as 'conservative populism', thrive when the uneducated male battler believes he has been abandoned.[32]

Economic and social indicators that emerged from government reports and the Australian Bureau of Statistics in the late 1990s, especially in Eden and Bombala, revealed communities under severe stress. Unemployment rates were considerably higher than state or national averages. Hospitals and services were limited, there was a large percentage of unskilled workers, and incomes were generally low. In Eden, for example, only 2 per cent of the population earned over $50 000 per annum. Every social and economic indicator suggested the region was 'relatively disadvantaged compared with State averages'.[33]

One of the few causes for optimism, expressed in reports commissioned by the government in the 1990s, was the Eden fishing industry. Eden has long been one of New South Wales' major fishing ports. Together with the timber industry and tourism, the fishing industry forms the backbone of the local economy. Today, several hundred people are employed full or part-time in the industry, with Eden supplying much of the fish to the Sydney Fish Markets. But fishing is not only important to the town's economy. It also forms the core of the community's folklore. Stories of whaling and fishing are the scaffold of the community's identity. The Eden Museum was established in 1931 immediately after the end of shore-based whaling to preserve and house the memories of the industry.

The canning of fish began in Eden shortly after the Second World War with the expansion of the commercial fishing industry. Tuna had been canned in Eden from the early 1950s, the ownership of the local cannery passing from Greens to Kraft in 1961, and then to Heinz in 1974. With the disappearance of protective tariffs in the 1980s, the Eden cannery came under increasing pressure from cheap tuna imports from countries such as Thailand. Workers rallied to the threat with a media campaign to 'Buy Australian Tuna'. But by the mid-1990s there were already rumours that the plant would be forced to close down. In June 1997, after a $2 million upgrade, the cannery's 230 workers were reduced to 150 in the name of efficiency and global competitiveness. As they had done in 1995, many of those who remained agreed to work fewer hours in order to save the jobs of their friends.[34] But only two years later, in May 1999, Heinz announced the closure of the cannery. In the words of Neville Fielke, the managing director of Heinz Watties in Australia, the 'tuna canning plant was not globally competitive'. Already believing themselves to be under siege from indigenous claims to land, both spiritual and material, government policies demanding cutbacks in the logging industry, and environmentalists, the working class of Eden now had another enemy to face — globalisation.

Press reports relayed the shock in the local community. Job losses totalled 12 per cent of Eden's workforce, 145 in all. Many who lost their jobs had worked at the cannery for more than a decade. Some were couples or families. A hundred and fourteen of the workers lived in Eden, while thirty-one lived in nearby areas. By any measure, the closure of the cannery was a devastating blow to a community already under considerable strain.[35]

When 300 people met at the Eden Fisherman's Club on 5 May 1999 to 'fight' the closure of the cannery, a decision they claimed was based on 'greed', many knew it was a futile exercise. Whereas government decisions could be reversed or amended, the decisions of corporate executives made offshore were final. Workers were left feeling powerless. As one worker told the meeting, 'they're not going to re-open it no matter what we do'. Speakers mentioned their fear at not being able to give their children 'a place to live and work in the future'. Signs were placed on the roads leading to the cannery — 'Keep our Cannery', 'Lives before dollars', 'Eden needs more jobs not less', 'No cannery no town'. Once again, the people of Eden felt they had been betrayed. Despite their efforts to succeed in the 'global economy', they had been discarded, still victims of forces beyond their control.

While local high school students organised petitions, council officials and representatives from the Chamber of Commerce travelled to Sydney to meet with Premier Bob Carr. The government explained bluntly that the local economy 'must be restructured'. Glenda Orland, 'Corporate Communications Manager' for Heinz Watties, might have been more accurately described as 'Retrenchment Communications Manager'. Insisting that the decision was not reversible, she reminded workers that the company's primary responsibility was to ensure a 'return to shareholders'. This explanation may have brought comfort to investors, but it did little for the people who had built their lives around the social networks formed during many years working at the cannery.[36] Bev Walker, a long-time cannery employee, tried to explain why: 'This global stuff means nothing to us … The company put in a new system and we got it up and running. They put in new targets and we got them too. Now they've turned around and [deserted us]. I am bitter, of course I am, this has really torn the heart out of [Eden]'.[37]

This 'global stuff' meant that employees bore the brunt of economic change which followed in the wake of deregulation. Being told they were not 'efficient' and were unable to 'compete' in the global market shattered their assumptions about civil society and the economic system in which they lived. Losing their jobs in such a brutal manner also made them question their purpose in life. For the twenty-six men and women who worked at the cannery and were over 50 years of age, there was no new career in waiting. No retraining scheme or redundancy payout could take away the loss of identity and pride they had suffered. Yet the emotional and financial suffering caused by unemployment was not a simple tale of poor whites in distress. Aboriginal people had worked in the cannery since it was established in the late 1940s. While the number of Aboriginal workers had declined in the final decade of the cannery's operation, the Aboriginal workers that remained faced the same dole queues and social consequences as their non-Aboriginal colleagues.

On 9 July, the last day of the cannery's operation, Channel Nine's *Today* program broadcast live from the cannery. Wreaths were placed on the gates. Some workers pleaded for the battler's hero, Dick Smith, to come to their aid. Eight months later the cannery was sold, the future site of a major tourist resort.[38]

Since 1990, the cannery employees had published their own journal, *Fish Tales*, a monthly newsletter containing staff and community news that was distributed widely throughout the town. Rhonda Gallagher, who worked in the cannery from 1988, until its closure in 1999, wrote in the final edition:

> Eden is a wonderful place to live and the cannery has been a great place to work. Many lifelong friendships have been formed, some employees are the third generation of their family to work here … Eden people have also been very proud of our cannery, it is part of our town's history … The Heinz company has said that we are not globally competitive … but the plant is productive and efficient … and the workers are loyal and conscientious.

Together with her friend Denis Peters, Rhonda Gallagher produced a small book commemorating the history of the cannery and those who worked there: *Greenseas: The Way We Were.* Photographs of golfing days and family picnics organised by employees break the text. In Eden, the cannery had been one basis for constructing both history and community. Gallagher's book concludes with a photographic roll call of the 144 workers who lost their jobs in 1999. Like snapshots of the casualties of tragedy or war that sometimes appear in the press, the cumulative effect of these photographs is to convey the human cost of retrenchment. The faces are the faces of the town of Eden, but they are also the faces of many people in regional Australia who have lost their jobs in the name of global competition. Unknown but familiar, they are the faces of communities under threat.

Writing on the subject of local history, Australian historian Graeme Davison recently observed that:

> community is always in the process of disappearing [and is] constituted as a subject of history more by the nostalgia of those who mourn its passing and the testimony of those who attest its persistence. How can we continue to believe in ideas of community, locality or neighbourhood in a society where all the big decisions are made out of town?[39]

Perhaps many people in Eden–Monaro have asked themselves the same question. Yet while they harbour deep fears for the future of their communities, their belief in 'community' is much more than nostalgia or wishful thinking on the part of a vocal minority. Retrenchments in the timber and fishing industries, the closure of banks and the threatened closure of public hospitals have only deepened the

THE GREENSEAS TEAM OF 1999

*Sue
Walker*

*Steven
Bell*

*Chris
Jones*

*Ken
Campbell*

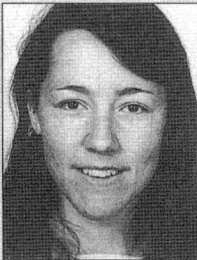

*Theresa
Dykhoff*

*Heather
Matthews*

*Jillian
Edwards*

*Helma
Luimes*

30 - Greenseas Cannery, Eden

'Save our Jobs, Save our Town'. Retrenched cannery workers, Eden, 1999.
[By permission of Rhonda Gallagher, Eden]

conviction of residents that their 'community' is real, both in its history and in its living social networks. Their 'community' is constituted by their presence at rallies and public meetings, by their participation in local politics, by their local press and media and by their profound attachment to place. This community, despite its difficulties, is proud of its survival, and while it may be a community under threat, it is a community nonetheless.[40]

Since the first European settlers came to the region in the 1830s, non-Aboriginal society in south-eastern New South Wales has identified strongly with narratives of the forgotten victim, narratives that have only been reinforced by recent events. These stories have changed over time, but at their heart is a common refrain:

We are not the colonisers.

We are not the receivers of the spoils of war.

We are not living on stolen ground.

We are the victims of neglect.

We are the battlers.

We are the people of 'the forgotten corner', waiting for Eden to arrive.

confrontation

8

NEW HISTORY, NEW POLITICS

> Exploration, exploring the past! We students in the camps
> seminar considered ourselves radical explorers. We tore open
> the windows and let in the air, the wind that finally whirled
> away the dust that society had permitted to settle over the
> horrors of the past … It was evident to us that there had to
> be convictions … The more horrible the events about which
> we read and heard, the more certain we became of our
> responsibility to enlighten and accuse.
>
> BERNHARD SCHLINK,
> *The Reader*, 1997[1]

Bernhard Schlink's novel *The Reader*, published in 1997, tells the story of a young German and his much older lover Hanna. They fall in love shortly after the Second World War, when the boy is barely 15 years old. In the early 1950s, when the affair is over, the boy, now a young man enrolled as a legal student, observes the trials of concentration camp personnel responsible for the Holocaust. On the first day of the trial, he is shocked to find that Hanna is one of the accused. As a former member of the SS, she served as a camp guard in Auschwitz until early 1944 and in a smaller camp near Cracow until the winter of 1944–45. As an SS guard, Hanna was responsible for the 'selection' process — as more and more transports of Jewish prisoners arrived at the camp, Hanna decided which Jews already resident in the camp would be sent to the gas chambers. Hanna's former lover struggles to come to the terms with the fact that he once loved a woman who was guilty of such horrible crimes.

> I wanted simultaneously to understand Hanna's crime and to condemn it. But it was too terrible for that. When I tried to understand it, I had the feeling I was failing to condemn it as it must be condemned. When I condemned it as it must be condemned, there was no room for understanding … I had to point at Hanna. But the finger I pointed at her turned back to me. I had loved her.[2]

The Reader explores the related themes of history, injustice, guilt and recrimination through the prism of generational divide and love remembered. As the story progresses, Schlink slowly reveals the complex range of human emotions and intellectual contradictions associated with any attempt to pass judgment on the past — from denial and pity, through the irreconcilable and competing desire to both condemn and understand Hanna's crime, to eventual resignation.

In both post-Nazi Germany and post-apartheid South Africa, there was a particular point in time when political regimes, and the racist beliefs which underpinned them, were defeated and discredited. Shortly afterwards, the citizens of both countries were confronted with a public trial of their recent history. It was in this context that the process of confrontation and historical understanding began — a revolutionary moment when, through a controlled process of legal interrogation, public confessions and formal statements, the past could be assessed in different terms. The narrator in Bernhard Schlink's novel, who is many ways representative of the German nation at large, is forced to confront a different history in one cathartic moment.

Australia has seen no 'cathartic' moment when the history of Aboriginal dispossession has been suddenly exposed; there has been no Nuremberg Trial, no Truth and Reconciliation Commission as White Australia came to an end, no ideology abruptly giving way, no Wall falling, no point when the past suddenly fell away. Instead, the process of confronting the past in twentieth-century Australia has been gradual. Beginning in the 1960s, and continuing through a succession of pivotal moments over the next four decades — the Bicentenary in 1988, the *Mabo* decision in 1992, and perhaps the closest Australia has come to a truth commission, the political controversy surrounding the Stolen Generations in 1997 — the process of confronting the history of Aboriginal dispossession continues to the present day. Throughout this period, as I showed in earlier chapters, narratives of acknowledgment have continued to coexist with narratives of denial, forgetting and evasion. But the 1960s and 1970s did see the end of Stanner's Great Australian Silence, which had reigned since the time of Federation. Critical histories of the Australian frontier emerged together with an increasingly politicised Aboriginal resistance. And in the public commemoration of 'founding moments', such as the Cook Bicentenary in 1970 and the Bicentenary in 1988, these new forms of history and politics helped to create what is now a familiar dilemma — how can we celebrate our history in the knowledge of what happened to Aboriginal Australians?

If there was one point when a more critical view of Australian history began to emerge in Australia's public culture, it was probably 1970. This was not a catharsis, or the sudden exposure of a grisly past, but perhaps it did see the beginning of a 30-year period when a sense of moral crisis emerged concerning the legitimacy of the Australian nation. The Cook Bicentenary was the first occasion in Australia's history when political resistance on the anniversary of a founding moment forced non-Aboriginal Australians to question the 'Australian Story'. Unlike 1938, when the Aborigines Progressive Association declared 26 January a Day of Mourning, and the mainstream press remained largely unmoved, in 1970 the broadsheet press was willing to embrace a more critical view of the past.

When Queen Elizabeth II sat beside her ministers and esteemed subjects to watch the re-enactment of Captain Cook's landing at Kurnell on 29 April 1970, she saw Aboriginal men and women dressed in brown trunks and corroboree paint acting out the performance of a story which had been told by white Australia for almost two hundred years. Cook's Tahitian interpreter stepped ashore and offered the Aboriginal people beads. Cook stood in his boat and fired a musket shot into the air. Aboriginal men rushed forward to throw rocks, but as one prepared to throw a spear another shot was fired, wounding one tribesman in the leg. The men retired and Cook walked ashore, taking 'possession of the east coast of Australia in the name of the King, naming it New South Wales.'[3] The re-enactment, screened nationwide on television, was described by a headline in the *Age* the following day as 'guilt-edged'.[4]

In February 1970, Asher Joel, chairman of the Captain Cook Bicentenary celebrations, was forced to defend the celebrations in much the same way as Jim Kirk, chairman of the Bicentenary Authority, would be forced to do on the occasion of the Bicentenary in 1988. 'We are not trying to commemorate the taking over of a continent', said Joel, 'we are recreating the birth of a country … We are going to direct attention to the achievements of the past 200 years'.[5]

With signs of a united federal Aboriginal political movement already evident, the poet Kath Walker, Queensland secretary of the Federal Council for the Advancement of Aborigines and Torres Strait Islanders (FCAATSI), led the protests against the 'offensive' commemoration of Cook's landing in April 1970.[6]

On the day of the landing at Kurnell on 29 April, FCAATSI marked the occasion as a day of mourning, just as the Aborigines Progressive Association had done in 1938. 'We intend a silent, dignified vigil of protest', said Walker. 'Those who cannot afford to wear black clothes will be asked to wear black armbands or bows'.[7] In Hobart, on the day of the centenary celebrations, students wearing black armbands demonstrated against the Tasmanian government's refusal to grant Truganini's last wish to be buried at sea.[8] In Melbourne, more than 150 people marched from Captain Cook's Cottage in the Treasury Gardens denouncing Cook as an invader and calling for Aboriginal land rights.[9] In Sydney and Canberra, the wearing of red headbands to symbolise the spilling of Aboriginal blood, as well as black dress and black armbands, were common features of vigils and protests. In the words of Kath Walker, the wearing of black dress symbolised both the genocide committed against Aboriginal people since the white man arrived and their present disadvantage.[10]

It was significant that Walker, a poet, should employ the black armband as a metaphor for the historical experience of her people. The collection of poems that she published in 1964, *We are Going*, bore the same spirit of mourning and resistance carried in her political protest. In the poem 'We are Going', she lamented the fact that Aboriginal people had become 'strangers' and outcasts in their own land, but she also insisted that the real strangers were the whites who rubbished sacred land as they hurried 'about like ants'. As a theatrical device, Walker's use of the black armband in 1970 proved effective, eliciting responses from the authorities and the press that would be echoed again in 1988 and beyond.

When the celebrations were over, broadsheet editorials began to display a new sensitivity to the Aboriginal perspective on the Cook Bicentenary. The *Age* stated that 'from the Aborigines' point of view the past 200 years had ... been ... bitter shame filled years', and admitted that the emerging truth of 'white brutality' on the frontier had at last stirred the 'white Australian's conscience'.[11] The *Australian* went even further, providing a text that bore a striking resemblance to Prime Minister Paul Keating's Redfern Park Speech twenty-two years later. Haunted by the 'dark side of the Endeavour' and the 'genocide' of Aboriginal Australians, the *Australian* accepted that 'Aborigines' mourned the coming of Cook as a symbol of 'death':

> We came bearing Christianity ... we also brought rum and smallpox, revolvers and Martini-Henry Carbines to slaughter men, women and children who speared the cattle we released on their land. And when we couldn't kill them we smothered them — withholding education, banning and banishing them ... They were easy victories, and we are still winning them — every time we shut our eyes, turn our backs, comfort ourselves with the myth that we are the world's most egalitarian people ... The Aboriginal concept of land is much deeper, more meaningful than ours ... Should we celebrate our nationhood while ignoring the schism dividing us?[12]

By any measure, this editorial is extraordinary for 1970 Australia. Its mea culpa tone included castigation of European culture, even going so far as to suggest that Aboriginal spirituality and sense of belonging to the land was superior to that of white Australians — finally throwing the hands up in resignation as if nothing could be done to redeem the situation. This contrite response to the history of dispossession would be repeated frequently over the next thirty years as a confession of responsibility and guilt, accompanied by self-flagellation, the head hanging low as if asking for forgiveness, full of remorse and sympathy.

After the Day of Mourning protests in April 1970, this version of Australia's founding moment was now so discredited it could no longer sustain critical attack.[13] The white man's sacred site of Kurnell was now the site of Aboriginal mourning where wreaths of remembrance were thrown into the sea.[14] In 1988, there would be no government-sponsored re-enactment of Phillip's landing at Sydney Cove or the arrival of the First Fleet. The founding moment could not be re-enacted because it was considered to be 'offensive' to Aboriginal Australians. A sense of paralysis had been created — it was as if there was no longer an opening sentence for Australian history. Aboriginal protesters, staging their own re-enactment, threw 'Phillip' into the waters of Sydney Harbour.[15]

Siding with the Aboriginal protesters who had declared 26 January 1988 a Day of Mourning, the *Sydney Morning Herald* claimed that the 'great unsettled issue' was 'the relations between European and Aboriginal Australia ... [and] only when Australians are reconciled with this aspect of their past, will the process of building a genuine Australian culture be credible'.[16]

Throughout the 1990s, with the High Court decisions in *Mabo* and *Wik* and a succession of public inquiries into the past and contemporary disadvantage of Aboriginal Australians, this question remained at the heart of the political and social movement for reconciliation, and of Australian federal politics. It was at the centre of the extraordinary community response to the release of the Human Rights and Equal Opportunity Commission's 1997 report into the Stolen Generations, *Bringing Them Home*, a response which historian Anna Haebich has described as a 'tragic dirge recounted around the country'.[17] It also helped to explain the marches for reconciliation that took place across Australia in May 2000. Over time, a considerable number of Australians had come to believe that Australia's identity and moral legitimacy as a nation would remain tarnished and incomplete until reconciliation between Aboriginal and non-Aboriginal Australians could be achieved.

Having explored the historical identity of non-Aboriginal Australians in south-eastern New South Wales in the previous chapters, I turn now to the history of Aboriginal people, particularly in the period between the early 1960s and 2000. In doing so, I am not setting out to write the history of one group in society. Instead, I hope to show that in the last decades of the twentieth century, the history of Aboriginal Australians became the vital issue affecting the national identity of non-Aboriginal Australians and the moral legitimacy of their nation. The history of one is the history of the other. I also hope that my local focus might illuminate the national story.

I want to address the key issues affecting our historical understanding of this period by asking a series of questions. Who was responsible for creating the sense of moral crisis that had so clearly come to characterise Australian politics by 1997? How had the process of confronting a more critical view of Australia's past occurred? How, for example, did the interaction between non-Aboriginal and Aboriginal activists and Australian historians assist this process of confrontation?

How, in turn, did this create tension in local and regional government, as it did in the theatre of Australian federal politics?

This history begins not in 1960 but 1860. This is because for Aboriginal people on the south coast of New South Wales, history is not something that can be compartmentalised as the specific domain or responsibility of previous generations. There is no tidy line that can be drawn between the past and the present.

The past lives in the person of every Aboriginal person. History is us, the country is us, 'we are all one'.

'WE ARE
ALL ONE'

I really get cross when people say, 'Oh, what are you
on about? You don't come from here anyway!' That
really sticks in my craw. I always say, 'Look, that's
not important. I'm Koori, that's it!'

MARY DUROUX,
Moruya, 1997[18]

In 1904, William Lunney walked from Bowral in the Southern Highlands of
New South Wales to Bega on the south coast, a distance of more than 300 kilometres. Towards the end of his journey, approaching the small village of Tilba Tilba
about 70 kilometres from Bega, he wrote later in his journal: 'the road passed over
a range of low hills — rather lovely except for the presence of Aborigines several
of whom I met on the road … at different intervals and I was always pleased when
I had passed them safely'.[19]

In his long trek down the coast, Lunney saw no other Aboriginal person. Only
a hundred years after Aboriginal societies had thrived along the south coast, it was
possible to travel for weeks without seeing one Aboriginal person. Lunney was
unaware at the time, but his sighting of 'Aborigines' was explained by the fact that
he had passed by Wallaga Lake, the first Aboriginal reserve to be established by the
NSW Aborigines Protection Board thirteen years earlier in 1891. It was at Wallaga
Lake that Guboo Ted Thomas, one of the leaders of the fight to declare Bega's
Mumbulla Mountain an Aboriginal sacred site in the late 1970s, remembered seeing his uncle shoot over the head of a Protection Board officer who was trying to
remove children from the reserve.[20]

By the 1860s, the traditional life of Aboriginal people on the far south coast had
been devastated. That decade saw the largest influx of settlers into the area, with the
break-up of the large squatting runs in favour of the smaller holdings
of free selectors. Aboriginal people, with their right to land unrecognised, came
to live either on the fringes of white society or on the reserves at Wallaga Lake
on the south coast north of Bega, and Lake Tyers on the north-east coast of Victoria.

The bureaucratic solutions to the 'Aboriginal problem' devised by the NSW Aborigines Protection Board, established in 1883, emerged within a settler culture which had long believed it was the duty of 'civilised' society to control the movement and behaviour of Aboriginal people. Long before the reserve at Wallaga Lake was staffed and managed by the Protection Board in 1891, the settlers were keen to 'round up' remaining 'Aborigines' onto mission stations or gazetted reserves. This was their way of tidying up the business of conquest. Once Aboriginal people could be removed from sight, they might be forgotten more easily. In 1887, the *Bega Standard* called for the rounding up of the last 'flock of Aborigines' about the Bega Reserve:

> The effort being made … to localise the Wallaga blacks on the reserve at that lake [is] to induce them to make it their home; and to arrange that the

Aboriginal People at Wallaga Lake, New South Wales,
photographed by William Corkhill, c. 1900.
[TT828, By permission of National Library of Australia]

children should have inducements to remain there, in place of tramping the country with their parents to get undesirable knowledge of the world at races and other country gatherings. The object has so far been accomplished ... Other attempts have been dignified by the title of missions: this is simply an attempt to home the blacks.[21]

Occasionally, press reports described corroborees, such as one that took place at Wallaga Lake in 1900, but these were often portrayed as little more than quaint theatre for the amusement of whites. In April 1900, one journalist complained that in performing their corroboree the 'Aborigines' at Wallaga Lake had not paid enough attention to 'dressing', unlike the corroborees of 'the old tribal days'. Reports describing Aboriginal people living on the fringe of town usually referred to them as 'remnants' or presented them as tragic figures bereft of hope. One year later, in 1888, the *Standard* reported on the death of one of oldest 'Aborigines' in the area, Queero:

Queero was the oldest and one of the few remaining members of his tribe, and was supposed to be about 65 years of age, as Mr. Underhill, senior, rec- ollects him as a boy of about 8 or 9 years of age, when he first arrived at Eden in 1832 with the Messrs Imlay. Often when asked his age, he would reply that he was a big boy when Captain Cook arrived ... Queero's lubra, Sally, is still alive, and is in a most deplorable state, being imbecile, nearly blind, and unable to move, lying in a miserable little camp at the lake, and presenting a most emaciated appearance. Jimmy and poor old Sally have been supplied for some time with government rations of tea, sugar and flour ... It is deplorable there is not better provision made for the amelioration of the sufferings of these poor outcasts.[22]

In the last half of the nineteenth century, various attempts were made to 'home' Aboriginal people: government-run stations, missions run by the churches, and reserves gazetted by the government for the exclusive use of partic- ular groups.

Sue Wesson has emphasised the diversity of Aboriginal experience during these years in Eden–Monaro. In Gippsland, for example, 'missions and informal camps were the usual places of abode, whereas on the far south coast there was only one mission and both formal and informal camps were important. On the Monaro there were no staffed mission stations'. At Delegate a reserve was gazetted in 1892, but with little assistance from government, most of the twenty or thirty Aboriginal people who lived on the reserve had moved to Wallaga Lake by the 1920s.

In spite of the government's attempts to control their movements, Aboriginal people adapted to state coercion in creative ways. Peter Read has shown how they used stations such as Wallaga Lake as drop-in centres while they moved up and down the coast, sometimes continuing traditional patterns of movement, sometimes travelling elsewhere and forging new alliances. As they moved about in search of employment, or visited family and friends, they made informal camps of their own. Many of the places in which they lived, whether government-managed stations or roadside camps, were on traditional campsites and continued to be places of deep cultural significance.[23]

The history of Aboriginal people between 1860 and 1960 reveals how the draconian and racist policies of a colonial power can sow the seeds of resistance and liberation for oppressed minorities. With every government attempt to eradicate 'the Aboriginal problem' between the 1880s and 1960s, Aboriginal people found new ways to ensure the survival of their culture. The history of their oppression is also the history of their success at subverting the colonial power's intention to witness their extinction.[24]

An Aboriginal family, photographed on the south coast of
New South Wales, c. 1900.
[By permission of Rene Davidson]

As the government pushed in one direction, seeking to control the movement of Aboriginal people, the colonial economy demanded a seasonal and itinerant labour force, encouraging the continuation of some pre-contact patterns of movement. Looking for work up and down the coast kept Aboriginal families one step ahead of government authorities. This helped to explain the enormous fluctuation in the population of staffed reserves such as Wallaga Lake throughout the twentieth century. In the 1920s, Aboriginal families would move each year to Eden from Wallaga Lake for the whaling season.[25]

Although the station manager at Wallaga Lake refused to allow Aboriginal people to speak their own language, and continued to discourage the practice of traditional culture at every opportunity, Aboriginal people turned the concentration of large numbers of people at Wallaga to their own advantage. Over time, Wallaga Lake became a 'repository' of cultural knowledge, a place where Aboriginal elders could pass on their knowledge to younger generations. Although the NSW Government had the power to remove Aboriginal people from towns, reserves, schools or informal camps, and frequently did so, they responded by creating new networks of belonging.[26]

The destructive impact of NSW Government policies motivated some Aboriginal people to forge alliances with others living in the north and west of the state, who were experiencing poor living conditions and similar mechanisms of state control. People from Wallaga Lake and Eden became tied through marriage and family with those from La Perouse near Sydney and Kempsey on the north coast of New South Wales. Sue Wesson has claimed that as early as the 1870s Aboriginal people on the Monaro and the south coast thought of themselves as one people. Their way of describing their relationship with one another left little doubt — 'we are all one'.[27]

Like other areas in New South Wales, Aboriginal people at Wallaga Lake lived as wards of the state, every aspect of their life being potentially subject to government control. Wallaga Lake was also a closed community; unauthorised visitors were not welcome. And like William Lunney, who wrote of his shock when he saw 'Aborigines' near Wallaga during his walk down the coast, few non-Aboriginal Australians would have wanted to go to an Aboriginal reserve. They preferred to see white skin on the beach.

One of the most pernicious forms of state control was the removal of Aboriginal children from their families. In 1994, an ATSIC report on the indigenous population of Eden–Monaro found that 12.4 per cent of Aboriginal people aged 25 and over had, as children, been taken away from their family by government authorities. Some had been removed with the consent of their mothers and fathers, while others had been removed without their consent.

After the passage of the NSW Aborigines' Protection Act in 1909, the freedom and movement of Aboriginal people was restricted severely. Men were forced away from Wallaga Lake in search of work, and the removal of children, according to Sue Wesson, became 'commonplace'. The policy of the Protection Board was to ensure that 'full blood Aborigines' stayed on the reserve, while 'half castes' and the 'almost white' were to be sent into the white community where their colour would slowly be 'bred' out.[28] The annual report of the NSW Protection Board in 1919–1920 referred to the steps being taken to remove 'quadroons and octoroons' from the reserves:

> The elimination of these people of lighter caste presents in many instances a difficult problem seeing that they have been reared among Aborigines all their lives, and all their connections and interests are with Aborigines. However, it is hoped that by a *gradual process of elimination* that problem will eventually be solved.

In the following year the Board stated that 'the process of gradually eliminating quadroons and octoroons [was] being *quietly* carried on' (my italics). The continuation of the policy of 'disassociating the children from camp life' would, it believed, 'eventually solve the Aboriginal problem'.[29]

Aboriginal children who attended government schools lived under constant threat of expulsion. One complaint to the headmaster, perhaps from the parent of a white child concerned about the uncleanliness or unacceptable behaviour of an Aboriginal pupil, and the Aboriginal child would be removed from school. Fortunately, Wallaga Lake had its own school until 1965, but any child who had been removed from a government school and did not live at Wallaga was denied an education.[30]

From 1908, many Aboriginal children and infants from the far south coast and the Monaro were sent to Bombaderry Babies Home near Nowra, and from 1911, at 14 years of age, some Aboriginal girls were sent to Cootamundra Girls' Home. Boys between 7 and 17 went to Kinchela Boys' Home from 1924. Girls who were sent to Cootamundra eventually found themselves farmed out as domestic servants for families in Sydney, while the boys went from Kinchela to work as farm hands in various capacities. The knowledge of parents concerning their children's whereabouts varied greatly, as did the experience of the children. Sue Wesson's research on Aboriginal families has found that 'all far south coast and Monaro families have a member who was stolen or sent into service, at a children's home or some other institution'.

But regardless of whether Aboriginal children were removed with or without their parents' consent, the broader patterns of racism in Australian society had created a situation in which Aboriginal people were deemed to be the property of the state and inferior in every way. Throughout these years, as Anna Haebich has shown in *Broken Circles*, the policy of the NSW Government 'moved uneasily between models of forced dispersion of Aborigines into the wider community as in Victoria, and segregation in centralised institutions as in Queensland'.[31] In south-eastern New South Wales, no Aboriginal community on the south coast has been left untouched by the policy of child removal. Everyone knows someone who was separated or forcibly removed from their family.

In addition to the various government policies intent on controlling their movements, conflicting demands were made on Aboriginal people by the rural economy. Between 1920 and 1975, Aboriginal people from all over New South Wales worked up and down the south coast in a range of seasonal occupations: bark-stripping, clearing land, corn-pulling, potato-digging, pea-picking, sleeper-cutting, and working as timber mill hands. Many of these forms of employment had been established in the late nineteenth century.[32] With their presence on the farmers' land tolerated only until the end of the season, Aboriginal people often worked for rations and lived in humpies with no sanitation or running water. In 1965, Bega had a permanent population of 200–250 Aborigines living in shacks and humpies along the riverbank, or on farms in the bush. Those who worked for local farmers had no unions to protect them and no minimum wage or conditions. They lived at the mercy of their employers. Others lived in the bush, some along the coast to the south of Eden, where they fished for lobsters and abalone, either trading their catch for provisions or selling the fish to the local cannery.[33] As late as 1973, a *Canberra Times* report claimed that seasonal Aboriginal workers on the south coast were being poorly treated. The paper seemed shocked that 'Aborigines' near Bega were 'living in the open'.

When Aboriginal people did attempt to come indoors, they were cordoned off from the white community, barred from hotels, forced to sit in a separate section of the cinema, and segregated from the settler community at every possible opportunity.[34] Between 1943 and 1964, NSW governments attempted to reward Aboriginal people whom the Aborigines Welfare Board deemed to be 'deserving' and 'superior' with exemption certificates, otherwise known as 'dog tags', which ostensibly afforded them similar citizenship rights to other Australians. The dog tag was yet another bureaucratic device aimed at exerting control over the behaviour of Aboriginal people and depriving those who failed to meet the Welfare Board's standards of their basic human rights. In the eyes of the government, Aboriginal people could only be accepted as equal citizens if they shed their culture. In New South Wales, one culture was legislated as becoming the other, constantly being moved from one place to the next, sometimes 'dispersed', sometimes concentrated, but all the time disparaged for being what it was — Aboriginal.[35]

The coexistence of cultures was unthinkable, as was any hint of fraternisation between them. In February 1954, a young Bega man, Harry Burton, was fined £10 for 'having wandered in the company of an Aborigine'. Police claimed that Burton and Lorna Thomas, an Aboriginal woman, had been seen lying on the banks of the river 'embracing'. Burton told the police that he had been living with Thomas for three months on the riverbank and was astonished to find that their cohabitation was unlawful.[36] But for the local authorities, the law was their servant, implemented indiscriminately, and often sanctioned the treatment of Aboriginal people as chattels of the State.

The memories of Aboriginal people on the far south coast recorded in the 1990s by Lee Chittick and Terry Fox reveal the trauma Aboriginal people suffered at the hands of the NSW Protection Board (renamed the Aborigines Welfare Board in 1941), and the strength of their determination to ensure the survival of their culture. The oral history of Aboriginal people on the south coast also shows how the links between people from the north coast, the south coast and the west of the state grew stronger as the decades passed. Like all memories, they are fractured and varied, and there is sometimes a tendency to long for the past, to invest it with a sense of perfection that it could never have possessed. At other times there is an understandable tendency to interpret past experience through the political consciousness of the present. But the new social and political links built between Aboriginal people throughout New South Wales in the twentieth century did form the basis of what they now believe to be a feature of the period after the 1960s, the period when they began to 'get their rights'.[37]

Aboriginal memories of the period between the 1930s and 1960s vary enormously, sometimes recalling oppression, at other times remembering fondly the sense of solidarity they experienced living on the road. They remember still the stories of frontier violence, of ancestors who lost their lives at the hands of the early settlers, and being left to 'fend for themselves' at Delegate reserve on the Monaro. Telling the story of the shooting of his grandfather, Jeff Tungai from Bega recalled: 'They didn't care much about blackfellas in them days. They'd shoot 'em'.[38] Others such as Bill Johnson, also from Bega, recalled how the managers of the farms where Aboriginal girls were sent to work as domestic labourers 'treated the Aborigines like they were nothing'.[39]

Conducted before the release of *Bringing Them Home* in 1997, the interviews recorded in Chittick and Fox's *Travelling with Percy* demonstrate that the narrative of the Stolen Generations existed within Aboriginal culture before the release of the report. The memory of being taken away from family and friends as children is etched deeply into the lives of Aboriginal people on the far south coast. Sometimes the authorities threatened to break up Aboriginal families as a way of controlling their movement patterns, as Percy Mumbler remembered: 'When I was young and roamin' around with my mother and father … the manager of Wallaga Lake sent the letter up to the manager at Roseby Park and told the manager that we got to go home to Wallaga or otherwise they'd send us away to the homes'.[40] Doris Kirby, from Pambula, remembered being sent to Cootamundra Girls' Home in the late 1960s by the 'Welfare Board', while her brothers and sisters were sent to other homes in Sydney and Taree: 'I was sent away to Cootamundra Girls' Home when I was about 4. This was the late '60s. I don't know what happened, I was never told … Mum and Dad didn't want it … we were just taken away by the Welfare board'.[41]

Memories of children as young as 12 years of age being dispersed to white families as domestic servants, and an intrusive state apparatus that pushed its way into every corner of the lives of Aboriginal people, has left a feeling of resentment. Guboo Ted Thomas remembered the way in which Aboriginal children were taught to hold their own identity in contempt: 'When I went to visit the children's home at Bomaderry, the kids would say, "Oh, here comes a blackfella." The kids were blacker than me but the matron would say to them, "You're not black; you're white now"!'[42]

Sandy and Norm Patten from Narooma speak of the days when their mother wore the 'dog tag'. This tag allowed her to walk the streets of Narooma after 6 pm. Police would not tolerate Aboriginal people without the tags on the streets. 'They would say to people who weren't exempt from the [Aborigines Protection] Act, "Go Back to your house!" Or "Go back to your mission"!' As young children in the late 1950s, Sandy's family camped with many other Aboriginal families on the banks of the Bega River. 'That would have been 1958 or '59. You had to go to the police station to get your rations. They had a store there. We'd go down with mum and get a bag of flour, a tin of powdered milk, half a bag of sugar, half a bag of tea'.

Sometimes the course of a person's life could be determined on the whim of a sympathetic white. Sandy and Norm's mother was greeted with a petition from residents soon after moving to Narooma in 1957:

> They knocked on our mother's door and said, 'We have a petition here. We want you and your family to move back to the mission'. But it didn't work that way because Mum owned the land and the house. And the sergeant at the time, a bloke named Bill Dudley, he come down and he removed all them people and said, 'Look, Mrs. Patten owns her house. Leave her and her family alone'. And that policeman, he's our best friend today, he just lives up the hill. He's in his seventies, he's retired now.[43]

Despite the racism, the oppression, the denial of basic human rights, and a state bureaucracy that seemed incapable of leaving them alone, many Aboriginal people today look back on aspects of their earlier life with fondness, even nostalgia. Those who resent the fact that they were taken from their families also speak of their years at Cootamundra Girls' Home as 'happy ones'. The men who speak of the 'dreaded times' in the 1940s and 1950s when families 'had to move constantly from one area to another to keep away from the Welfare Board' also point out that this was one way of retaining their freedom and independence. Working in sawmills or picking beans at least allowed them to 'get away from the mission thing'. Back at Wallaga Lake, they would need to seek the permission of the manager merely to 'go and dig tussocks' on a nearby farm.[44]

Aboriginal pickers and their families on the south coast lived in deplorable conditions, in makeshift shanties, or in tents on riverbanks, and finally, by the late 1950s, in the huts white farmers saw fit to offer them on their land. Yet while they had protested against the Protection Board's work for rations regime during the depression in the 1930s, between this time and the early 1960s, the era of assimilation, there was no industrial action by pickers, almost all of whom were Aboriginal. Many Aboriginal people were born into this life and knew nothing else. They adapted where necessary to the coloniser's economy in order to survive.[45] If times were good, they could still earn well above the basic wage, at least while the season lasted. As Jeff Tungai recalled, when he travelled around picking beans he would jokingly taunt his mates: '"Pick away boys. Make the white man rich. Keep him goin', getting' richer and richer and he'll have the money and we'll have none" ... But you couldn't stop 'em! They wanted to work for the white man'.

And work they did. They worked to escape 'the mission' and they worked for the white farmers, some of whom were considerate and some of whom were merely interested in fattening their monthly cheques. Looking back on these years today, many Aboriginal people long for the 'carefree' lifestyle of the 'pickin' times'. From within the walls of their suburban homes, they see a time when there were no possessions, when they had 'just a few clothes' and money was not the sole object of life; a time when journeying was still part of everyday life. Sandy and Norm Patten probably put it best: 'They were the best days of our lives. We used to meet all the Kooris, do everything together. And you always had a place to stay ... even though ... Koori people were picking beans and working hard, there was a lot of caring and sharing and happiness among them'.[46] From this itinerant lifestyle and the massing of vast numbers of Aboriginal people near Bega — up to 400 in some years — emerged the seeds of 'the unity of the Koori people'.

Like many Aboriginal people interviewed by Chittick and Fox, Mary Duroux spoke of the 1960s and 1970s as a time when Aboriginal people first struggled in a coordinated fashion for land rights. This was as much a cultural and spiritual fight for survival as a political struggle.[47] One of the most interesting aspects of this period is the reason why this shift in Aboriginal consciousness occurred. Why, for example, after decades of enduring the state's attempt to control their lives, occasional resistance, or avoiding it as best they could, did Aboriginal people in south-eastern New South Wales politicise their resistance in the way they did in the 1960s and 1970s? While Aboriginal people on the south coast had always resisted government policies, especially since the 1920s, the politics of Aboriginal resistance on the south coast did not transcend the 'local' until after the 1960s. Nor did it reach the non-Aboriginal community in the way that it did between the early 1960s and the 1990s.[48]

Aboriginal people had resisted government attempts to rezone land at Wallaga Lake in 1949 and had also campaigned for better housing in the 1950s, but their political rhetoric shifted markedly in the 1960s and 1970s. On the south coast of New South Wales, the first signs of this shift began to emerge in the early 1960s. Between 1964 and 1970, there was a divisive community debate in Bega and Eden over a plan to house Aboriginal families in the heart of the white man's sacred ground.

9

'FRIENDLY BUT FIRM DISCRIMINATION'

THE FIGHT FOR ABORIGINAL HOUSING IN BEGA,
1960–1970

Houses in town for the Aborigines are out of the
question, there are no empty ones to be had.

SHIRE CLERK,
Bega 1965[1]

God made [the Aborigine's] skin black, and God made me; so
anybody who would deny him help is a hypocrite — but a high
class residential standard would be too much of a contrast to
what they are used to. It is just too much to ask … I regard
myself as a decent citizen and a fair one … but to just come out
of the blue and say, 'Your next block will be inhabited by
Aborigines is really a blow'.

BEGA RESIDENT
commenting on a proposal to house
Aboriginal families in the town of Bega, 1967[2]

I used to live in a tent for eight years at Bega with my family
because we couldn't get a house — eight of them, eleven with
the three grandchildren. We had just one tent.

EILEEN PITMAN,
who with Margaret Dixon and others fought for
Aboriginal housing in Bega in the 1960s[3]

In late December 1961, the South Coast Labour Council, in conjunction with the Aborigines Advancement League, decided to conduct a survey into the living conditions of Aboriginal people between Wollongong and the Victorian border. As part of this survey, they sent a small delegation to Wallaga Lake, Bega, and other towns on the south coast of New South Wales. The party consisted of Joe Howe, a Port Kembla wharfie and Trades and Labour Council delegate, Helen Hambly, Dick Hunter, an Aboriginal rigger from Broome, and Ray Peckham, an Aboriginal man from western Victoria. Hambly, Peckham and Hunter were members of the Communist Party of Australia and travelled widely throughout New South Wales in the early 1960s enquiring into the state of Aboriginal communities.[4]

The Labour Council's survey would be one of the first steps in breaking down the wall of racism and indifference that had hitherto characterised the attitudes of settler communities towards Aboriginal people on the south coast. It would also be the first in a series of protests throughout the 1960s, originating largely from church groups, the union movement and the liberal Left, which were concerned with the poor quality of Aboriginal housing in and around Bega. Housing would become the first issue in the 1960s to draw the attention of non-Aboriginal Australians in south-eastern New South Wales to the plight of Aboriginal people.

Once this process of questioning began, the edifice of racism began slowly to crumble. The living conditions of Aboriginal people could not be explained without reference to the whole history of indigenous–settler relations. Exposing discrimination in one area would ultimately lead to the exposure of a different kind of history.

Perhaps the conclusions of the Labour Council's report were already evident in the general statement which prefaced the report's findings. The council believed that Australia's 'Aborigines' were 'second rate citizens', and that they had been kept 'deliberately' in a 'humiliating condition' by governments, both Liberal and Labor. Consistent with Communist Party policy at the time, the report also alleged that Australian governments had tried unsuccessfully to destroy Aboriginal people, 'a National group with a nationality, history, and culture in their own right'. When the council's members visited Aboriginal communities on the south coast, they first explained where they were from:

> Whenever we went to see the Aboriginal people, we had the same experience … Our first explanation would … be 'We are not from the Aborigines Welfare Board … we are from the Aboriginal Advancement League, from the Unions, [and] we … broke the barrier … the people had heard of some Union battles on their behalf.

Precisely which 'union battles' Aboriginal people had heard of is unclear. But unions in New South Wales had supported Aboriginal political organisations since the 1920s. The findings of the Labour Council's report were damaging. They found there were no permanent employment opportunities for Aboriginal people in towns on the south coast. Seasonal bean-picking appeared to be the most common form of employment, and Aboriginal people usually worked 12-hour days on fixed rates of pay. When the picking was over they would be 'destitute' for nine months of the year. The living conditions of the majority of pickers were described as 'appalling'. It was not uncommon for two families with several small children to be living in milk sheds or barns 'not fit for fowls', some of them less than '10 foot square'. There were no facilities and no sanitation. After visiting Wallaga Lake, the Labour Council delegation found the residents fearful that the Welfare Board would sell their land, just as it had done with a large section of the reserve in 1949.[5]

They concluded that 'racial discrimination on a similar scale to South Africa' operated on the south coast, before appealing to the ALP, the Communist Party, churches and humanitarian organisations to campaign for better housing, education and employment for Aboriginal people. Demanding that the NSW Government repeal the Aborigines Protection Act, they couched their final appeal in the language of universal human rights:

> Our Aboriginal people have been hampered in their just fight to be treated as human beings in accordance with the Charter of Human rights, as endorsed by the United Nations. Through bitter experience they see Governments ... and employers as their enemies. They are unionists, some of them ... they are part of the Australian Labour movement ... We in our Unions, do not practise discrimination. Our Aboriginal people are fighting for freedom in common with the African people, American negroes and others ... Greet our Aborigines as friends ... Your co-operation will end discrimination.

In this rush of outrage in 1961, it was possible to see some of the major themes that would characterise Aboriginal protest and resistance over the next three decades. The role of the union movement and church groups would prove crucial in highlighting the plight of Aboriginal people. Non-Aboriginal activists, motivated by the new political and social agendas of the 1960s, often alerted Aboriginal people to the most appropriate forms of legal and political resistance. They also helped to place their struggle in an international context, and to show that the struggle of Aboriginal Australians had much in common with the civil rights struggle of African Americans and all those who suffered under the apartheid regime in South Africa.[6] Finally, they gave them hope that change was not only needed but also possible. Yet there were also tensions.

Keeping in mind that Aboriginal people on the south coast today have largely positive memories of the 'picking times' between the 1920s and the early 1960s, it is possible that the concern over Aboriginal housing and wages was initially felt more strongly within sections of the non-Aboriginal community than it was within Aboriginal communities. This is not to suggest that Aboriginal people were not involved, or to imply that Aboriginal people did not already know of the discrimination to which they had been subjected. But it does point to important questions. At what point in the 1960s and 1970s did outrage over the living conditions of Aboriginal Australians on the far south coast broaden to a more comprehensive political movement? At what point did the vast majority of Aboriginal people believe they could change the circumstances of their lives?[7] The story of the politics of Aboriginal resistance in south-eastern New South Wales in the late twentieth century provides some answers.

In 1965, four years after the Labour Council's report, the Australian political scientist CD Rowley visited Bega and the south coast. Rowley was yet to publish his seminal work *The Destruction of Aboriginal Society*, but he had already begun research on various case studies of Aboriginal communities which would eventually form the basis of *Outcasts in White Australia: Aboriginal Policy and Practice*, published in 1971. As part of a broader project studying Aboriginal societies in Australia, Rowley had come to Bega to examine the social and economic conditions under which Aboriginal people lived, and the policies of local and state governments that affected their lives. He offered a first-hand account of the housing made available to Aboriginal people by white farmers during the picking season. While there were some examples of adequate housing, most pickers and their families lived in undesirable conditions. Rowley saw the tin sheds with cardboard walls and earth floors, and visited large families living in cramped conditions dominated, as he said, by 'the typical indestructible Aboriginal grandmother'. At one point during his travels, an Aboriginal woman who mistook him for a welfare officer struck Rowley. 'She was drinking from a flagon.' One of her children had recently been taken away by the Welfare Board.

Rowley's research was not limited to Aboriginal communities but extended to the settler community. In describing the regional situation of Aboriginal Australians, he explained their predicament by placing it in a national and international context. He wrote of the way in which some farmers spoke of Aboriginal people in terms of 'animal husbandry', threatening to 'clear the lot'. They displayed, said Rowley, 'the typical love-hate relationship of the colonial plantation manager who expresses contempt for the "native" but can talk about little else'.[8]

Rowley may well have been encouraged to visit Bega after reading reports in the *Canberra Times* in 1964. Indeed, he refers to some of these reports in *Outcasts in White Australia*. In what was to become a common feature of the moral outrage expressed over the living conditions of Aboriginal people in the 1960s and 1970s, reporters from the *Canberra Times* made the three-hour journey from Canberra to the south coast, interviewed one or two Aboriginal people, photographed their shanty dwellings, asked a few local residents to explain the situation, then returned to the city. In Canberra, they wrote of the shameful state in which Aboriginal people were living 'on our doorstep'. When their readers walked out onto their lawns the next morning to pick up their copy of the *Canberra Times,* they were confronted with images of squalor which affronted their sense of morality and fairness. Although Aboriginal activists in New South Wales had been taking their complaints to the press from the beginning of the twentieth century, non-Aboriginal journalists, academics, and political activists had never questioned the treatment of Aboriginal Australians in the way they did in the 1960s. The politics of embarrassment was under way.

The proximity of the south coast of New South Wales to the national capital tended only to make the issue of Aboriginal rights more striking, as the *Canberra Times* wrote in 1964:

> The time has come to ask whether Australia can tolerate these conditions any longer … So long as we continue to tolerate conditions like the Aboriginal camp at Bega, only 100 miles from the Federal Capital, we are not in a very strong position either to criticise racial discrimination in other countries or to answer attacks on our own racial policy … The Aborigines are our people just as much as the whites: they have the same rights to decent houses, decent jobs, and schools for their children. No one pretends that this is an easy problem. We are dealing with the legacy of 150 years of callous indifference and lack of understanding.

Journalists who worked on a paper which reported daily on the civil rights movement in the United States, and who were often sympathetic to the civil rights agenda, also highlighted international criticism of the White Australia policy and the racial discrimination practised against Aboriginal Australians. In September 1964, the *Canberra Times* drew attention to the visiting Kenyan Minister for Justice's observation that the White Australia policy was creating a 'bad impression of Australia overseas'. At the same time, in Federal Parliament, some members of the Labor Party were comparing Australia's treatment of indigenous people to the apartheid regime in South Africa. When Kim Beazley Snr did so in September 1964, he relied on the Australian anthropologist WEH Stanner as his authority. When the *Canberra Times* wanted race politics in the United States explained to an Australian audience it often commissioned academics such as political scientist Geoffrey Sawyer to write longer articles.[9]

The electronic media, together with the postwar politics of human rights in the United Nations, were helping to create the end of the 'domestic' political arena. Every 'domestic' issue was potentially capable of being brought before the eyes of an international audience. By extending the public sphere, the media were extending the public space in which 'shame' could be experienced. Confronting images of Aboriginal people living in poverty and desperation would make many Australians feel ashamed. But knowing that people in other nations could see the same images created another form of shame — the shame that others might think less of us because we had allowed racial discrimination to continue.

In the early 1960s, media technology was beginning to alter the framework of political debate. The street marches in the United States led by Martin Luther King were having an impact on the politics of race in Australia. Television had created a new reality, bringing the images of protest into Australian homes. By doing so, it not only spread the philosophies of the civil rights movement more widely but also created a new theatre in which politics was played out. In the 1960s, politics became a performance art, a fact that was not lost on Charlie Perkins when, as the leading participant in the 'Freedom Ride' in 1965, he stood in a swimming pool at Moree, holding the hands of Aboriginal children who had been denied entry to the pool after school hours. Perkins stood for the benefit of the television cameras and for the benefit of his cause. The image, screened nationwide on Australian television, would convey powerfully the fundamental injustice of racial discrimination.[10]

In Bega, events in the United States were causing concern. The editor of the *Bega District News*, writing shortly after the Freedom Ride in western New South Wales in early 1965, described the demands of Martin Luther King as 'terrifying in the extreme'. He saw danger ahead for White Australia:

> An anxious national conscience is stirring like never before in the Union's history ... It is not long since the American negro, like the Australian Aborigine, was docile and more inclined to drift around in the sun, without ambition, because opportunity for dark people just did not exist in a white man's country ... America's racial unrest portends the pattern of struggle for civil rights that our own country is fast approaching, if allowed to drift without sensible action, although the rather inert looking groups we see in these parts ... may remain listless and inoffensive for many years ... The recent students' freedom bus tour in northern NSW, based on inspiration rather than sound knowledge of the complex nature of the problem of the coloured Australians, nevertheless, is an example of what will develop once the organisation for the integration of the aborigine begins to expand — and expand it will![11]

In late August and early September 1964, the *Canberra Times* ran a series of articles on the living conditions of Aboriginal people in the Bega area. It was this series of articles that led Charles Rowley to visit the area in 1965. The 'scandal' revolved around an Aboriginal community living in roadside camps near Stoney

Creek, 6.5 kilometres north of Bega.[12] A white farmer had applied to the 'Eden Pastures Protection Board' for a lease on the land occupied by 'the Aborigines'. AB Jauncey, the much lauded pioneer historian of Bega, a 'gentleman of the old school', was also president of the local Progress Association, and he campaigned vigorously on behalf of the farmer to 'evict the Aborigines'. In Jauncey's eyes, the camp was a 'menace' to local residents. 'The Aborigines', he said, 'indulge in petty pilfering, terrorise passing motorists, and are considered generally undesirable'. A conference was quickly planned by Mumbulla Shire Council to discuss 'the Aboriginal problem'.[13]

In Bega, feigning concern for the welfare of Aboriginal people now became a useful way of arguing that they should be moved on 'for their own good'. After having lived in close proximity to the Aboriginal camp for three years, without having once voiced concern for their well-being, the farmer who had applied for the lease on the land became suddenly troubled by the poor conditions under which Aboriginal people were living. He claimed he was 'appalled' and 'shocked' that 'Aborigines' were 'living in humpies … and using blackberry bushes for toilets'. Planning to build a house near the site of the camp, he insisted he needed to 'consider his wife and children'. He was supported ably by the Reverend Canon Whiting, an Anglican minister who lamented that after 200 years of settlement by the 'white man', 'Aborigines' had still not learnt how to use proper sanitary facilities and keep themselves clean. The minister should have known; after all, he was a 'University graduate with an honours degree in anthropology'.[14] Meanwhile, the secretary of the Eden Pastures Protection Board stated that 'there was no record of the Aborigines having been given permission to camp on the three acre block'. Other residents claimed that 'the Aborigines' were to blame for the conditions. The onus of segregation is on their shoulders', said one man. 'They do not want to mix with the white people.'[15]

When the *Canberra Times* sent their reporters to Bega, they returned a few days later claiming they had been 'disgusted' by the 'squalid and primitive' conditions under which some fifty Aborigines were living at Stoney Creek. The camp's occupants were seasonal workers and their families. The picture painted of the humpies by the reporters was grim. They were small, dirty and cramped, with roofs of tin or carpet held down by stones, surrounded by wrecked cars and the detritus of the white man's rubbish dump. There were no facilities. Children played near the open toilets. Aboriginal people told reporters they had gathered there because 'there was no other place to go'. One man, Des Pickalla, 64 years of age, had allegedly been evicted from Wallaga Lake because he had failed to pay his rent of £1 per week.[16] In a mixture of genuine concern and paternalism, the *Canberra Times* editorial decried the fact that the children at the camp did not attend school: 'left alone to grow up, dirty and illiterate, in their shanty encampments they will inevitably repeat the fatal pattern of their fathers … in some cases it may be better to take the children away from their families altogether in order to educate them in better surroundings'.[17]

Because the camp was not a formal Aboriginal Reserve, the Aboriginal Welfare Board insisted the 'problem' was one that belonged to local government, in this case Mumbulla Shire Council. But the attitude of the council was not encouraging. In an official report on the 'Aboriginal problem', Mumbulla Council stated that 'generally speaking, the Aborigine is socially unacceptable'.[18] Although the motives of the *Canberra Times* reporters writing on the Stoney Creek camp differed from that of the local farmers, who wanted 'the Aborigines' moved on 'for their own good', both parties agreed the camp should go, one because the camp's presence was a source of moral and political embarrassment, the other because it wanted the land for its own ends.

In early September, after considerable debate, the manager of the Wallaga Lake reserve, and a Welfare Board officer, visited the Aboriginal people living at the camp. They had come to persuade them to move to Wallaga Lake. Squatting under trees by the side of the creek, the Aboriginal elders conferred. There, they decided, allegedly for 'the good of their children's education', to move at once to Wallaga Lake. The *Canberra Times* reported jubilantly that the 'sordid camps' would go. Humpies and 'all signs of occupation' would be demolished.[19] Charles Rowley made the astute comment that 'Bega Municipality, having no Aborigines in town, [now] formed a nice microcosm of the Commonwealth, enjoying its absence of racial strife because the cause was excluded'.[20] But the *Canberra Times* had also been instrumental in ensuring the exclusion of Aboriginal people from the Bega community. Well-meaning moral outrage sometimes produced the same results as the racist policies of the Welfare Board. Nonetheless, both Rowley and the reporters from the *Canberra Times* had helped sections of the non-Aboriginal community to begin to view Aboriginal Australians in the same moral framework they applied to themselves — to see Aboriginal people as human beings equal in every respect. In this way, they helped to make outrage and shame possible.

By highlighting the problems of Aboriginal people in Bega, the metropolitan media had also provoked a response from the local Member of Parliament. In early September 1964, the man who had employed Aboriginal men on his farm to dig up tussock grass, Jeff Bate, local farmer and member for Macarthur, led the Tilba district branch of the Liberal Party in requesting the party's State Council to eliminate constitutional discrimination against Aboriginal people.[21] The digging of tussock, however, would continue.

Despite Rowley's conclusions, the exclusion of the 'Aboriginal problem' from the township of Bega would not last for long. Within less than three years, and only six weeks before the 1967 referendum, the residents of Bega were confronted with the possibility of Aboriginal families living next door. The thought of black faces on the other side of the paling fence would prove unsettling for many people in Bega.

In mid-1966, the Aborigines Welfare Board began negotiations with the Anglican Church with the aim of purchasing land in the centre of Bega. The Board had earlier been frustrated in its attempts to buy land in the town. Once vendors realised the Board intended to use the land to build homes for Aboriginal families, 'they withdrew [the land] from sale'.

In late April 1967, one month before the referendum, the Board announced it had succeeded in purchasing the land from the Anglican Church. It planned to build fourteen homes on the site for Aboriginal families. The community debate that followed this announcement offers an insight into the shifts in race politics that were beginning to occur in the 1960s, not only on the south coast of New South Wales, but Australia-wide.

In 1967, Bega had recently received a new Anglican rector, Reverend Frank Woodwell. Woodwell, then in his early thirties, had previously been at Goulburn and Cooma where, in 1961, he had earned the ire of local authorities by campaigning for better housing and employment opportunities for 'immigrants in the town'.[22]

For Woodwell, Christianity was first and foremost a lived faith. Praying for the less fortunate was not enough; it was also necessary to provide material, social and political support to those in need. He came to Bega carrying a different understanding of Christianity, and a different vision of Australian society. In many ways he represented the liberal face of the more radical and urban politics of the 1960s. His clash with the old guard of Bega's rural oligarchy in the local council and the town's press was symbolic of the wider generational and political confrontations occurring in 1960s Australia.

Between 1942 and 1965, 250 Aboriginal families had been placed in housing commission homes throughout New South Wales, although many of these families were still subject to close supervision.[23] But in Bega, the idea of housing Aboriginal families close to town proved novel. The first editorial in the *Bega District News* on the day of the announcement betrayed the shock of many in the town. The whiteness of the Bega valley was under threat. The editor claimed Bega was 'not large enough' to accept the move without 'grave concern'. Aboriginal people would be moving into Bega's 'prime domestic area'. 'Ghettoes' would be formed and property values would be affected. Bega was also 'limited in employment opportunities'. 'Few white members of the Australian community', said the editor, 'elect to take up residence among the Aborigines, and when they are forced to, it is only natural that they should suffer some confusion'.[24] But the 'confusion' was only just beginning.

The Mayor of Bega, Alderman DB Goldberg, pleaded the case of the Bega community, a community imagined as separate from the Aboriginal community. He spoke of his 'surprise, concern, and disappointment'. The people of Bega had not been consulted. He warned that 'Aboriginal people would have to be educated to live in a house' and 'be trained in elementary domestic science'. But his fears went far beyond poor domestic standards:

> Perhaps this experiment may have been launched in an area less elite than the one selected where, by gradual process, the hereditary characteristics, instinct, established habits and behaviour common to their race may be thrown off … and in due course they may learn to adopt standards of behaviour more acceptable to the white community.

In other words, not until Aboriginal people were willing to give up their culture and identity would they be acceptable as citizens. And if they were to give up their culture, they should work towards this goal in 'less elite' areas, anywhere but the town of Bega.[25]

The Reverend Frank Woodwell holding the sign he found in Howard Avenue, Bega, in 1967
[By permission of *Canberra Times*, 3 May 1967]

In his sermons at St John's Church in Bega, Frank Woodwell spoke of the 'prejudice' and 'discrimination' in the community, and urged his parishioners to counter the 'unchristian' response, and vote Yes at the May referendum to remove 'the elements of discrimination in the Constitution'.[26] At this point, after hearing of the crisis in Bega, the *Canberra Times* decided to focus on Bega as part of a series of feature articles on Aboriginal communities in the lead-up to the referendum on 27 May. On 3 May, the front page of the *Canberra Times* carried a photograph of Frank Woodwell that did not appear in the local press. Woodwell had found a sign fixed to a corner post in Howard Avenue, one of the streets planned in the proposed subdivision. 'Printed in black ink, on the back of a calendar which had been pasted on to cardboard', was the racist slur 'Coon Avenue'. Below was another photograph showing a drunken Aboriginal woman lying on the footpath.

While the *Canberra Times* saw Woodwell's discovery as yet another example of the Bega community's attempts to exclude its 'unwanted neighbours, Bega's Mayor Dudley Goldberg thought otherwise: 'We don't want a *colony* out there … We don't want a separate Aboriginal community in the town … What's the point of having these homes if the Aborigines have no permanent jobs? Where are they going to work? … They are nomadic, they won't settle down' (my italics).[27]

The Mayor was unaware of his talent for historical irony. He could only see Aboriginal people as he had seen them all his life. They were occasional visitors to the town, not permanent residents. When the Mayor said there were no jobs he meant there were no jobs for 'Aborigines'. When he said Bega didn't need a 'separate' Aboriginal community, he meant he preferred them to be individually assimilated into the white community or a distant 'community', out of sight and mind.

Meanwhile, reporters from the *Canberra Times* visited Aboriginal families living in the bush. This was one of the few examples of Aboriginal voices being heard. The bulk of debate was an argument within the non-Aboriginal community about where Aboriginal people should be housed. When a reporter wrote of his visit to the bush home of Joseph and Cecilia Bond, it was accompanied by a photograph of their house on Reedy Swamp Road.

In this house the Bonds lived for twenty-five years. While the image may have proved shocking to readers of the *Canberra Times*, it was not shocking to Joseph and Celia Bond. Joseph did not want to move: 'Even if they offer me a home I won't shift. For 14 years I have been waiting for a house that was promised to me and I still haven't got it … [but] those families that move in … will adjust to them. You don't need an education to live in a house'.[28]

In an effort to combat what it saw as outside interference in the town's affairs, the *Bega District News* ran editorials and opinion columns condemning the plan to house Aboriginal families in the heart of Bega. The racism expressed in these articles was breathtaking. One week before the 1967 referendum, the paper ran an article by Dan Weeks of Bega:

Now that Bega's and Australia's … sad problem has been brought out into the open, we should take a close look at the problem … No reputable citizen could have any objection to an educated African Indian or Asian family as neighbours, when their ideals of citizenship and accepted behaviour are the same as our own. … Everywhere in the world [violent] clashes [between different races] take place, except in fortunate Australia; fortunate because our hardy pioneers decreed that the Chinese miner and the Kanakas … return home. And home they went, leaving us a homogenous population — but not quite. The Australian Aborigine was also present including a large number

Joseph and Cecilia Bond standing in front of their house, Bega, 1967.
[By permission of *Canberra Times*, 4 May 1967]

who ranged [on the far south coast]. Some of these remnants of the original tribes … [have preferred] to live in any sort of wretchedness within reach of the picture theatre or the hotel. But although they have number[s] of bright and well-dressed children, we never see any of them at Sunday school or school … These poor remnants have no future at all as modern people know it, and they seem totally unfitted to take their places with other folk … [But one day I hope to see] many, many little dark faces marching along behind the [school] band — please God — like everybody else.[29]

While Weeks' diatribe offered a perfect example of the racist dimensions of assimilation, Woodwell was preaching a different gospel in St John's Church. There, he held up the 'Coon Avenue' sign as an example of the racism his congregation was being asked to fight. Many of his parishioners would no doubt have been readers of their local paper. But once seated in the pews at St John's, they were told another version of history. Speaking just days before the referendum, and refusing to apologise for the church's stance in wanting to house Aboriginal families in the town, Woodwell offered a different account of what the white man had done to Aboriginal people:

Since the white man came to this country, [the original Australians] have been deprived of their opportunity to live on the same footing as those who took this country from [them] … A start must be made in Bega if our consciences are to be purged of the shame that is ours, through the dreadful line of the human demarcation that is condemning a section of the human race to a deplorable state of physical, social and mental degradation.[30]

For Woodwell, achieving equality for Aboriginal people in Bega was one means of purging his conscience of a shameful history. Woodwell's moral language, steeped in the Christian imagery of sin, was, like the language of the journalists who wrote for the *Canberra Times*, one which had come to Bega from outside the community, a language carried by people one local resident described as 'city theorists'. But it also bore a new sensibility towards Australian history and contemporary politics. In what would become a common feature of Aboriginal protest between 1960 and 2000, specific calls for justice were legitimised by linking them to a wider history. Woodwell linked the campaign for Aboriginal housing in Bega to a Yes vote in the 1967 referendum. But the moral justification for his cause was the deep sense of injustice conveyed by the history of Aboriginal dispossession.[31]

After one university student from Canberra visited Bega during the time of the housing crisis, he reflected on the attitude of Bega's residents towards Aboriginal people. His comments, published in the local press, would prove to be typical of the new attitudes towards Aboriginal issues emanating from university campuses in the 1960s.

The attitude of Bega people towards the Aborigines is one of indifference; and these people, together with Australians in general, would be content to live alongside poverty, injustice and inequality ... No one questions whether white residents are legally married. No one questions the ... morality of a white householder who comes home drunk ... It is the responsibility of the [Bega] community to take a little more initiative than the customary 'Uncle Tom' gestures such as the Christmas party for Aboriginal children every year.[32]

In south-eastern New South Wales, this new emphasis on racial equality mingled with traditional attitudes which assumed the inferiority of Aboriginal people. In the wider community there was no consensus over the precise meaning of terms such as 'assimilation'. Although the era of government-initiated assimilation was now coming to an end, many people believed differently. Once governments began to leave behind the old management policies of the Welfare Board and introduce policies influenced in part by political events beyond Australia's shores, new ideas came down from a metropolitan class of policy-makers to isolated regional areas where traditional attitudes held sway. This resulted in an extraordinary clash of ideas, not only concerning Aboriginal people, but social mores and values in general.

On Saturday, 27 May, the day of the national referendum, the issue of Aboriginal housing still preoccupied local government and the press on the far south coast. As the editor of the *Bega District News* wrote, the people of Bega were 'well conditioned to cast a vote in tomorrow's referendum'. Advocating a Yes vote, and echoing Prime Minister Harold Holt's appeal that a No vote would 'injure Australia's reputation as a fair minded people', the editor admitted that 'Australia as a nation' would have to 'answer to the world for its treatment of the native people'. At the same time, he insisted that if the referendum returned a Yes vote, Commonwealth powers would have to be used 'to the fullest advantage'. In this sense, he urged his readers to vote Yes because the Commonwealth government would then have the power to tidy up the 'Aboriginal problem'.[33]

This reasoning was nowhere more obvious than in the way the referendum result was reported in Bega, a town which had the distinction of recording the second highest rejection vote in Australia, just behind Kalgoorlie.[34] Twenty-two per cent of people in Bega voted No on 27 May 1967, compared with the national average of 9.03 per cent. The headline in the *Bega District News* on the Monday after the referendum, 'Majority Favour change in Aboriginal Control', suggested that the Yes vote was seen as reinforcing the perception that Aboriginal people were to be controlled by government. Under no circumstance was the resounding Yes vote in the referendum seen in Bega as the first step in a wider campaign to address the inequality of indigenous Australians. Mindful of the American civil rights movement, the editor of the *Bega District News* warned 'Aboriginal intellectuals' not to 'provoke racial hatred' because they felt — 'justifiably or not' — that they were 'suffering segregation'.[35]

The referendum debate in Bega revealed that in broad terms there were two different approaches to Aboriginal issues in the non-Aboriginal community. One was the dominant and traditional racist language of exclusion and condescension, led most notably by the local press and local government. The other was the moral language of inclusion and universal human rights led by the Reverend Frank Woodwell. As the *Bega District News* and the local council attempted to stir community anger and opposition to the proposal to house Aboriginal families in Bega, Woodwell and his allies attempted to argue that Aboriginal and non-Aboriginal could live side by side.

While some residents spoke of the need of solving the 'Aboriginal problem' with 'friendly but firm discrimination', others were willing to be persuaded by Woodwell, often linking the history of the frontier to contemporary calls for justice.[36] As one resident, who lived in the street earmarked for Aboriginal families, remarked: 'Australians have booted the Aborigines out of areas when it suited, and their land had been taken away from them ... And as for the proposed housing area being elite, [it is bounded] by a swamp, slaughter yards and a Department of Main Roads Depot'.[37]

To his credit, Woodwell was able to gather a large crowd of supporters at a public meeting in Bega in August 1967, and managed to get a motion passed in support of housing Aboriginal families in the centre of town. Although Aboriginal people were present at this meeting, there is no public record of them having spoken. On the surface at least, this debate about the question of where Aboriginal people *should* live was one conducted within the non-Aboriginal community. But although newspaper reports failed to report on the views of Aboriginal people in Bega, indigenous oral history demonstrates that several Aboriginal people, Margaret Dixon and Eileen Pitman being just two, worked closely with Woodwell and other non-Aboriginal supporters.

Four days after the local council voted to reject the Welfare Board's proposal to 'concentrate' Aboriginal people in Bega, Woodwell and his supporters, both Aboriginal and non-Aboriginal, formed the Bega Valley Aborigines Advancement Association (BVAAA). Two days later, after a meeting between the newly formed BVAAA, the Welfare Board and local councils, it was decided that there would be 'no mass housing scheme' in Bega. Instead, there would be one Aboriginal family housed in the town. The voice of the town crier had won. The *Bega District News* was euphoric, but it still had the audacity to warn of the danger in 'rushing one family into a cottage'. To do so, the editor claimed, would only encourage 'imported Aborigines' to 'squat' nearby.[38]

Margaret Dixon, the woman who had fought for Aboriginal housing with

Frank Woodwell, was the first Aboriginal person, together with her family, to reside in Howard Avenue.[39] Thirty years later, in 1997, she would lead the local community's call for an apology to the Stolen Generations.

Between 1967 and 1970, the debate over Aboriginal housing continued. Changes in the rural economy, such as increased mechanisation on farms, resulted in a sharp decline in the picking industry. The crisis in Aboriginal housing, exacerbated by increasing unemployment, arose in part because the non-Aboriginal community, which had previously tolerated fringe camps due to the need for seasonal labour, soon wanted Aboriginal camps removed when the economic need for such labour decreased. But the focus on the living conditions of indigenous Australians, which had become a regular fixture in the national media in the 1960s, also meant that the poor standards of accommodation farmers had earlier offered Aboriginal workers were no longer acceptable. ABC television documentaries, such as the *Four Corners* report on Aboriginal housing in Walgett screened shortly before the referendum in May 1967, made an impact on commentators in Bega.[40]

Analogies between Walgett and Bega were not difficult to draw. The non-Aboriginal community's opposition to Aboriginal people living in close proximity was strong in both towns. In 1969, Frank Woodwell claimed that thirty-four Bega citizens who were asked to rent or lease accommodation to Aboriginal people had all refused. In the same year Bega was described in a report issued by FCAATSI as the 'worst pocket of Aboriginal poverty in NSW'.[41] Yet despite the constant lobbying of the Federal Department of Aboriginal Affairs in Canberra by Woodwell and others, local councils in the area continued to resist any attempt to house Aboriginal communities in major towns. Instead, they issued Aboriginal families with eviction notices as a means of forcing them from their camps.

In 1969, Mumbulla Council decreed that bean farmers were to 'have all people off their land who were not satisfactorily housed'. When this decision was combined with the council's refusal to house Aboriginal people near the town, and their determination to remove all fringe camps, there were not many places left for Aboriginal people to go. After the referendum, local councils tried hard to place political pressure on the Federal Government to solve the 'Aboriginal problem'.[42] For many Aboriginal people, there were so few moments in their lives when the guiding hand of government authority was not reaching over their shoulder. Forced to move from one place to the next at the behest of local councils, they were treated as aliens in their own land.

In October 1969, Frederick Hewitt, minister for Child and Social Welfare in the NSW Liberal Government, visited the far south coast. With the usual optimism of the visiting politician from Sydney, he proclaimed that housing conditions for Aboriginal people would improve 'given 2 years', but in the meantime, he thought 'tents would be acceptable'. Indeed, conditions would improve, but in an unexpected way.[43]

When news first broke in 1967 that a major chip mill would be established at Eden, it was immediately seen as a means of providing employment for Aboriginal men. With 'gainful employment', Aboriginal people presented less of a threat to the non-Aboriginal community. They could be housed nearby, preferably closer to the chip mill than to the town.[44] For Woodwell and members of the BVAAA, the mill held a ray of hope. Lack of employment had been one of the most common arguments used to thwart the plan to house Aboriginal families in Bega.

After lengthy consultations with the Federal Minister for Social Services and Aboriginal Affairs, William Wentworth, and the newly established Commonwealth Office of Aboriginal Affairs, represented by Nugget Coombs, members of the BVAAA secured funding for what became known as the 'Kiah scheme'. Essentially, this involved the conversion of a former school site at Kiah, 12 kilometres south of Eden, into a caravan park. Six three-bedroom 28-foot caravans were to be provided for Aboriginal mill workers and their families. The old school house became the Aboriginal community centre. After the outcry in Bega, and the refusal of the local council in Eden to locate the caravans there, twenty-seven caravans at Kiah represented a triumphant success.

Ozzie Cruse, who had been involved in establishing the BVAAA, was the leader of the new community at Kiah. Speaking at the opening of the scheme, Cruse, a reformed alcoholic and evangelical Christian, quoted from the Bible, reminding his community that 'where there is no vision the people will perish'. His words were matched by Minister Hewitt, who used the opportunity to indulge in hyperbole of his own, trumpeting the scheme as an opportunity for 'Aboriginal people to take their rightful place as equal citizens of the Australian community'.

Like the reception of the Yes vote in the referendum, any attempt to correct the traditional policies of White Australia towards indigenous people was seen as a magnanimous gesture. The local press described the plan to house Aboriginal families in caravans as a 'Big Effort to Help the Aborigines'. But one 'big effort' was enough. Subsequent editions of the Eden *Voice* focused on the housing shortage in town, suggesting it was now the turn of non-Aboriginal people to receive government assistance.[45] Although the Kiah scheme helped to give Aboriginal workers greater financial independence, and demonstrated that the cycle of seasonal employment could be broken, it was phased out as soon as government-funded training grants dried up. Nor did Aboriginal workers receive priority for government housing in Eden, as they had been promised. But the Kiah scheme was still an important beginning, an example of positive cooperation between Aboriginal communities, employers and government.[46]

On the day the scheme was launched in 1970, Ozzie Cruse and his brother Percy were presented with two chainsaws. Thanking the firm who donated them, Cruse said they would be used in 'the best way possible'. The brothers were photographed proudly holding the new symbols of their inclusion in the Eden community. The chainsaws were a reminder to the Aboriginal workers of the purpose of the 'big effort' made by the people of Eden. The trees of the ancient forests around Eden were to be felled for the production of woodchips. As Cruse held his chainsaw aloft in 1970, he could not have foreseen that the object he was holding would soon become a symbol of the white man's reckless destruction of all that was sacred on Aboriginal land.

10

RAISING A
DIFFERENT FLAG

THE STRUGGLE FOR ABORIGINAL RIGHTS IN
SOUTH-EASTERN NEW SOUTH WALES IN THE 1970s

Percy Mumbler at the Upper Shoalhaven in the late 1970s.
Photograph by Lee Chittick. [By permission of Lee Chittick]

Right, this here land what we talk about today, we want the
rights for what the white man took from us. He took this
land by killing our people. And that's the only way he could
capture this land from us, is to kill our people and frighten
our people so our people will run away so they could put
their flag up. Captain Cook! … I'll fight to the last for my
people because this is our land. I want to know who give him
the rights that he owns [the land].

PERCY MUMBLER,
Wallaga Lake 1978[1]

Born sometime between 1905 and 1907, by the 1970s Percy Mumbler had
come to stand for the unity of Aboriginal people in south-eastern New South
Wales. Percy's father, Jack Mumbler, or Biamanga, was from the Delegate area on
the Monaro, while his mother Rosie Carpenter, or Gunaal, came from the lower
Shoalhaven on the south coast. Their marriage was an indication of the changing
patterns of association as Aboriginal societies adapted to colonisation.

Throughout the course of Percy's long life, until his death in 1991, Aboriginal
societies on the coast came gradually to think of themselves as one 'mob'. In the
early and mid-nineteenth century, the term 'Yuin' had never been used south of the
Bega River, but by the late 1970s terms such as the 'Yuin nation' were used to
describe all Aboriginal people living on the south coast of New South Wales. Percy
Mumbler was at the forefront of this change. He was one of the leading figures in
the fight to preserve Aboriginal sacred sites on Mumbulla Mountain north of Bega
from logging in the late 1970s, and he led the fight for Aboriginal land rights from
the late 1960s.[2] Whereas the major leader for Aboriginal rights in the 1960s had
been an Anglican minister, Frank Woodwell, in the 1970s Aboriginal leaders such as
Percy and Guboo Ted Thomas emerged to lead not only their own people but
non-Aboriginal supporters as well. By 1975, eight years after Woodwell had formed
the BVAAA in 1967, every office-bearer of the organisation was Aboriginal.[3]

If there was one major change in Aboriginal culture between 1967 and 1975,
it was the emergence of an 'Aboriginal consciousness' which bore tremendous cultural pride. Unlike the demonstrations of the Aborigines Progressive Association
in 1938, for Aboriginal leaders in the 1970s land was the fundamental basis of their
political demands and the central means of explaining their culture, both to themselves and to the non-Aboriginal community. The end of the 'white manager era'
and 'the pickin' times' on the south coast may have opened up possibilities of
greater economic independence for Aboriginal people, but the source of their
politicisation and increased cultural pride lay elsewhere.[4]

After 1970, the political links between Aboriginal people in New South Wales became stronger. Terry Fox, a close friend of Percy Mumbler, was the man who probably did more than most in the non-Aboriginal community during this time to assist Aboriginal people on the south coast in their struggle for land rights. Fox has written of how Mumbler and other Aboriginal leaders gained from their association with Pastor Frank Roberts, who helped form the NSW Aboriginal Land and Rights Council in 1970: 'Perhaps [the council's] greatest contribution, however, was to sharpen the thinking of its members, to shape their land rights rhetoric and to encourage their contact with left-wing Labor politicians and trade unionists. In other words, it politicised them'.[5]

As the decade progressed, the language of Aboriginal resistance would become more universal. A more cohesive and centralised political organisation led inevitably to a more 'national' rhetoric of protest. This does not mean that 'local' differences were submerged, merely that each local community, thanks to the efforts of both Aboriginal and non-Aboriginal activists, came to understand better what it shared with the experience of others. The colonisers had created their vision of the Australian people in their own image. But an Aboriginal 'people' were now emerging to contest that vision. By the late 1970s, at the same time the non-Aboriginal community was beginning to focus more attention on settler history, press releases from the committees of Aboriginal Land Councils in Sydney or Canberra appeared in the local press on the eve of 'National Aborigines Week': '[Australia Day represents] the beginning of dispossession of land, of deliberate murder, and of consistent attempts to break down Aboriginal custom, culture, laws and languages'.[6]

These national themes had emerged in the annual conferences of FCAATSI since 1963, and they were now informing the struggle for local identity and the politics of 'cultural survival'. This process was helped by the fact that government funding of Aboriginal political and legal organisations, both Commonwealth and State, became a regular feature of the political landscape after 1967, particularly after the election of the Whitlam Government in 1972. Government support increased the autonomy, scope and networking capability of indigenous politics, as did access to the existing communication networks and infrastructure of trade unions and the Australian Labor Party.[7] Aboriginal leaders travelled New South Wales in an effort to formulate shared objectives in the struggle for land rights, establishing the NSW Aboriginal Land Council in 1977, attending Land Council meetings, local and state branch meetings of the Labor Party, and union meetings.[8] The rhetoric of the Labor Party, steeped in egalitarianism and the principle of a 'fair go', appealed to Aboriginal leaders and their non-Aboriginal supporters. Speaking in 1997, Ozzie Cruse appealed to these instincts when he claimed the invaders had unfairly 'pushed a man out from his own backyard'. Now, he said, it was only just that Aboriginal people should receive 'land as a form of compensation from the Australian government'.[9]

The 1967 referendum had also created pressure for greater Commonwealth involvement in Aboriginal affairs, and an end to government-sponsored discrimination. In 1968, the NSW Government removed all discriminatory legislation, dismantled the Aborigines Welfare Board and began to close down homes such as the Cootamundra Girls' Home and remove managers from the reserves. With government more attentive to Aboriginal rights, Aboriginal leaders who had never been granted the privilege of speaking to the local council suddenly found themselves sitting at the same table as federal parliamentarians. This helped to open the door on a 'national' conversation on indigenous history, social disadvantage and land rights.

In September 1973, Ozzie Cruse, the south coast representative of the NSW Aboriginal Advisory Council, sat before a House of Representatives Standing Committee at Eden. In the room were members from both major political parties and the committee's special adviser, WEH Stanner. When the chairman, Mr Cross, opened the proceedings, he began by way of explanation: 'We are trying to inform ourselves about the situation of Aboriginal people and what their problems are'. Ozzie Cruse replied quickly, 'It sounds like an historical event to me. It is the first time that it has ever happened'. Agreeing with Cruse, Stanner claimed the hearings as an historical event: 'a committee of all members of all sides of Parliament have gone round to hear you say for yourself what you think the problems are'.[10]

The encounter was providing an opportunity for cultural exchange. At one point, the chairman asked Cruse why Aboriginal people seemed reluctant to leave home to pursue a tertiary education:

CHAIRMAN: Is there something in the Aboriginal love of family, home life or something that makes him not want to leave his family?

CRUSE: Yes ... there are home ties, unity. It is not in the European.

CHAIRMAN: It is in the European.

CRUSE: Not in the proper sense. You make laws for us to say, 'You can only have your family in your house', but we do not keep those laws ... It is not in the Aboriginal to send a second cousin ... out into the open.[11]

As non-Aboriginal members of Parliament were confronted with Aboriginal perceptions of their own culture, indigenous leaders were forced to come to terms with the coloniser's bureaucracy and conflict resolution mechanisms. Inevitably, divisions would arise among Aboriginal leaders as to whether land title should be vested in local Aboriginal communities, or in bodies such as the NSW Aboriginal Lands Trust, created by the NSW Government in 1972. The Trust was to hold the title to all Aboriginal reserves in the state, and Aboriginal communities would apply to lease the land from the Trust.[12]

Cruse, for example, saw the Aboriginal Lands Trust, to which he had then forwarded his nomination, as a means of keeping land in Aboriginal hands in perpetuity. If Aboriginal people were to move from the area, the land would remain in the hands of the Trust. Others, such as Percy Mumbler, saw the land as inseparable from their own being, as it had been for his father, and as it would be for his children, and their children. Perhaps Cruse had more faith in the white man's bureaucracy. But Mumbler would eventually prove that title to land could be vested in local Aboriginal communities.

In March 1983, the NSW Government passed the Aboriginal Lands Rights Act, which transferred the title deeds of existing reserves to local communities. As Terry Fox has shown, this Act was 'accompanied by the Crown Lands [Validations of Revocations] Act which validated the illegal seizure, between 1913 and 1969, of the great majority of New South Wales reserves. On the south coast, this amounted to approximately 90 per cent of the originally reserved land area'. Despite this injustice, in February 1984, Wallaga Lake became the first Aboriginal community in New South Wales to receive title deeds to what remained of their traditional lands.[13] But this success was the result of more than a decade's struggle.

In 1972, the erection of the Aboriginal Tent Embassy in Canberra, only 270 kilometres north-west of the far south coast, acted to galvanise Aboriginal politics, especially in New South Wales. Percy Mumbler and other Aboriginal leaders travelled to Wollongong for land rights marches in 1972, while Aboriginal people resident at Brown's Flat near Nowra, immediately to the south, held rent strikes, and a branch of Pastor Frank Roberts' Land and Rights Council was established at Wallaga Lake the following year. The Tent Embassy, and the unfurling of the Aboriginal flag in front of Parliament House, had an enormous psychological impact on Aboriginal politics. For the first time there was a national site of Aboriginal protest visible in terms the coloniser could not fail to understand. The Embassy was a catalyst for a more coordinated approach to Aboriginal protest. Demands for land rights and justice in every Aboriginal community now had a national and international face. But the new dialogue that had opened up in Aboriginal politics was not just a case of national bodies dictating to a provincial fringe. National and state-based Aboriginal organisations, political parties and trade unions were in turn influenced by Aboriginal people who came from communities such as Wallaga Lake.[14]

Max Harrison, a member of the ALP and a colleague of Percy Mumbler in the struggle for land rights, remembers when he travelled with his mates up to Sydney for a state Labor Party Conference in the late 1970s:

> That was in the Sydney Town Hall, and we had Aboriginal issues runnin' hot for three years in succession … [At one meeting] I can remember getting' a standin' ovation, more than what old Nifty Wran got. I spoke on land rights and there was about to be a division within the party meeting and I said, 'I'm glad to see that everyone has sat down and stayed still because I don't want my words just to fall on sympathetic ears. I want everyone to hear it. I see a

lot of old returned diggers here and I wonder why they wear those badges. What did they fight for? … All those old fellas sort of looked down at their badges. And I said, 'You fought because you were scared of someone taking your land'… I knew then that I got my point across.[15]

From the 1970s, at the meetings of political parties and trade unions, academic conferences and religious gatherings, non-Aboriginal Australians would sit and listen to speeches such as those made by Max Harrison. Even if they disagreed, or had heard the refrain many times before, they knew it was their turn to listen. But the close personal relationships that developed between many Aboriginal activists and their non-Aboriginal supporters during these years helped to lay the basis of a new kind of politics, and ultimately, perhaps, of reconciliation.

Terry Fox was a Catholic priest who came to live at Wallaga Lake in the early 1970s. More than any other person, Fox helped Percy Mumbler emerge as a major political force in Aboriginal politics in New South Wales. Just as the relationship between the Methodist minister Ted Noffs and the young student Charles Perkins proved crucial in assisting Perkins' emergence as a national Aboriginal leader in the 1960s, Terry Fox's friendship with Percy Mumbler was integral to the political success of indigenous campaigns on the south coast. Every Easter, Fox would drive Percy, Jack Campbell and Ted Thomas to Canberra for the annual FCAATSI meeting. There they met Aboriginal people from the far north of Australia and other areas in New South Wales. It was through Fox that Mumbler and others first came to have contact with Pastor Frank Roberts' Land and Rights Council in the early 1970s. Together, they travelled to all areas of the state. Through Fox and his connections with the NSW Labour Council, Mumbler, Thomas and Campbell attended anti-uranium marches and anti-nuclear rallies. Finally, in 1978, Fox, together with Aboriginal activists Max Harrison and Mervyn Penrith, joined the Australian Labor Party in an effort to push for Aboriginal land rights within the party's structure.[16]

In the 1970s, the land rights movement became a political struggle increasingly informed by a broad national network of Left politics largely suspicious of national governments, militarism and consumer culture. The traditional, the spiritual, the local, and the natural environment were exalted over the modern, the secular, global capitalism and the urban environment. The former represented innocence almost lost at the time of colonisation, the latter represented the forces that had brought indigenous societies to the brink of extinction. On a personal level, friends like Terry Fox and Percy Mumbler were sharing the experience of learning about a different culture. Years later, Fox revealed that one of the most profound and moving moments in his relationship with Percy was hearing him sing 'Danny Boy' in his own language. As Mumbler opened Fox's eyes to Aboriginal culture, Fox showed Mumbler and others the means of making effective political protest within the framework of the coloniser's power structures: the law,

Parliament, and peaceful political organisation. In 1979, shortly after Mumbler and Ted Thomas had succeeded in halting the logging of Aboriginal sacred sites on Mumbulla Mountain, the philosophies of Terry Fox and Percy Mumbler were on graphic display at Wallaga Lake. The Mumbulla Mountain dispute was the first time Aboriginal people on the south coast had come together as a united political force, forming the 'Yuin Tribal Council' at Wallaga Lake.[17]

In February 1979, the NSW Legislative Assembly Select Committee on Aborigines came to Wallaga Lake to hear the views of Aboriginal leaders such as Percy Mumbler. The Committee itself was of historical significance. Kevin Gilbert and Marcia Langton were the first Aboriginal Australians to sit on a NSW Government joint parliamentary committee. Never before, as the editor of the *Bega District News* wrote, had 'a parliamentary select committee met with Aboriginal people in their own environment … a straggling collection of poorly maintained timber and fibro cottages', but a 'prime piece of real estate' nonetheless.[18] Wallaga Lake was the committee's first port of call, and the sense of historical occasion was not lost on the Labor chairman, Maurice Keane, who opened proceedings by claiming optimistically: 'the whole climate is different to what it used to be … White Australians … are more sympathetic and more aware of Aborigines' importance to Australian history'.[19]

Shortly afterwards, a framed portrait of Percy's father, Biamanga, fell on top of Bill Knott's head. Knott was one of the committee members sympathetic to the Aboriginal cause. Percy was disappointed that his father had fallen on the wrong man. Under a large marquee, with photographs of Mumbulla Mountain hanging inside, the committee members sat behind a wooden table in front of an audience that consisted predominantly of Aboriginal people. At the rear of the marquee were the television cameras. Although the focus of the committee hearings ranged widely and included matters such as health, housing and education, much of the attention fell on two issues: logging on Mumbulla Mountain and the community land claim on Wallaga Lake. The language of indigenous leaders such as Guboo Ted Thomas was direct. Aboriginal people were tired of being seen as a welfare problem: 'It is a political problem between the black owners of the land and the white invaders and destroyers. And the key to solving that problem is not better welfare … it is land rights, self-determination and just compensation. Nothing else will work'.[20]

Thomas conveyed the anger of the Wallaga Lake community. They had not forgotten the local council's theft of part of the reserve in 1949 to build holiday cottages. As a result, their traditional burial grounds had been desecrated. Thomas went on to emphasise the sacredness of Mumbulla Mountain, drawing on an analogy that had been used by Aboriginal activists since the early 1960s, and one that was also used by Terry Fox: 'you have your cathedrals in Sydney where you worship. It is the same for Aboriginal people. We have it in the bush'. He explained that the Europeans' sense of the sacred was defined by the commercial value of the environment. Only Aboriginal people could see a tree as 'sacred'. Percy Mumbler's evidence was powerful and emotional. In his words it is possible to see a lifetime's grievance, anger and frustration pouring out in one moment, the moment when the white man first came to sit at the table and hear the perspective of those he had displaced:

> Brothers and sisters, when I talk about these things it chokes me to think … [but] what I have to say is mighty strong. I am not going to beat about the bush. I am going to come out with it. These are the gentlemen I would like to get a go at and to let them know what we want today in this country … Our brothers and sisters came before Captain Cook put his foot on this earth and came here to control our people and be ignorant of our people in Botany Bay. He came with guns and ammunition, not with spears [and] … he saw our brothers and sisters in the wild country. They are still here today, from the south to the north, from the east to the west; they still go on today, our brothers and sisters, and they will never die out. This land is ours and we must stand up and fight for it … We do not want any of this half way stuff. We do not want to be asked how much land we would like. A couple of acres or something like that. [We] want the full rights to this land, to do what [we] want with it and to go where [we] want to go … This is our country … We want to be free wherever we go. We do not want to be chained or tied up. We do not want to be accused of trespassing on our own land. We are living like dogs. We are no better off today than we were in the past. We want decent homes in which we can live with our families. We want a fair go in this country.[21]

For the dispossessed, there is no dividing line between the actions of past generations and those of the present. The documentary evidence of past injustice is present in everyday life, present in the emotions and thoughts of their people, present in their flesh and blood. For this reason, and because of their shared historical experience, Aboriginal people could think of themselves as proud survivors — 'one people'. When the committee asked Max Harrison his address he replied, 'Australia, because I go all round Australia. I go round to see my people'.[22] When Terry Fox rose to address the committee, he read from prepared notes. Describing himself as a 'cultural interpreter', he explained his position as a non-Aboriginal Australian, and his decade-long association with Aboriginal people: 'I have something of the spirit of these people and what they think and feel. At the same time, being a white person, I am able to communicate these things more effectively to white people because I can think in their rather legalistic way'.

Fox, the 'cultural interpreter', then began an impressive survey of the history of Aboriginal people since 1788, both in Australia and on the south coast of New South Wales. He began by quoting Charles Rowley: 'no adequate assessment of the Aboriginal predicament can be made so long as the historical dimension is lacking'. The contemporary political demands of Aboriginal people, Fox argued, could only be understood by understanding their recent history:

> What happened when the white people came to these parts? [Aboriginal people] were dispossessed of their land and had no say in it. They were dispossessed without any treaty. Their dispossession was accompanied by various forms of violence and disease … it is something that we as white people should be ashamed of … there is no greater situation of injustice in Australia than that of the Australian Aborigines. We are living with an immoral situation, as long as these people are denied their heritage, and part of their heritage is their line of culture.

Fox understood the importance of the moment, stressing repeatedly, as did others who gave evidence before the committee, that there was 'a real movement … towards a cultural revival amongst these people'. He also knew how many years his friend Percy Mumbler and others had struggled for their rights, and for that reason alone perhaps, he gave an oration of tremendous intellectual and emotional power. When he came to the particular position of the Aboriginal community on the south coast, he was able to illustrate the injustice that had been done like few others:

> Up until 1821 [when the first whites came to settle on the coast near Nowra], for every 100 000 acres of land on the south coast the Aborigines had effective control of 100 000 acres. By 1900 … the white people had 99 700 and the Aborigines had 300 acres. That is pretty bad. Today it is ten times worse than it was at the turn of the century. The Aborigines have lost 90 per cent of the land that was left to them at the turn of the century. That is disgraceful and immoral, and it is time we reversed this process.[23]

By the time the Select Committee handed down its findings in 1981, Bernard Smith had given his 1980 Boyer Lectures, *The Spectre of Truganini*. In the final pages of the committee's report, Smith was quoted with great approval and at great length:

> The select committee agrees with Professor Smith when he states the crucial challenge to our culture lies in its capacity to come to terms with the continuing Aboriginal presence. For the greater part of our history we have attempted to put it out of sight and out of mind but, during the past 50 years

or so … it has become part of our cultural experience.[24]
Bernard Smith's representation of Australian history as a 'locked cupboard', in which was hidden the act of 'genocide' that Australians betrayed with a 'guilty awareness', resonated with the evidence the Committee had heard at Wallaga Lake and elsewhere in New South Wales. Like Fox and Smith, the Committee members believed that the moral legitimacy of Australia would always be in doubt until Aboriginal people gained land rights and reparations. They had to 'win', or Australians would lose as a result. The same language was present in the Wallaga Lake land claim addressed to the NSW Government, which accompanied the report.

> Sooner or later, the Aboriginal people of NSW, and of all Australia, must be compensated for all the land taken from them and lost forever …
>
> When the white people came just a couple of hundred years ago, they took our land from us, using the gun, poison and disease to help them. It was then, not in 1978 with the bombing of the Hilton Hotel that terrorism came to these shores. Today most white people in Australia are wealthy, but most Aborigines are poor. White people today are still profiting from the sins of their grandfathers, while we are still suffering from the sins committed against our grandfathers.[25]

In 1984, a satisfactory compromise was reached between the NSW Government and indigenous claimants, and the Wallaga Lake sites were saved. In the evidence of Percy Mumbulla, Ted Thomas and Terry Fox before the Select Committee, in the quoted words of Stanner, Rowley and Bernard Smith, which were endorsed by the committee, and in the wording of the Wallaga Lake land claim, there was a common thread. Non-Aboriginal interpretations of Australian history were both reflecting and influencing Aboriginal understandings of the past. The work of anthropologists, historians, political scientists, lawyers and journalists was being taken up by political activists as a means of reinforcing indigenous oral history and legitimising political change. Blackfella history and whitefella history were beginning to tell the same stories.

The critical histories of the frontier that emerged in the 1970s were being quoted in parliaments, the media, government reports, and on the front line of political negotiation. They were inspiring activists like Fox to fight for Aboriginal rights. When Aboriginal leaders such as Ozzie Cruse addressed government committees, they now came armed with the legal and political history of discrimination and injustice suffered by Aboriginal people, expressed in terms the coloniser could understand — that of documentary evidence and legal argument. As Aboriginal leaders travelled more widely and listened to the experiences of their people in Queensland and the Northern Territory, they returned to their own communities informed by a broader history, often drawing on the work historians had carried out in the north of Australia.

When Ted Thomas first wrote to the NSW Government in 1979, he compared the situation of his people at Wallaga Lake to that of Aboriginal people in Queensland. He spoke not only for the Wallaga Lake community but also for Aboriginal Australians. And he spoke as an Aboriginal leader who had learned from the experience of indigenous Americans. The struggle of local communities for land rights and justice was one shared by others. The local struggle was the national struggle; the national struggle was the international struggle. It was not only the isolation of rural communities that had come to an end in the 1960s and 1970s, but also the isolation of Australia. The result of these changes was that Aboriginal people in south-eastern New South Wales had, by the late 1970s, begun to convince the NSW Labor Government and sections of the non-Aboriginal community that they should 'get their rights', especially to the land that had always belonged to them.[26]

Working together, at a time when racism was being challenged overseas and the White Australia policy had finally been abandoned by Australian governments, Aboriginal leaders and their non-Aboriginal supporters had helped to create a crisis of moral legitimacy for the Australian nation. Throughout the 1980s and 1990s, this crisis of legitimacy remained unresolved. In south-eastern New South Wales, it reached a climax in 1997 with the release of the Human Rights and Equal Opportunity Commission's report *Bringing Them Home*.

11

'A VERY
HURTING THING'

APOLOGISING FOR HISTORY

[As the] gins and children stood around the fire ... one of the
party asked a black woman if she would sell her child ...
She appeared quite alarmed and putting her child on to
her back made off as fast as possible into the bush.

OSWALD BRIERLY,
Journal, Twofold Bay, December 1842

I can see no further improvement in the condition of the
Aborigines of this district ... The tribes belonging to the
coast between Moruya river and Twofold Bay ... have an
insuperable dislike to parting with their children ... If schools
were established in the district ... the children would be
permitted to attend ... provided [their] parents and friends
were sometimes allowed to visit ... [Then] the dislike of
parting with the offspring would ... gradually wear off,
[after which] the children could be removed ...
and finally separated from their tribe.

JOHN LAMBIE,
Crown Lands Commissioner, Eden–Monaro 18471

There is never one moment when the past dissolves completely, leaving a new
landscape in its wake. Between the late 1960s and the Bicentenary of settlement in 1988, non-Aboriginal society in south-eastern New South Wales, as in
many areas in Australia, was confronted with an alternative reading of settler history. In newspapers, on television and radio, in schools and colleges, greater public space was granted to the views of Aboriginal people and their supporters.
Although the formal political process of reconciliation in Australia did not begin

until 1991, the task of reconciling history began much earlier. From the moment an indigenous perspective on the history of European settlement began to infiltrate non-Aboriginal communities in the late 1960s, the need to reconcile 'their' story with 'our' story arose. For many residents in the area, the debate over the Stolen Generations in the late 1990s represented the culmination of a three decades long struggle to come to terms with a different view of their past.

In 1969, in preparation for the Bicentenary of Captain Cook's 'discovery' of Australia, a historical thanksgiving parade took place in Bega. Stewart Jamieson, a former Australian diplomat, spoke at the Bega festival homecoming dinner at the War Memorial Hall. In his speech he referred to historian Alan Moorehead's book *The Fatal Impact* and reminded his audience what Cook had left for his successors in Australia: 'that fearful and sometimes terrifying problem of conscience we face with the Aboriginals'. While Jamieson returned to his home town speaking of Aboriginal Australians as a 'problem of conscience', many people in Eden–Monaro continued to find ways of denying the historical injustice suffered by Aboriginal people. On the eve of the 1967 referendum, one article in the Bega press attempted to mix acknowledgment with denial:

> In Victoria every schoolboy knows that the Aborigine, whenever he showed fight to defend himself … [was] hunted down by dogs and shot out of hand. Not content with that, some of the early pioneers poisoned the creeks and water holes so that whole families perished together … This sort of discrimination was practised in other areas as well. But it was never done on the far South Coast [of New South Wales].[2]

Believing that the deliberate murder of 'Aborigines' happened everywhere but in the Promised Land of the Bega Valley was a strategy employed on the Monaro as well. Almost a decade later, Laurie Neal, one of the better local historians of the Monaro, tried to answer the same question:

> If Hancock's [estimate] of 1500 years of Aboriginal occupation on [the] Monaro was correct … then in less than 6 generations we have virtually wiped out a population which took 600 generations to build up … Why? Disease, loss of land [and] hunting grounds … Although on the Monaro there was no evidence of the Europeans shooting Aborigines it did occur in other areas.[3]

'Everywhere else but here' was one way of trying to reconcile the dispossession of Aboriginal Australians with the need for a glowing account of the region's history. Another way, which proved popular during the Bicentenary celebrations in 1988, was to admit that 'our ancestors made mistakes' before concentrating on the more important task of celebrating the achievement of the pioneers in building 'a country in which we obviously enjoy living'. This approach has much in common with the strategy adopted by conservative Prime Minister John Howard after his election in 1996: acknowledge the 'blemishes' of the past in the opening paragraph of the nation's historical narrative, before the deluge of 'heroic achievement' colonises the remainder.

In 1988, the year of the Bicentenary, the national media offered broad coverage of the indigenous perspective on the celebrations. Under the headline 'to celebrate or mourn', the local press in Bega published the demands for a 'sovereign treaty' that appeared in Judith Wright's book *We Call for a Treaty*. But coexisting with the willingness of some to listen to an indigenous view of Australian history was another, quite different rhetoric — aggressive, unapologetic and glib. In Bombala, the Australia Day address was given by the local dignitary, Mr Tony Garnock. In front of a large crowd gathered for a memorial dinner, Garnock offered his response to those who would mourn on 26 January 1988:

> Unfortunately too much controversy and bad blood exists in our fair country today, and we should dispel it by getting a few facts straight. We should be inordinately proud of our country's achievements over the past 200 years … At the same time we should feel no shame about our forebears' treatment of the Aborigines. These, our British antecedents, were severely deprived as pioneers, a hardy and gentle folk, and not inhumane as too often accused … We should feel no shame about our treatment of either the genuine or pseudo Aborigines, who have more privileges and handouts than their white brothers these days. We bear no blame for anything done in the past. This is history … Inevitably the weaker elements were overpowered … The process of colonisation is merely an extension of the old tribal battles for territory — and these were bloody enough … Land rights in the great majority of instances are a complete nonsense. When their own tribes overran each other, the vanquished were hardly in a position to claim rights from the victors … The radical hybrids like Charles Perkins should not be tolerated in public office, just in deference to some communist inspired United Nations organisations … Let us be proud of our British heritage … The British majority have nothing to be ashamed of, and should dominate our culture … We are all Australians now — there is a place for all breeds'.[4]

Published in full in the *Bombala Times*, Garnock's address elicited no letters of complaint and no editorial objection. Instead, it was accepted as fair comment. The rhetoric of Pauline Hanson's One Nation party is present here eight years before Hanson gave it a party-political face. The sentiments are familiar. Insularity, refusal to accept that Australia has responsibilities to a global community, suspicion of supra-national organisations, and an eagerness to defend the heritage of the early settlers. Settlers, like Hanson's battlers, were represented by Garnock as victims, while Aboriginal Australians were seen as the beneficiaries of government largesse. Any injustice they may have suffered was merely a necessary part of the march of history, a superior race stamping on the face of an inferior race. Garnock's vision of Australia is dependent upon the eradication of Aboriginal culture. His Australia must make a choice — a choice between a history of shame and a history of pride.

To explain the hatred and racism expressed in Garnock's address is not a simple task. But part of the reason may lie in the fact that many Australians, especially those who live on land their family has held for generations, deeply resent being told they are living on bloody and stolen ground. There are no highways of asphalt or neon billboards to distance them from the frontier. Having created a history denuded of an indigenous presence, they react defensively when told they have assisted in cultivating a culture of forgetting.

Many local histories published in the 1990s continue to bear testimony to the absence of Aboriginal Australians in local communities. In 2000, the publication of a collection of interviews of long-time residents of Towamba, the village in which I live, demonstrated how little knowledge of Aboriginal culture and history there is. When asked about 'Aborigines', residents often shrugged their shoulders in ignorance. The one significant exception, an interview with Leo Farrell, resulted in Leo's bald statement that 'there was some pretty bad things happened. [At Nungatta] they shot all the blacks … They were thought of like roos and vermin'. Other local histories, such as Klaus Hueneke's recently published *People of the Australian High Country*, contain the following statement: 'The Aborigines have gone, wiped clean like a teacher's blackboard, and were not available for this oral history, not even in the form of descendants'.[5]

Historical narratives such as this demonstrate a degree of defiance. Despite the fact that 'the Aborigines' have not 'gone', some local historians still prefer to believe they have become 'extinct'. Today, traditional narratives of pioneer history continue to coexist with more critical narratives. Many people are not willing to have their beliefs about the past questioned. To some extent, this explains their evasive strategies of denial and their shock when the High Court's *Mabo* decision was handed down in 1992. Shortly after the decision, Peter Cochrane, the National Party member for Eden–Monaro, voiced the opinion of many in the area:

> Only genuine full blood Aborigines should be eligible [for] land claims … [There are] very few indigenous people left in Australia, the majority of land claim proponents are multi racial descendants of the Irish, English and Scots, [but] … the slightest hint of Aboriginality allows them to join the land claim bandwagon … Australian freehold landowners should not be intimidated by bogus land claims by pseudo indigenous groups … Two hundred and five years of productive toil by landowners will not be relinquished without strenuous resistance.[6]

Again, Cochrane's views represented an aggressive defence of the theft of Aboriginal land. The settlers had broken the line of the traditional Aboriginal owners. Cochrane did not care to ask how the line had been broken. He was merely interested in denying Aboriginal people their right to land by relying on arguments that were more than a century old; there were 'none left', and those that were left were illegitimate because they were not 'full blood' and they were 'not from round here'. Like many regions of Australia after the *Mabo* decision, the people of Eden–Monaro were fearful that their land would be the subject of Aboriginal native title claims. In June 1993, the *Eden Magnet* expressed its relief with a front-page headline: 'No Freehold Land Claims'. Aboriginal leaders did their best to assuage community concern, attempting to explain their attachment to land in terms the non-Aboriginal community could understand. Danny Chapman, the South Coast representative on the NSW Aboriginal Land Council, stated that native title claims would apply to Crown land, national parks and state forest, because 'that's where our churches are'.[7] Members of the clergy also worked hard to allay the fears that freehold land would be claimed. As this knowledge seeped slowly into the community, the more positive effects of *Mabo* began to emerge.

In January 1993, the Aboriginal Land Council opened in Bega. The council's administrator, Vivienne Mason, drew on *Mabo* for inspiration at the opening ceremony, saying that it showed the land had always been occupied by Aboriginal people who had their own 'laws and beliefs'. In Eden, one of the leaders of the Aboriginal community, Ozzie Cruse, responded to the *Mabo* decision by working together with local high schools. The local Land Council organised educational programs explaining the meaning and ramifications of the High Court's decision.

Mabo also provided a pretext for designing school programs on the indigenous history of Eden–Monaro and contemporary Aboriginal culture. Cruse pointed proudly to the fact that in 1968 there were only two Aboriginal families in Eden, whereas in 1993 there were fifty. By 1993, the International Year of Indigenous People, the quantity, content and tone of stories relating to indigenous people in the local press had shifted dramatically. *Mabo* had vindicated the long-held belief of Aboriginal people that they had a right to their land. Legally, morally and historically, it provided institutional recognition of native title and supported the integrity and validity of Aboriginal culture. Land councils in Bega and Eden gave the Aboriginal community an official status, and served as a source of positive information. After *Mabo*, Aboriginal people were seen more often in the local media. They were photographed at local schools, or seen helping out in various community projects. *Mabo* also helped to give them a platform from which they could explain their political campaign.[8] By the end of the Hawke-Keating Labor government in 1996, a series of events had combined to create the perception that reconciliation was a pressing political and social issue — the political controversy surrounding the Bicentenary in 1988, the High Court's *Mabo* decision in 1992, and its *Wik* decision, handed down nine months after the election of the Howard Government in 1996, and a succession of inquiries and reports such as the Royal Commission into Aboriginal Deaths in Custody in 1991. Together, these events demonstrated that there was a history to reconcile, and helped to create a sense of moral crisis surrounding relations between Aboriginal and non-Aboriginal Australians.

In the late 1990s, as in many cities and towns in Australia, the people of Bega were deeply divided over one question. In May 1997, The Human Rights and Equal Opportunity Commission released its report *Bringing Them Home: the National Inquiry into the Separation of Aboriginal and Torres Strait Islander Children from their Families*. In the months following, governments, churches, community organisations and individuals across Australia debated the question of whether to apologise to Aboriginal people for the hurt and damage Australian governments had caused by removing Aboriginal children from their families.

In Bega, the debate centred on the local council, a body which in 1997 comprised a number of aldermen who vehemently opposed issuing a formal apology to Aboriginal people on behalf of the local government. The tensions in this regional debate mirrored the tensions in the parliamentary theatre in Canberra. What began as a question about apologising for the policies of child removal soon came to be seen as a much broader issue. The debate over the Stolen Generations became a debate on how non-Aboriginal Australians should come to terms with the entire history of their relations with Aboriginal Australians. Inquiring into the history of child removal policies brought related aspects of indigenous history into the public domain — theft of land, frontier violence, denial of fundamental human rights, and the long history of racist policies legislated by 'democratic' governments.

Bringing Them Home also raised the question of 'forgetting'. Australians who were shocked by the knowledge that Australian governments had been removing Aboriginal children up to the late 1960s were forced to confront the way in which settler Australia had excluded the stories of Aboriginal Australians from 'Australian' history. The willingness of many Australians to apologise for the removal of Aboriginal children from their families represented, in part, a desire to apologise for not knowing — the sea of coloured hands erected in front of Parliament House, each one an emblem of sorrow and empathy, the sorry books placed in workplaces across the nation that invited Australians to sign and address their personal expression of sorrow, the official apologies of local and state governments — all of these represented an apology for the whole history of denial and oppression as much as an apology for the specific policies of child removal.

In Bega and Eden, the debate over the Stolen Generations in the late 1990s revealed how the non-Aboriginal response to Aboriginal history had become the defining moral and political issue in the community.

In late December 1996, the Bega Valley Shire Council had been asked to endorse a joint motion passed by the House of Representatives in Federal Parliament. In response to domestic and international concern over the right-wing views expressed by Pauline Hanson, and their increasing popularity, both major parties believed it was necessary to reaffirm the core values of Australian society. The motion declared the Parliament's commitment to 'equality regardless of race, colour or creed, reconciliation with the Aboriginal people and a commitment to a culturally diverse Australia and racial tolerance'.

In Bega, the motion was not put. The Mayor, and other councillors, complained that the issue was one for federal and state politics only. Present in the public gallery were around twenty Aboriginal people who were especially keen to see the council demonstrate its commitment to racial equality. This would be the first of several visits they would make to the council over the next three years. Three days later, a special meeting of the council 'erupted' in 'bitter' accusations. Mayor Tom Collins had again tried to rule the motion out of order on the grounds that it was not a matter for local politics. On this occasion, however, he failed. The motion declaring the council's commitment to racial tolerance and reconciliation was passed. As many in the public gallery left the council chambers, they remained unconvinced. Aboriginal spokespersons insisted the council was 'racist'. At one point in the debate, Councillor Hopkins revealed his dislike for the Governor-General, Sir William Deane, 'the judge that divided Australia with the Mabo decision and had made three speeches denigrating Pauline Hanson'. He then turned and looked directly at the Aboriginal people in the public gallery before pleading: 'We are concerned over how you have been treated but it is not our fault'.[9]

Well before the release of *Bringing Them Home*, the burning issue in the council was the question of how local authorities should respond to the historical injustice suffered by Aboriginal people. At the same time, another phenomenon was emerging. Just as Federal Parliament's declaration of Australia's commitment to racial equality was a response to international criticism as much as domestic concern, the initiative of local councillors in Bega to support the Parliament was also a regional response to a national and international issue. The Mayor's attempt to create a regional sphere of politics detached from a wider national framework failed. Just as 'national' politics was now conducted in the daily theatre of the international media, local politics could no longer be isolated from national politics. The globalisation of communication technologies was breaking down the barriers that had previously existed between town, city, nation and 'overseas', with politics being framed increasingly by metropolitan concerns and values. Equally, and paradoxically, the economics of global 'free trade' was enlarging the social and economic divide between urban and rural areas. The tension created by these forces was creating fertile ground for the rise of right-wing populism.

When the council in Bega came to debate its response to *Bringing Them Home* in August 1997, councillors could no longer hide behind the veil of domestic politics. The removal of Aboriginal children from their families was an issue which affected every region in Australia. Bain Attwood has described how, in the three decades between 1970 and 2000 a gradual process of 'narrative accrual' had seen the work of indigenous writers, academic historians, novelists, film-makers, playwrights, feminists and journalists constitute the Stolen Generations narrative as a site of 'collective memory' for Aboriginal Australians. With the release of *Bringing Them Home* in 1997, this narrative had become central to the identity of Aboriginal Australians. In turn, three decades of increased political activism by Aboriginal people and their non-Aboriginal supporters had begun to alter the way Australians were remembering their past. Just as Aboriginal people, imbued with a greater sense of cultural pride, mourned their historical experience in settler Australia as one of subjugation and oppression, non-Aboriginal Australians began to question the moral legitimacy of their national past. For both Aboriginal and non-Aboriginal Australia, the past was being reimagined.[10]

On 15 August 1997, the front-page headline of the *Bega District News* reported that the 'Bega Valley Shire [had] No Regrets'. The council had refused to

Council workers trying to remove the shame, Bega 1997.
[By permission of Bega District News, 19 August 1997]

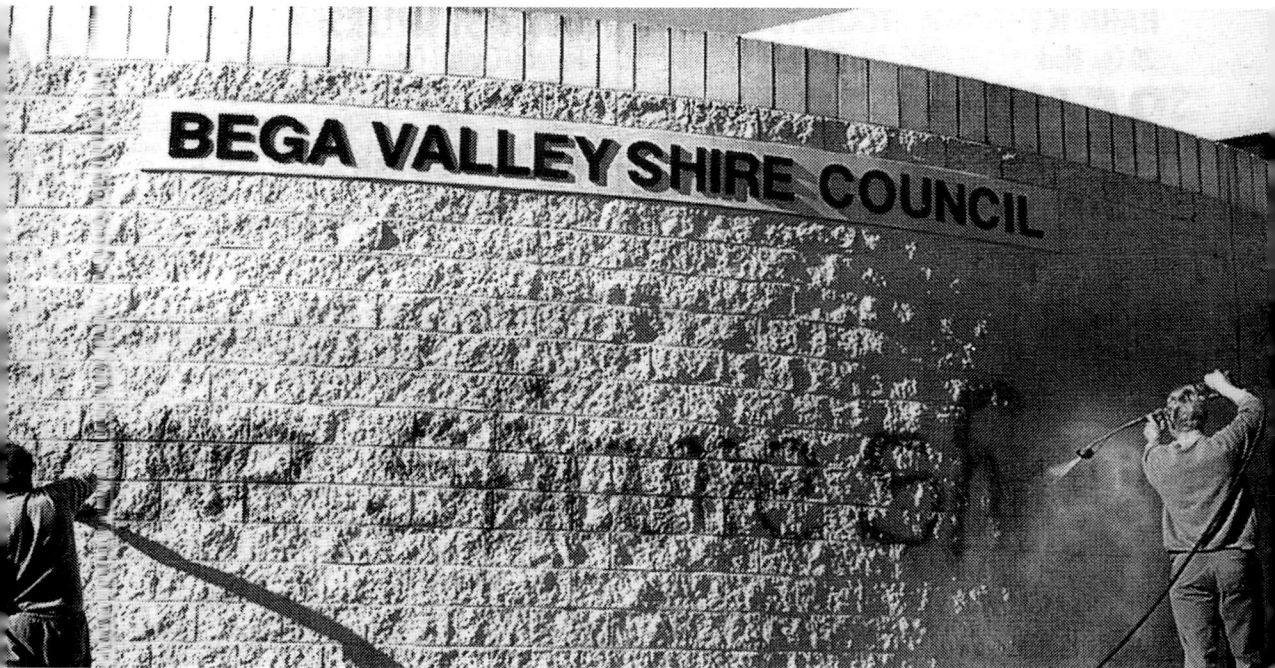

support an 'expression of regret' to the 'stolen generation'. Mayor Tim Collins explained that to do so would be to say 'they were all wrong, although the whole community believed they were doing the best that could be done'. Older councillors saw the motion as an attempt to 'stir up trouble', while others claimed that the council's failure to express regret suggested that it supported the forced removal of children from their parents — something 'the Nazis did'.

Among the many Aboriginal people in the public gallery was Margaret Dixon who, together with Frank Woodwell, had fought for Aboriginal housing in Bega in the 1960s. Denied the opportunity to address the council, Dixon left the meeting in tears. She told waiting journalists how her younger brother and sister had been taken to Nowra police station when she was a teenager, and 'put on a train out of Bombaderry'. The editor of the *Bega District News* was plainly embarrassed by the council's actions: 'Why is regret so difficult?' he asked. 'This is a practice that occurred in the Bega Valley as recently as the early 1970s, well within the memory of every member of council … [It is] a shameful situation'. 'Shame' was a term which gradually came to characterise the vocal community response to the council's stance.[11]

Only a few days later, the words 'Shame! Shame! Shame!' were sprayed on the front wall of the council chambers in red paint. Scrawled on the entrance door to the council were the words 'racist fools'. Condemning the act of graffiti, the editor of the *Bega District News* was forced to admit he agreed with the sentiments expressed. Letters to the editor in local papers were largely critical of the council's policy. Unlike the 1960s, Aboriginal voices were now prominent. Sean Burke, the administrator of the Bega Aboriginal Land Council, attempted to clarify the issue:

> Our governments, both Commonwealth and State, were responsible for the forced removal of Aboriginal children from their families. Non Aboriginal children were also removed if they were assessed to be in situations of neglect. Aboriginal children were removed because they were Aboriginal — that is the big difference … [The Council are the] representatives of the Aboriginal people of this Shire as well as the non-Aboriginal people.

Another letter, from Liz Doyle, presented a potted history of Aboriginal experience as remembered and related to her by Aboriginal people she had known and worked with:

> As the councillors debated the issue of acknowledging regret for the stolen children, my sense of shame at the ignorance and blatant racism of the majority of council members grew. I felt shame that these people … were speaking on behalf of me and my children, when most of them expressed opinions that were the antithesis to the attitudes of myself or any of the people with whom I work and mix. As the observers left the council chambers after the decision,

grief and shame were expressed in tears and words. All the members of the local Aboriginal community present spoke of personal experiences of their families being threatened with removal by welfare organisations. These were people who grew up in Australia at the same time as I did, people who had constantly lived with the threat of forced removal from their families while I lived a blissful childhood in this country free of terror and martial law. I have worked with the local Aboriginal community as an adult education teacher for the last 10 years. In that time I have heard stories from every family I have met which reveal the fear and uncertainty of the lives they spent as the children of itinerant workers; of constant moves to follow work in the fields of some of Bega's older families; of shanties and huts that they were permitted to live in while they worked for low wages; of camps by the tips which were on Crown land and therefore available to black families when there was no work; of fathers who travelled the country working as labourers wherever they could to support their families; and mothers who struggled in shanties and camps to feed, dress, clean and school large families of children. These are also stories of laughter, love and support from huge, loving extended families and some generous and kind white farmers … I asked myself how the councillors might have responded if the issue being debated was that of support for the Jewish victims of Nazi war crimes, if they would have been able to drop their personal politics and power games for one moment to make a genuine and humane statement to the people who sat waiting hopefully to be acknowledged.[12]

Sections of the non-Aboriginal community were trying to share and understand the grief of Aboriginal people. An 'urgent reconciliation meeting' was called. At short notice, 450 people gathered to discuss the issue, an extraordinary number in a town such as Bega. The report of the meeting, which appeared in the *Bega District News*, carried a front-page photograph of Margaret Dixon addressing the meeting.

For many that attended, the issue represented a moral crisis for the community. As with the national debate, the question of an apology had come to encompass not only an acknowledgment of injustice over the Stolen Generations but a much broader expression of sorrow for the history of Aboriginal dispossession. But there was a profound difference between the public discussion of *Bringing Them Home* and the political confrontation at the time of the 1988 Bicentenary. Meetings like the one in Bega saw the *public* airing of history in a way that had never been witnessed before. The audience watched the Human Rights Commission video 'Bringing Them Home', and they listened to Margaret Dixon tell her personal story. Her father had worked hard on vineyards, but the family had lived in humpies on the outskirts of towns. The authorities had taken her sister and brother: 'It's a very hurting thing to have a sister and brother taken away and not see them for a long time ... It cuts you to pieces'. Margaret had been reunited with her brother when he was 18, but hardly knew her sister, who lived in Yass. She had twelve children, and the authorities had threatened to take all of them away. Although her husband worked for the council, they still couldn't find a house. It was at this point that Frank Woodwell had come to her aid. Still, the residents didn't want them in the town and had it not been for Woodwell she would have been unable to find a house. When Margaret Dixon had finished, the meeting heard Harold Harrison tell how he and his brother had been grabbed, put in a car, and taken away from their family. Others like Sandra Patton told how she had been stolen from her family when she was only a few weeks old. Somehow her mother managed to get her back.

But for many in the non-Aboriginal community, there was a need to address much more than the policies of child removal. Roy Howard, a councillor who was too ill to attend, asked for his statement to be read to the meeting:

> It should never be forgotten that every landowner of broad acres and every owner of residential blocks of land in the Bega Valley has freehold title to property that as recently as 170 years ago comprised the happy hunting grounds of the Aboriginal people of the area and from which they were most cruelly and unmercifully dispossessed.

'It's a Very Hurting Thing'. Margaret Dixon leaves the public meeting at Bega, accompanied here by the headline on the front page of the Bega District News August 1997.
[By permission of Bega District News, 20 August 1997]

'It's a very hurting thing'

PEOPLE from all over the Bega Valley packed the Bega Town Hall on Thursday night to express their regret over the "stolen children".

The public reconciliation meeting was called by Cr Jack Miller earlier in the week after the Bega Valley Shire voted against endorsing a community expression of regret to the Aboriginal people of the district.

Cr Miller said that, given the short notice, he had expected about 50 or 60 people to attend and had been stunned as they continued to pour into the

To the indigenous people of the Bega Valley region:
We publicly and sincerely express our deep regret for the gross injustices perpetrated against you.
The forced and coerced taking of your children defies expression and justification. It occurred in every Australian State and Territory over successive generations.
It is paramount that we now acknowledge this abuse of power in our community, exercised by one race against another.
We are sorry that this has occurred and express our profound regret to you.
We join with many voices in Australia in calling for a future direction for this country where the heritage of the Aboriginal and Torres Strait Islander people is valued, the land is respected and where there is respect and justice for all its people.

Rights Commission video, "Bringing them Home", and to hear Mrs Margaret Dixon tell her

permission to address the Bega Valley Shire Council two weeks ago.

When Mrs Dixon was a

community (regardless of their wishes), detribalised Aborigines were to receive an education and

years Aborigines received no housing or unemployment benefits and although her father worked hard in vineyards and on farms, the family had to live in humpies on the outskirts of towns.

Mrs Dixon said her sister and brother had been taken by the authorities.

"It's a very hurting thing to have a sister and brother taken away and not see them for a long time," she said.

"It cuts you up inside, tears you to pieces."

She was reunited with her brother when he was 18 and maintained a good relationship.

•Mrs Margaret Dixon weeps at the reconciliation meeting as she tells of her separation from her brother and sister.

Before the meeting closed it passed the following resolution:

> To the indigenous people of the Bega Valley Region:
>   We publicly and sincerely express our deep regret for the gross injustices perpetrated against you.
>   The forced and coerced taking of your children defies expression and justification. It occurred in every Australian State and Territory over successive generations.
>   It is paramount that we now acknowledge this abuse of power in our community, exercised by one race against another.
>   We are sorry that this occurred and express our profound regret to you.
>   We join with many voices in Australia in calling for a future direction for this country where the heritage of the Aboriginal and Torres Strait Islander people is valued, the land is respected and where there is respect and justice for all its people.[13]

The editorial in the *Bega District News* stated that the meeting, and the public remembering of the history of Aboriginal people, had been an 'emotional experience', 'part of a learning process'. The Bega Valley, it claimed, was now 'ready for reconciliation'.

It was only the recounting of the historical experience of war that had cut so deeply and resulted in so much public display of emotion. The public meeting in Bega was not a government-sponsored Truth and Reconciliation Commission, as in post-apartheid South Africa, but it served the same function. Aboriginal people rose to address the meeting and offered public testimonies, airing the personal pain wrought by discrimination that had been hidden for years. The non-Aboriginal community had never listened in silence to the stories of Aboriginal people as they did in 1997. This was history as healing, the public telling of a national 'shame'.

The resolution issued by the meeting at Bega also demonstrated the willingness of Australians in the 1990s to embrace symbolic declarations of community or national intent. The Bega resolution was the local version of the 1996 motion passed in Federal Parliament. It also bore some similarity to the formal statements of reconciliation issued by the Council for Aboriginal Reconciliation in May 2000, which spoke of the need for 'the peoples of Australia' to 'heal the wounds of the past'. For many Australians there was a need to out the past, acknowledge the history of injustice suffered by indigenous Australians, apologise, and declare 'where we stand', be it through local declarations of reconciliation or new preambles to the Australian Constitution. Symbolic political statements were not a propaganda exercise emanating from the elite theatre of federal politics in Canberra. They were bound inextricably with Australian history and signalled the yearning for settlement of some kind — a ritual for healing. They also mattered to local communities and touched the everyday lives of ordinary Australians.[14]

Between 1996 and 2001, conservative governments in Australia succeeded in framing the politics of reconciliation as a choice between two alternatives: wallowing in guilt and mourning for the actions of past generations — 'navel gazing' about the past — or being proud of Australian history and addressing the present-day disadvantage of Aboriginal people.[15] Contrary to the views of some in conservative politics, however, policy relating to indigenous Australians did not have to be a mutually exclusive choice between 'practical' measures and 'feel good' statements or apologies, a choice between soft and hard reconciliation. In Bega, both were crucial and inseparable in the minds of those people who desired reconciliation. Polarising the debate in this way is to place a real obstacle in the way of reconciliation.

As the crisis in Bega dragged on throughout 1998, it began to attract the attention of the national media. In the space of three weeks early that year, John Herron, the Minister for Aboriginal Affairs, and Aboriginal leader Mick Dodson, both visited Bega. While Herron spoke of the government's vision of 'practical' reconciliation, Dodson drew attention to the council's failure to 'endorse an expression of regret to the Aboriginal community'.[16] On the same day as Dodson's visit, an 'expression of regret' was again lost in the council. The tone of editorials in the local press and in the community now shifted from embarrassment to anger. Annoyed by councillors who claimed that an apology was not the responsibility of local government, the editor of the *Bega District News* insisted that the time had come to recognise that 'Australia had an official policy of genocide' towards Aboriginal people. Letter writers such as A. Powell were able to explain exactly why local government was responsible for apologising to indigenous people:

> Throughout this century, local government administrators and representatives have actively implemented the policies of the state. Being in a position to exercise control or discretion over planning matters, land allocation, land use, health and building codes, local government representatives and officials in the Bega Valley, both in the past and present, have either participated in or been responsible for the destruction of Aboriginal people's houses [as occurred at Wallaga Lake in the 1950s and 1960s], the dispersal of people from town camps and other communal areas, removal of children and adults from their communities on 'health' or other grounds, and obstructing attempts by Aboriginal organisations to exercise their legislated rights in relation to claims over vacant Crown Land. In this context, it is worth noting that many thousands of hectares of vacant Crown Land have been handed over, gratis, to Daishowa's woodchip mill [via its Australian agent, NSW State Forests] compared to the hundred-odd acres granted over 15 years to the local Aboriginal Land Councils.[17]

The longer the debate continued, the more bitter the fight became. In March 1998, Margaret Dixon was reminded of the indignity of the 1967 'Coon Avenue' insult. In a repeat of events in 1967, the words 'Coon Cave' were scratched into signs on the front window of the new office of the Bega Aboriginal Land Council. But unlike 1967, this action did not represent the feelings of a majority of citizens. By early 1998, it was clear that the council no longer had the confidence of the community. When it voted for a third time against endorsing an expression of regret, shortly after the inaugural National Sorry Day in May 1998, it was to be one of the council's last decisions.[18]

Twelve months later, Harry Woods, the NSW Minister for Local Government, sacked the Bega Valley Shire Council. Woods appointed administrator Rod Calvert for an interim period until a new council could be elected. Although the NSW Government had not removed the council solely because of its failure to apologise to the indigenous community on the south coast, it was significant that Calvert's first act as administrator was to adopt a motion of 'sorrow and regret' in relation to the stolen generations. Speaking in the council chambers, he then called for the community to move to the next step in reconciliation, a meaningful memorandum of understanding. Calvert said his reasons were twofold. The council had become out of step with the majority of local, state and federal governments. And in Bega, they were 'out of touch with the feelings of the general community on reconciliation'.

Hearing these words, the public gallery erupted in spontaneous applause. It was September 1999, almost eighteen months since the first motion expressing regret had been put before the council. Although Calvert had not used the word 'apologise', for those Aboriginal people and their supporters, both inside and outside the council, many of whom had campaigned so long for some degree of moral justice, Calvert's use of the words 'sorrow and regret' was like the walls of a dam breaking.

A hundred and seventy years after the first settlers rode on horseback into the Bega Valley, invading Aboriginal land with little consideration for the rights of the people they would displace, the people of the Bega Valley expressed their 'profound regret' for the 'gross injustices' that had been perpetrated against indigenous Australians.[19]

Sometimes political labels wear. The words that first capture the energy and hope of those advocating change become jaded, and their frequent use in public debate seems only to empty them of meaning. But in south-eastern New South Wales, 'reconciliation' is still the right word. In local communities, for both Aboriginal and non-Aboriginal Australians, the desire for 'reconciliation' is still present.

conclusion

LOOKING FOR
BLACKFELLAS' POINT III

When the Reverend Frank Woodwell removed the 'Coon Avenue' sign from a Bega street in 1967, he must have felt that it would be a long time before Aboriginal people would be accepted as equal members of society on the far south coast of New South Wales. In 1967, many people in the sarea remained determined to exclude Aboriginal people from society. The resounding Yes vote in the national referendum in May that year offered little indication of the difficulties that lay ahead. The gulf in cultural understanding between Aboriginal and non-Aboriginal people was vast. The struggle for Aboriginal rights, land and social equality would continue throughout the next three decades, as would the struggle of the non-Aboriginal community to come to terms with the history of Aboriginal dispossession. Yet despite the fact that these political and social challenges remain incomplete today, two stories in particular reveal how much further Australians have travelled down the road of 'shared cultural understanding' since 1967. Perhaps there is no better symbol of the progress made than the story of an old willow tree in Bega.

In 1998, the Bega Valley Shire Council ordered that the old willow on the corner of Gipps and Bega Streets be cut down. Aware that the willow had been a long-time meeting place for Aboriginal people in town, and that it was listed by the local Land Council as a significant site, the council went ahead regardless, claiming that the tree was a threat to 'public safety'. Here was a familiar story — decisions that affected the lives of Aboriginal people were taken without dialogue or negotiation, and with local government officials seemingly incapable of showing any respect for indigenous culture. This was the same council body which had refused to endorse an expression of sorrow and regret to the Stolen Generations. Many people saw the council's removal of the willow as being symptomatic of the ageing oligarchy's disdain for Aboriginal people. After a sympathetic press reported strong protest from indigenous leaders and others in town, the council was forced to apologise to the indigenous community for cutting the old willow down. One week later, Mark Cannadier, the man responsible for taking the decision to remove the tree, was photographed together with John Dixon, an Aboriginal council worker, planting a

Charlie Thomas holding Barry Davidson, Eden, c. 1920.
[By permission of Rene Davidson]

blue gum seedling where the willow once stood. For the press, the planting of the blue gum was a symbol of the spirit of reconciliation.[1]

Two years later, at the time of the Sydney Olympics, another example of this spirit was on display in Bega. Like many towns in Australia, the running of the Olympic torch through the streets of Bega in September 2000 was an event of enormous symbolic importance, imagined as an opportunity for 'ordinary' Australians to become extraordinary, if only for a few minutes. The torch runners of Bega represented the universalism of the Olympic movement and the Australian spirit. Shops and businesses prepared to close down to witness the event.

On 5 September 2000, the *Bega District News* reported that Aboriginal people were planning to boycott the Olympic torch rally being held on their 'traditional lands at Bega and Merimbula', because there was no indigenous runner. John Dixon, the man who had planted the blue gum seedling in 1998, helped distribute flyers throughout the town that made the anger of Aboriginal people clear 'Aboriginal people here in the Bega Valley do not receive a fair and equitable share of the resources, including jobs, major events, and the media coverage of this fact'. As Dixon said, 'the white fellows were getting greedy' again, and Aboriginal people were not getting their 'fair share'.[2]

When the Olympic torch was finally carried through the streets of Bega, Aboriginal people were there to witness the event. Standing in the crowd of onlookers, together with John Dixon's family, was Chris Allen of Tantawangalo. Allen had been chosen as one of the torch runners. But after hearing that there was no indigenous runner, he had given up his place to Craig Dixon. This act of selflessness and goodwill was rightly written up in the press as a positive example of the spirit of reconciliation. The following issue of the *Bega District News* carried the photographs of all the torch runners on its front page. Among them was the indigenous runner, Craig Dixon, a Bega High School student in Year 11. Inside was a photograph of the Dixon family and Chris Allen standing together.[3]

These stories demonstrate the determination of many people today in south-eastern New South Wales to reconcile with Aboriginal people and build an inclusive society. And this determination is reflected in many ways. It is evident in the positive reporting of indigenous initiatives and programs in the local press; it can be seen in the social networks built between Aboriginal and non-Aboriginal women, and the involvement of Aboriginal leaders in education programs in local schools. And it is present every time the Aboriginal flag is flown in the streets of towns on the south coast. Compared to the 1960s, Aboriginal people today have a far greater and more positive public presence in the everyday life of local communities. This 'presence' is a direct result of the political agitation of Aboriginal and non-Aboriginal activists since the 1960s. But the story of the willow tree in Bega, and the running of the Olympic torch, also show how the political struggle of Aboriginal people to be visible in mainstream culture is constant and ongoing.[4] Although the history of the campaign for Aboriginal rights since the 1960s is a vindication of the capacity of political organisation and protest to effect political change, the need for continuing political agitation remains. The moment when ignorance and racism falls away has not been reached.

When 800 people walked across Bega River Bridge in May 2000 as part of the national marches for reconciliation, Donnal Aldridge, from the Bega Land Council, reminded local communities that reconciliation would not occur without due *recognition* of Aboriginal culture and history.[5] Recognising history, and the political and social consequences of that recognition, is in large part what this book has been about.

When I began *Looking for Blackfellas' Point*, I set out to understand how a different kind of historical understanding might affect not only my own relationship with the land in which I live, but the political landscape of local and national communities as well. I have tried to show that the way in which we create and remember history plays a crucial role in determining our local and national identities and our political agendas. By constituting history, we set the framework within which politics takes place — our historical imagination reflects what we believe to be possible today. This is why the critical histories of the Australian frontier which emerged in the 1960s and 1970s helped to feed a new kind of politics in Australia and ultimately, through the dissemination of this history, created a new political landscape in which 'reconciliation' came to be seen as necessary and desirable. The history we remember creates the political and social presences which constitute our public culture. Therefore, the need to retain and repeat a critical history of the settlement of the Australian colonies remains imperative today. By remembering the history of frontier violence and the government-sponsored oppression of Aboriginal people, we maintain a history which underscores the need for political, economic and social justice. This is not to suggest that the remembering of different histories is an instant panacea for political conflict or for continuing Aboriginal disadvantage such as high unemployment, low income and poor health and social dysfunction, but it does help to bridge one gap between 'us and them'.[6]

As for my personal relationship with the land at Blackfellas' Point, my knowledge of the history of the frontier, and the way in which Aboriginal people were dispossessed of their land, leaves me feeling ambivalent about the land I own, and any attempt we might make to 'celebrate the nation'. While the knowledge of this history does not render me illegitimate, the only practical response is permanent remembering and continued political agitation. Until Aboriginal people can be satisfied that they possess a greater sense of political, economic and social justice in Australia, my sense of ambivalence about the nation remains.

On the south coast, one of the most contentious issues for Aboriginal people today is fishing rights. Speaking in an interview given in 1992 in Narooma, Vivienne Mason offered an example of how the knowledge of the history of indigenous land use can help underwrite present-day political demands for indigenous rights, in moral if not in legal terms.

> That's what the coastal Koories have survived on for thousands of years, and now … Koories who have applied for fishing licences … [have been] refused, an abalone licence costs close to half a million dollars. Ronny [her husband] often speaks of when they were growing up on the coast and the gubbas [white people] didn't know what abalone were, they had no idea. They would watch the Koories diving for the abalone and when asked what they were, the Koories naturally told them … Over the years the Japanese got hold of it and now it's a million dollar export market. Yet the Koories are being hounded and chased by fishing boats and threatened by the fishing community because they're gathering their own food.

One of the most remarkable features of Aboriginal people today is that despite their historical experience since 1788 they have not lost their belief in the capacity of human agency to create history anew. In south-eastern New South Wales, indigenous leaders freely admit that this understanding of history has not been something entirely of their own making.

In the same interview in 1992, Vivienne Mason spoke proudly of her grandfather, Joseph Sutton, who was involved in the first Aboriginal rights march in Sydney in 1938. At the same time, she was acutely aware of the contribution made by non-Aboriginal historians, anthropologists, linguists and archaeologists to the same struggle to which her grandfather devoted much of his life.

> The best thing that has come out of this research [whitefella stuff] is that Koories are learning and passing their knowledge on to the kids and letting the older members of the community know what their ancestors did. No-one has done any work on the Koorie culture down here, from an Aboriginal point of view … A lot of the people down here didn't know much about their tribal background and going through this research we have found that it was actually the white people who saved our history for us. We've learnt from them. If they hadn't recorded a lot of it, our history would have been lost, not our culture but our history. Through doing this research we have finally located our tribal areas, our clan areas, the names of the people who were here and the groups' tribal names … The white man has taken our culture and history away from us but he has actually given it back in what he has recorded.

What 'the white man' has 'given back' can sometimes be confronting for Aboriginal people, especially in its personal content and manner of delivery. Recalling how Mason came to know the identity of her grandmother, Brenda Ardler, also of Narooma, explained why.

> I was in my late 20s ... when a lady ... turned up at my door ... She had done a bit of investigating and digging around at Canberra and the archives, and she approached me with a photograph, and informed me that she was under the suspicion that a lady with the name of Jenny Adgery had married my Grandad, and I [have] believe[d] from that day onward that was my grandmother.

The giving of history has involved confrontation for both Aboriginal and non-Aboriginal Australians. Yet it has also laid the groundwork for the politics of reconciliation by taking the first and most important step: giving back a past which might have been lost and thereby creating the possibility for the remembering of different histories. And it is this possibility, afforded by the work of historians and political activists over the last three decades, that must be one of the first steps in achieving reconciliation. The struggle to make these stories an essential part of the fabric of our historical memory is ongoing. The recent publication of a history of the Bega Valley, funded by the Bega Valley Shire Council as part of the Centenary of Federation celebrations in 2001, shows why. When discussing the history of relations between early settlers and Aboriginal people, the authors, Helen Swinbourne and Judy Winters, do not acknowledge that conflict or violence occurred. Their explanation for dispossession rests on the introduction of disease and inevitable decline. Frontier violence is mentioned only once in the text, and then only as a form of denial. Commenting on a false report of a massacre at Twofold Bay in the *Sydney Gazette* in 1828, the authors exclaim; 'there was no massacre'.[7] Reconciliation can never be achieved until the silences and denial in our history come to an end.[8]

In *Sacred Places*, Ken Inglis remarked that the 'monuments missing from the landscape can be as significant as those erected'. Inglis drew attention to the fact that throughout Australia Aboriginal people are 'nowhere commemorated by the monumental form most attractive to Europeans in the nineteenth century' — the war memorial. In south-eastern New South Wales, the story is the same. The monuments to the fallen are the usual effigies of stoic diggers, footnoted by the roll-call of the local war dead, the necessary sacrifice binding the community in a history of suffering. But missing from the memorials and cenotaphs is any mention of the indigenous dead, those Aboriginal men and women who lost their lives defending their land, their people and 'their way of life'. Remembering these 'fallen' Australians in the form of a monument or special place is essential if history is to be a bridge to shared cultural understanding.[9]

While there are no names of particular Aboriginal warriors who might be commemorated in Bega, Eden or Bombala, there are many well-known Aboriginal leaders who have made important contributions to the life of local communities in southeastern New South Wales. There is also a history in need of public remembering.

This book has offered ample evidence of the violence committed by sealers and their gangs at Eden in the early nineteenth century, of the violent conflict between settlers and Aboriginal communities around Bega in the 1830s and 1840s, and of the mass poisoning and shootings of Aboriginal people near Bombala and

The road to Parliament House, 2001.
An excavator prepares the way for Commonwealth Place in Canberra. Reconciliation Place, which is to be positioned behind Commonwealth Place, is not planned as a memorial but as a place where visitors will be able to contemplate artistic images that relate to four major historical themes: Separation, Native Title, the 1967 Referendum, and Strength Service and Sacrifice. There will also be formal acknowledgment of indigenous culture and a 'welcome to country' statement in the language of the traditional Aboriginal landowners, the Ngunawal. There will be no mention of frontier conflict.[10] [Mark McKenna]

Pambula during the same period. Yet even more important than the names and dates, and the numbers killed, is the remembering and public acknowledgment that such things occurred. When the loss of Aboriginal life and land becomes a shared and visible loss in the public space of our culture, we take one step towards building a more inclusive society. As Noel Pearson remarked in an address to the National Press Club in Canberra in 1993, to deny the racist inheritance in Australia and the havoc it has wrought for Aboriginal people is to fail to understand Australia. 'It is after all, the baggage that your forefathers and ... all those who have loved you and whom you loved have given you. It is a troubling inheritance. Because to deny it is to deny something of yourself'.[11]

Talk of the need to 'acknowledge' frontier violence or 'the truth about our history' is commonplace. More rare is to encounter someone suggesting the form this acknowledgment should take. Two Australian historians have tried. Henry Reynolds has attempted to include the Aboriginal war dead within the Anzac tradition, while in 1998 Ken Inglis suggested that the loss of life on the Australian frontier could be remembered by the erection of a monument at the Australian War Memorial in Canberra.[12] My personal view is that the public remembering of frontier conflict should steer well clear of any connection with Anzac Day or the existing rituals associated with the commemoration of Australia's war dead. We should not feel the need to legitimise Aboriginal history by telling it as a whitefella story, least of all by making it 'fit' into the Anzac legend. The Aboriginal 'fallen' were not Anzacs. They did not die for King and country, adventure, in the trenches at Gallipoli, or the mud fields of Flanders. Their sacrifice was not for the Australian nation; it was to stop the settlers invading their land, to protect their country against the forces that would ultimately lay the basis for the Australia we now know. Theirs was a sacrifice that was fundamentally different from that of the settlers who were sometimes their enemies, and who also lost their lives. It deserves to be remembered in its own terms, in all of its complexity, and for what it was rather than for what some of us would like it to be. Remembering the Aboriginal 'fallen' in the same public space as the Anzacs would exalt their sacrifice and play down their resistance. It would only assist in the creation of a depoliticised history, one in which every story could be incorporated into the Anzac legend. Far better to see the erection of monuments and plaques in cities and towns which tell the local stories of Aboriginal resistance and the nature of the frontier wars — if that is what Aboriginal people want.

On the south coast, small steps could be taken. In Eden, the history of whaling that dominates the public memory through the whale museum could be broadened to include other aspects of the town's history. While there is extensive knowledge of the role played by Aboriginal people in the whaling industry, there is no detailed recognition of Aboriginal resistance to the sealing gangs in the early nineteenth century, or of the frontier wars in the coastal hinterland which continued into the 1840s.

Equally, there is a need to remember much more than a history of violent conflict and tragedy. Another way of acknowledging different histories in the area would be to adopt a system of shared naming for important landmarks. Signs could be posted which explained the origins of both indigenous and settler names. Mount Imlay could then also be known as Mount Ballun, as it was for hundreds of years before Dr George Imlay came to Twofold Bay. The names of Oswald Brierly and his friend Budgenbro (Toby), could be remembered as well. Their friendship could be celebrated.

The struggles of all those who have fought for Aboriginal rights, especially since the 1960s, could also be commemorated in some form. The efforts of Frank Woodwell, Margaret Dixon, Percy Mumbler, Ozzie Cruse, Guboo Ted Thomas and Terry Fox are all more than worthy of public acknowledgment. If the history of the pioneers of settlement can be commemorated throughout the area, then the history of the pioneers of Aboriginal rights should be remembered as well.

Walking into the Bega Family History museum in 1999, I encountered a mausoleum of pioneer ephemera. Inside, history was represented as the spoons, saucepans, fireplaces, jam jars, biscuit tins, tools, evening dresses, furniture, buggies and commodes of the pioneer generation and their descendants — a complete stage set for the performance of a pioneer burlesque. Portraits of earlier generations, some unnamed, peered over my shoulder as I walked through the main hall of the museum. In the office, separated from the pioneer ephemera, were a few portraits of local Aboriginal people and 'King Billy's' cane.

King Billy was allegedly the grandson of Biamanga, an early Aboriginal elder in Bega. In February 1957, when Governor-General William Slim visited the centenary Bega Show, King Billy, riding a white horse, was introduced to Slim. The Governor-General asked him how long he'd been in Bega. 'We've always been here', said King Billy — 'we own the place'. Yet King Billy's obituary, published in the *Bega District News* in 1962, claimed that 'he was one of the few remaining pure Aborigines. His breed is dying now ... almost gone'.[13]

If the Bega Family History museum is a museum of the people of Bega rather than of non-Aboriginal people only, with adequate funding it could be rearranged to include Aboriginal people both as a people with a unique culture and as pioneers who helped develop the area. There is a long history of cooperation between Aboriginal people and settlers in Bega. It would be helpful to acknowledge, for example, that Aboriginal people led the pioneers to their land, often out of pride — they wanted to show the white man how beautiful their country was. In 1844, George Robinson was approached by a Bega Aboriginal who insisted Robinson visit his country. 'Good place', the man said, 'budgery good place by and by you see'. When one of the old Monaro pioneers, Bernard O'Rourke, was interviewed in the 1890s, he was asked who 'opened the country up?'

'Why, it was the blacks, and nobody else, who opened up the country,' he said. 'Who else would have opened it up? … They led you and me and everyone else here and there' … 'The blacks … would yabber about a big fellow station out there and the settlers, desirous of increasing their territorial possessions, would … go after them'.[14]

For those interested in marketing positive history, there would be wonderful stories to tell of bravery and cooperation at times of natural disaster. In May 1851, floods devastated much of the far south coast and the lives of seventeen settlers in Twofold Bay and Bega were lost and many of their homesteads wiped out. With the waters of the Bega River rising rapidly, many settlers climbed to the top of their huts to escape the water. Aboriginal men dived into the river and swam to rescue people clinging to branches of trees or floating on ricks of wheat. On one occasion a 'blackfellow' named 'Captain' swam over a mile together with his gin with a tinder box fastened 'to his hair on the crown of his head … without getting it wet' to supply a fire light for stranded settlers.[15] A plaque commemorating Captain's bravery might allow people the opportunity to dwell on the history of cooperation between Aboriginal people and settlers. At every point in our history, there have been occasions when white and black have cared for and nurtured one another. One of my favourite photographs, taken during the last years of whaling in Eden during the early twentieth century, is one of an Aboriginal whaler sitting atop the carcass of a shark, holding a white child. The Aboriginal man, Charlie Thomas, holds the child close and tight.

The public remembering of different histories can be broader in other ways as well. Throughout south-eastern New South Wales, for example, there is little public awareness of the history of extensive cooperation between the Chinese community and Aboriginal people. The role the Chinese played as pioneers on the south coast could be remembered — clearing the land, developing businesses, mining, fishing and establishing market gardens, especially in Bega. As the list of pioneers gets longer — indigenous Australians, Maori and American whalers, German, French, Chinese and British settlers — and the connections between them unfold, the exclusivity of terms like whiteness, blackness, invaders, settlers and pastoralists, begins to break down.[16] There is a shared history because the history of each group contains the history of others.[17] The history of 'roads' in south-eastern New South Wales is another example of this phenomenon.

In my research, I came across many examples of settlers acknowledging, often unconsciously, that the pioneers didn't only build roads, they also *found* roads and *widened* them. Long before the pioneers 'discovered' the south coast, Aboriginal people travelled along an extensive network of 'roads' connecting their ceremonial and camping sites. These roads were approximately 4 feet wide and were maintained by regular firing.[18] When I looked closely at some of the early journals and records, I found comments such as the one entered by Oswald Brierly at Twofold Bay on 13 August 1843: 'Messrs Brown and Browning started [last Tuesday] to find a road to Monero [*sic*] ... they *found* a road' (my italics).[19]

There were also other discoveries. In the National Library, I was surprised to find a letter that described how corroborees had taken place on the river flats close to Blackfellas' Point. In the papers of the local historian Harry Wellings, I found a letter addressed to Wellings from JG Stephensen at Manly, dated 18 October 1958. The letter contained yet another parable of 'the first white child':

> My mother was the first white child born at Towamba ... on December 5 1850 ... Our grandfather was in charge of Towamba for Ben Boyd, head-stockmen. We believe it was the only house there then. The remains of their old cottage was across the river ... old fruit trees there in our time at Towamba. Granny often told us of the wild blacks from the tablelands meeting the coastal tribes and holding corroborees on the flats where Bollman's farm was in our time. Granny sat up all night and watched them while grandfather was away with cattle to Boydtown, all the company she had was a tame black gin.[20]

From the same hill on which I stood in 1993, when I first saw Eureka and Blackfellas' Point, I now look down the river and see the flats where the corroborees took place. I can see the point across the river where Stephensen's grandmother 'sat up all night' watching, and I can imagine the light of the fires, the voices, and the sounds of the night bush mingling with the theatre of dance and song. The letter Stephensen wrote to stake his grandmother's claim to being 'the first white child born' at Towamba has for me become a way of connecting myself to a time when roads led to different happenings and different possibilities. Aboriginal people had performed corroborees on or near this site for thousands of years. And they had moved along this same river valley on their way to and from the Bogong moth festival on the Monaro plains.

In 1842, Ben Boyd, Oswald Brierly and Toby rode past the same river flats on their way up to the Monaro. Brierly drew many of his sketches nearby. The road that lies only 70 metres from where my house now stands follows the line of one of the many Aboriginal roads from the Monaro plains to the south coast. In 1882, a visitor to the area remarked that the road, 'for a greater portion of the way goes up and down the hills, just in the old track originally formed by the blacks'.[21] This was the road that was 'found' by Benjamin Boyd's men in 1843 and quickly became Boyd's stock route. Boyd's teamsters came past carrying produce that eventually found its way to London. In 1848, Boyd's Melanesian slave labourers passed by, looking for the first opportunity to bolt into the bush. The free selectors who came in search of their plot in the 1860s walked on these roads as well, as did the group of federal parliamentarians in 1902 who had come to south-eastern New South Wales to assess the claims of Eden–Bombala to be the national capital. Like the Aboriginal people who moved from the Monaro to the coast in winter, the politicians dreamt of a capital city with access to a coastal retreat.[22] The logging companies that moved into the Eden forests in the 1970s also travelled along ancient Aboriginal tracks. They built their wide-open roads on the ridges where traditional campsites were most likely situated.

Today, around the beaches of Twofold Bay that swell with holiday-makers every Christmas, the visitor is greeted by the telltale signs of the leisure coast: caravan parks, resorts and billboards line the highway promising peace and relaxation. In the forest nearby, gum trees are festooned with the bright plastic ribbons of real estate agents — 'Land Sale! Sea views! New Homes available now!' — harbingers of the growth and development to come.

The road to Towamba, NSW, 2001.
[Mark McKenna]

On the same beaches, deep beneath the sand, along the coastal dunes, the ancestors of the Aboriginal people of Twofold Bay are buried. Their bodies were placed in shallow graves, sitting upright, with their legs and arms folded in front of their chest and tied with string, facing east to the sea.[23]

notes

ABBREVIATIONS
USED IN NOTES

ABC	Australian Broadcasting Corporation
AIAS	Australian Institute of Aboriginal Studies (earlier title)
AIATSIS	Australian Institute of Aboriginal and Torres Strait Islander Studies
ANU	Australian National University
ATSIC	Aboriginal and Torres Strait Islander Commission
BDN	*Bega District News*
CUP	Cambridge University Press, Cambridge
HRA	*Historical Records of Australia*
HRNSW	Historical Records of New South Wales
JRAHS	*Journal of the Royal Australian Historical Society*
MUP	Melbourne University Press, Melbourne
NLA	National Library of Australia, Canberra
NPWS	National Parks and Wildlife Service
OUP	Oxford University Press, Oxford
SMH	*Sydney Morning Herald*
SUP	Sydney University Press, Sydney
UNSW	University of New South Wales
UQP	University of Queensland Press, Brisbane

page vii

1   WG Sebald, *The Rings of Saturn*, Harvill Press, London, 1999 [1998], p. 125.

2   Louis De Freycinet, *Reflections on New South Wales 1788–1839*, Horden House, Sydney, 2001, pp. 199–201.

INTRODUCTION

Looking for Blackfellas' Point I

1   *Pambula Voice*, 20 April 1894.

2   Brian Egloff, *A Report on an Investigation of Places of Cultural Significance to Aboriginal People in the Southern Portion of the Eden Woodchip Agreement Area*, NPWS, Canberra, 1987, p. 6.

3   Judi Hearn, *Bermagui by the Sea*, Bermagui Historical Society, 1996; J Liston, *The Thaua Language: An Aboriginal Pictionary from the NSW South Coast*, Canberra, n.d. (AIATSIS).

4   Inga Clendinnen, 'True stories and what we make of them', in Michelle Grattan (ed.) *Essays on Australian Reconciliation*, Bookman Press, Melbourne, 2000, p. 253.

5   Don Watson, *Caledonia Australis: Scottish Highlanders on the Frontier of Australia*, Vintage, Sydney, 1997 [1984].

6   Claire Schofield, *Bombala: Hub of Southern Monaro*, Bombala Shire Council, 1990, p. 30.

7   H Wellings in *Eden Magnet*, 20 June 1931. Products from Eden–Monaro were displayed at a Universal Exhibition in London, 1862–63.

8   *A Survey of the Cultural History of Biamanga [Mumbulla Mountain] and the Biggah (Bega) Area, May 1999*, Students of the Land Conservation and Restoration Certificate II Course, Coast Train Bega, p. 27.

Looking for Blackfellas' Point II

9   *Candelo and Eden Union*, 23 June 1887. See also D Byrne, *The Mountains Call Me Back: A History of the Aborigines and the Forests of the Far South Coast of New South Wales*, NSW Ministry of

Aboriginal Affairs Occasional Paper No. 5, June 1984, pp. 4–6; DG Parbery, *Fabric of a Family*, self-published, 1992; Rev. WB Clarke, *Researches in the Southern Goldfields of NSW*, Reading & Wellbank, Sydney, 1860, p. 188. See also Joan Kent, *Eden CRA Region: Overview Thematic Forest History (non-indigenous)*, NPWS, Sydney, 1997, pp. 5–7; H Gibbney, *Eurobodalla: History of the Moruya District*, Library of Australian History, Sydney, 1980, p. 11; *Regional Histories of NSW*, Heritage Office and Department of Urban Affairs and Planning, NSW Government, 1996, p. 116.

10 *BDN*, 15 October 1931.

11 Mark McKenna, 'A half way house: the claims of Eden–Bombala', *New Federalist*, 3, June 1999, pp. 63–6; Also *Age*, 23 September 1920; W Bayley in Moruya Examiner, 18 July 1942.

12 Kate Clery, a local historian from Towamba, has interviewed residents. See Kate Clery, *The Forgotten Corner Interviews*, Eden Killer Whale Museum, 2000.

13 See WA Bayley, *The Story of the Settlement and Development of Bega*, Brooks, Sydney, 1942, p. 102 on 'Cocky McLean' (NLA).

14 Egloff, *A Report on an Investigation of Places of Cultural Significance*, p. 5.

15 *Mount Dromedary: A Pretty High Mountain*, Forestry Commission of NSW, Sydney, 1987, p. 27; Dymphna Clark (ed.) *Baron Charles von Hugel: New Holland Journal November 1833–October 1834*, MUP, 1994, pp. 320–1.

16 ME Sullivan, 'A Shell Midden Excavation at Pambula Lake on the Far South Coast of NSW', *Archaeology in Oceania*, 19(!) 1984, pp. 1–15; Lampert and Hughes in *Archaeology and Physical Anthropology in Oceania*, 9(3) 1974, p. 228.

17 H Wellings in *Eden Magnet*, 1, 7 August 1931. See also Sue Wesson, *An Historical Atlas of the Aborigines of Eastern Victoria and Far South Eastern NSW*, Monash Publications in Geography and Environmental Science No. 53, Monash University, 2000, p. 98.

18 GA Robinson, Journal, 30 August 1844, p. 161. See also AW Howitt, *Native Tribes of South-East Australia*, Aboriginal Studies Press, Canberra, 1996, pp. 82, 513; Sue Wesson, *An Historical Atlas*, pp. 8–15. See also Sue Wesson, *An Overview of the Sources for a Language and Clan Atlas of Eastern Victoria and Southern NSW*, Canberra (AIATSIS), 1993.

19 Sue Wesson, *Alps Oral History Project*, Australian Alps Liaison Committee, 1994, p. 54 (held at AIATSIS); Robinson, Journal, p. 186; Sue Wesson, *An Aboriginal Whaling History Project*, NPWS, Sydney, 2001, p. 3; Valerie Attenbrow, 'Aboriginal Subsistence Economy on the far South Coast of New South Wales', BA (Hons), University of Sydney, 1976, p. 37. Also AW Howitt, *Native Tribes of South-East Australia*, Aboriginal Studies Press, Canberra, 1996, p. 83; Oswald Brierly, Journal, 14 August 1844, reports on his attending a corroboree of 'Monaro blacks'; Josephine Flood, 'The Moth Hunters: Investigations towards a prehistory of the south eastern highlands of Australia', PhD thesis, ANU, 1973 (MS 3919 NLA), p. 40; Richard Helms, *Anthropological Notes*, 10, 2nd Series, Proceedings of the Linnaean Society of NSW, 26 June 1895, pp. 387–407.

20 George Bennett, *Wanderings in NSW*, vol. 1, London, 1834, p. 273; Helms, p. 387; D Horton (ed.) *The Encyclopedia of Aboriginal Australia: Aboriginal and Torres Strait Islander History, Society and Culture*, Aboriginal Studies Press, Canberra, 1994, vol. 1, p. 1009.

21 Wesson, *Alps Oral History Project*, p. 54 (Interview with Ellen Mundy).

22 My conversation with BJ Cruse, Eden Aboriginal Land Council, 25 May 1999.

23 Wesson, *An Aboriginal Whaling History Project*, p. 207; *Eden Propeller*, 27 November 1903.

25 Wellings papers, NLA, quote from RH Matthews, 'Aboriginal Tribes of NSW and Victoria', paper read before the Royal Society of NSW, 5 October 1904. The Eden correspondent in *Bega Gazette*, 2 May 1868, is critical of the general consensus that Aboriginal people are useless as labour, and claims their whaling skill is an example of their intelligence. Also Wesson, *An Aboriginal Whaling History Project*, p. 13; JAS McKenzie, *The Twofold Bay Story*, Eden Killer Whale Museum, 1991; D Davidson, *The Davidsons of Kiah*, self-published, 1990, p. 65.

26 Verified from different sources: Wesson, *An Aboriginal Whaling History Project*, p. 23; my interview with Ellen Mundy, Bega, May 1999; 'No whales after big fly comes' recorded by Oswald Brierly, Journal, 10 September 1844. Also B Cruse et al., *Bittangabee Tribe: An Aboriginal Story from Coastal NSW*, Aboriginal Studies Press, Canberra, 1994.

27 Conversation with BJ Cruse, Eden Aboriginal Land Council, 25 May 1999.

28 Helms, *Anthropological Notes*, p. 388.

29 Wesson, *An Historical Atlas* pp. 155–7. Wesson points out that Robinson recorded no name for the language at Twofold Bay, only the borders. She claims the name Thawa came originally from GA Robinson; see for example Robinson's Journal, August 1844, p. 161.

30 Matthew Flinders' Journal 1798 in Tim Flannery (ed.) *Terra Australis: Matthew Flinders' Great Adventures in the Circumnavigation of Australia*, Text, Melbourne, 2000, pp. 8–11.

31 William Clarke's description of his walk along the coast in 1797, after the wreck of the *Sydney Cove*, in Michael Organ, *A Documentary History of the Illawarra and South Coast Aborigines*, Aboriginal Education Unit, Wollongong University, 1980, pp. 12–15. See also H Wellings, 'The Twofold Bay Aborigines', *Eden Magnet*, 1 August 1931.

32 Nicolas Baudin, Journal, translated by C. Cornell, foreword by Jean-Paul Faivre, Libraries Board of South Australia, Adelaide, 1974, p. 802. Portuguese reference in *Australians: Events and Places*, Fairfax Symes & Weldon, Sydney, p. 261. The entry on Eden claims the ruined blockhouse at Bittangabee Bay may have been built by Portuguese sailors in the 1520s. See also K Macintyre, *The Secret Discovery of Australia*, Picador, 1982 [1977], pp. 169–71; Lawrence Fitzgerald, *The Portuguese Discovery of Australia*, self-published n.d., pp. 121–3; H Rosenmann (ed.) *Dumont d'Urville: Two Voyages to the South Seas*, University of Hawaii Press, 1988, vol. 1, p. xxi.

33 Rosenmann, *Dumont d'Urville*, pp. 65–7.

34 Brierly, Journal, 20 December 1842. *Moruya Examiner*, 26 January 1888, editorial by Wolrab, alias Reginald Herbert Barlow. He claims he 'once heard from the lips of Coorall', an Aboriginal elder who'd died in the 1860s at over 80 years, that he remembered as a boy sitting on the beach with his tribe at Tuross Point and seeing 'the first white man ship'. Also Peter Porter (ed.) *The Oxford Book of Modern Australian Verse*, OUP, Melbourne, 1998, p. 24. Roland Robinson's poem 'Captain Cook', as related to him by Percy Mumbulla, explains the Aboriginal response to Cook at Batemans Bay. As Cook left, 'these wild kurris were runnin' out of the scrub … They were throwin' the clothes an' biscuits back at Captain Cook as his men were pullin' away in the boat'; see also AW Howitt, *The Native Tribes of South East Australia*, Aboriginal Studies Press, Canberra, 1996, pp. 442, 444; JSW, *Down the River and Other Papers*, London, 1884 (Mitchell Library 500/90), pp. 12–15. The author relates the story of sitting with 'Ramrod', who told him he remembered as a piccaninny seeing the first white man. Ramrod's tribe retreated to the bush and watched the man from a safe distance. His clothes were torn to rags, and he was footsore and weary. They watched as he devoured fish they'd left behind in their hurry to escape their camp-fire. The next morning, as he lay sleeping, the blacks attacked him, Ramrod's father wearing the trophy of his hand around his neck for some time. See H Wellings, *Eden and Twofold Bay: Discovery, Early History and Points of Interest, 1797–1965* (NLA), p. 20. Wellings also refers to the many 'aboriginal statements' and 'aboriginal records' which he draws on, some as early as the 1820s, to establish that in their stories, they spoke of ships in the sealing days and even before 1788, 'long before Bass came'.

PART ONE: DISPOSSESSION

I 'Without treaty, bargain or apology'

1 Godfrey Charles Mundy, *Our Antipodes: or Residence and Rambles in the Australian Colonies*, Richard Bentley, London, 1852, p. 226.

2 Henry Reynolds has demonstrated this undercurrent of concern in *This Whispering in Our Hearts*, Allen & Unwin, Sydney, 1998. See also Bain Attwood and Andrew Markus, *The Struggle for Aboriginal Rights: A Documentary History*, Allen & Unwin, Sydney, 1999, p. 2. Attwood implies that Reynolds has tended to construct a humanitarian tradition rather than provide the evidence to support the existence of one, and sides with Richard Broome's description of the humanitarian tradition as a 'thin strand'. John West's *History of Tasmania* published in 1852, is often quoted as an example of early recognition of the brutal dispossession of Aboriginal Australians.

3 *The Colonial Intelligencer: the Aborigines Friend, 1847–1848*, Aboriginal Protection Society, London, p. 44.

4 William Thomas, Assistant Protector of Aborigines, wrote in 1845 in the *Select Committee Report on Aborigines in NSW*: 'their indifference to prolong[ing] their race, on the ground as they state, of having "no country to call their own"'.

5 Dymphna Clark (ed.) *Baron Charles von Hugel: New Holland Journal November 1833–October 1834*, MUP, 1994, pp. 138, 461.

6 Ibid., p. 417.

7 *House of Commons Parliamentary Papers*, vol. 7, p. 1837. Report from Flinders Island contained in Franklin to Glenelg, 3 August 1837.

8 John Dunmore Lang, *Cooksland*, Longman, Brown, Green & Longmans, London, 1847, pp. 267–74. For similar comments also see Mundy, *Our Antipodes*, pp. 229–30.

9 Charles White, *The Story of the Blacks*, unpublished manuscript, n.d. (probably late nineteenth century) (NLA).

10 Ibid.

11 Ann Curthoys, 'Mythologies', in Richard Nile (ed.) *The Australian Legend and its Discontents*, UQP, 2000, pp. 11–41, p. 30. See also Henry Reynolds, *The Breaking of the Great Australian Silence: Aborigines in Australian Historiography 1955–1983*, Trevor Reese Memorial Lecture 1984, Australian Studies Centre, London; Ann McGrath (ed.) *Contested Ground: Australian Aborigines under the British Crown*, Allen & Unwin, Sydney, 1995, esp. Chapter 10.

12 Human Rights and Equal Opportunity Commission, *Bringing Them Home: National Inquiry into the Separation of Aboriginal and Torres Strait Islander Children from their Families*, April 1997, pp. 270–5; Senate Legal and Constitutional References Committee, *Healing: A Legacy of Generations. The Report of the Inquiry into the Federal Government's Implementation of Recommendations Made by the Human Rights and Equal Opportunity Commission in Bringing Them Home*, Parliament of the Commonwealth of Australia, November 2000. See also Mark McKenna, 'Metaphors of Light and Darkness', *Melbourne Journal of Politics*, Special Issue on Reconciliation, 25, 1998, pp. 67–84; Bain Attwood (ed.) *In the Age of Mabo: History, Aborigines and Australia*, Allen & Unwin, Sydney, 1996; Ann Curthoys, 'The politics of history: representing the past in Australia in the nineties', *Crossings* (Australian Studies Association) 20, June 1994, pp. 8–17.

13 A recent example is an unpublished lecture given by Noel Pearson at Australia House, London, 7 July 2000: 'Aboriginal Australians and the Common Law'. Pearson employed Reynolds as the only historical authority. See also the Council for Aboriginal Reconciliation's publication *Sharing History*, Key Issue Paper No. 4 1994, which relies heavily on Reynolds. In March 2000, when Aboriginal leaders Peter Yu, Pat Dodson, Lowitja O'Donoghue, Gatjil Djerrkura and Marcia Langton held an audience with the Queen in London to request her support for a British government apology to indigenous Australians, they took with them briefing papers written by Reynolds. See *SMH*, 25 March 2000. Government submission contesting the term 'Stolen Generation' in *SMH*, 4 and 5 April 2000. See Phillip Ruddock speaking at the UN in *SMH*, 23 March 2000. For the attack on Reynolds see Keith Windschuttle in *SMH*, 19 September 2000; R Evans and B Thorpe, 'The massacre of Aboriginal history', *Overland* 163, Winter 2001, pp. 21–40.

'Quietly, the Aborigines submitted'

14 Murray Bail, *Eucalyptus*, Text, Melbourne, 1998, pp. 24–5.

15 T Dunbabin, 'Whalers, Sealers and Buccaneers', *JRAHS*, 11, 1926, pp. 4–8; Stephen Martin, *A New Land: European Perceptions of Australia 1788–1850*, Allen & Unwin, Sydney, 1993, pp. 12–13, 18.

16 Kym Thompson, *A History of the Aboriginal People of East Gippsland*, Land Conservation Council, Victoria, 1985, p. 16; EJ Wakefield, *Adventures in New Zealand 1839–1844*, vol. 1, John Murray, London, 1845, pp. 312–14; *Daily Telegraph*, Historical Supplement, 14 April 1969; Sue Wesson, *An Aboriginal Whaling History Project*, NPWS, Sydney, 2001, pp. 8, 11; T Dunababin, 'Whalers, Sealers and Buccaneers', pp. 12–13.

17 *Sydney Gazette*, 22 July 1804, 27 October 1805.

18 H Wellings in *Eden Magnet*, 8 August 1931.

19 *Sydney Gazette*, 6 April 1806.

20 *Sydney Gazette*, 18 May 1806.

21 *HRA*, Series I, p. 660; King to Camden, 15 March 1806.

22 *Sydney Gazette*, 19 September 1812 (also in H Wellings, *Eden Magnet*, 1 August 1931); *Sydney Gazette*, 7 October 1815; *Sydney Gazette*, 23 June 1821; *Sydney Gazette*, 24 September 1828 (later claimed to be false); H Wellings, *Eden Magnet*, 1 August 1931; Captain Phillip P King, *Narrative of a Survey of the Intertropical and Western Coasts of Australia 1818–1822*, vol. 1, John Murray, London, 1827, pp. 4–6.

23 *Sydney Gazette*, 7 October 1815.

24 *Sydney Gazette*, 23 June 1821.

25 Lambie quoted in Sue Wesson, *An Historical Atlas of the Aborigines of Eastern Victoria and Far South Eastern NSW*, 2000, p.184. Joseph Phipps Townsend, *Rambles and Observations in NSW*, London 1849, p. 107, refers to stockmen taking Aboriginal women as common. Also letter to *SMH*, 24 June 1839; Robinson, Journal, 1844, p. 130: several white men had fathered children to Aboriginal women. On alcohol and its effects see *Illawarra Mercury*, 13 April, 12 May, 20 July, 30 August, 1857; *Goulburn Herald*, 30 June 1849; *Illawarra Mercury*, 13 April 1857; *Candelo and Eden Union*, 26 April 1883. On disease see Michael Young, Ellen and Debby Mundy, *The Aboriginal People of the Monaro*, NSW NPWS, Canberra, 2000, for example at p. 36; *Illawarra Mercury*, 24 March 1896; Josephine Flood, 'The Moth Hunters: Investigations towards a prehistory of the south eastern highlands of Australia', PhD thesis, ANU, 1973 (MS 3919 NLA), p. 44; Oswald Brierly, Journal, 10 September 1844; Robinson, Journal, 5 August 1844, p. 158, 7 August 1844, p. 162; Wesson, *A History of Aboriginal Involvement*, pp. 8, 10.

26 References on population and lifestyle change: WK Hancock, *Discovering Monaro: A Study of Man's Impact on his Environment*, CUP, 1972, p. 67; Sarah Colley, in *Archaeology in Oceania* 22, 1987, pp. 97–106; A Atkinson and M Aveling (eds) *Australians 1838*, Fairfax, Syme & Weldon, Sydney, 1987, p. 22. See also censuses taken by Lambie, Crown Lands Commissioner for Eden–Monaro 1842–48, for example 11 January 1842 and 2 January 1850; *Regional Histories of NSW*, Heritage Office and Department of Urban Affairs and Planning, NSW Government, 1996, p. 164. Wesson, *An Aboriginal Whaling History Project*, p. 3; Valerie Attenbrow, 'Aboriginal Subsistence Economy on the far South Coast of New South Wales', BA (Hons), University of Sydney, 1976, pp. 46–9; D Byrne, *The Five Forests: an archaeological and anthropological investigation*, NPWS, Sydney, 1983. Also Robinson, Journal, Entries at Bega and Twofold Bay, 1844.

27 Hancock, *Discovering Monaro*, pp. 68, 112. A similar example is Brian Egloff, *A Report on an Investigation of Places of Cultural Significance to Aboriginal People in the Southern Portion of the Eden Woodchip Agreement Area*, NPWS, Canberra, 1987, p. 13, where he refers to local newspapers as the 'more obscure sources'. Also Geoffrey Blainey, *A Land Half Won*, Sun Books, Sydney, 1995 [1980], pp. 77–8. Klaus Hueneke, *People of the Australian High Country*, Tabletop Press, Canberra, 1994, p. 265, relates the story of Richard Brooks, the first to settle on the Monaro, who was forced by hostile Aboriginal people to shift on several occasions. *BDN*, 17 May 1928, mentions a J Bourke who travelled from Melbourne to Yass in 1838 and found the natives hostile.

28 A Weatherhead, *Leaves From my Life: Being Fifty-Six Years Experience on the South Coast of New South Wales*, Eden Museum, Eden, 1984, p. 22. See also Robinson, Journal, 29 July 1844, p. 146; *Bega Standard*, 29 March 1904; *BDN*, 30 April 1928; W Bayley, *The Story of the Settlement and Development of Bega*, Brooks, Sydney, 1942, p. 13; *Bega's Century of Progress 1857–1957*, *BDN*, 1957 (NLA), pp. 4–5. See also the JA Perkins papers, NLA. These papers contain a collection of early newspaper articles on the history of south-eastern New South Wales; see for example one headed 'Cooma in 1835'.

29 'Recollections of Frank Buckland', in *Mallacoota Memories*, Merimbula and District Historical Society, 1980, p. 61; Baron Field, *Geographical Memoirs of NSW*, London, 1825, p. 460. There are other examples of early homesteads in the area being fortified against attack. See for example *Cobargo Chronicle*, 19 May 1933. A report refers to the old Tarlinton homestead: 'when it was demolished by the late Dan Tarlinton, bricks were found between walls and lining showing that every precaution had been taken against an onslaught by native tribesmen, who frequently

hiked from the tablelands to the coastal areas and had conflict with their southern brethren. It was a common sight to see the victor carrying a limb or an arm on the homeward journey … meat for the hungry en route'. The writer claims that Tarlinton's son Jim was once speared, 'and the Aborigine's reward was meted out to him with the aid of a tomahawk'. See also *BDN*, 4 June 1928, where a writer surmises that the high brick wall surrounding Boyd's Sea Horse hotel 'may have been intended as a defence against surprise attacks by the Aborigines … it is lowest on the seaward face and therefore was not intended as a protector against the weather'. Finally, see Townsend, *Rambles and Observations*, pp. 109, 111.

30 *SMH*, 26 June 1839.

31 Michael Organ, *A Documentary History of the Illawarra and South Coast Aborigines 1770–1850*, pp. xxxiv–xxxvi; *Sydney Gazette*, 18 February 1841.

32 *Eden Magnet*, 8 August 1931.

33 From 1845, whaling was used as an example of Aboriginal intelligence and cooperation. See for example *Well's Geographical Gazetter of the Australian Colonies 1848*, NSW State Library, facsimile edition, 1970. Also M Pearson, 'Shore-Based Whaling at Twofold Bay: One Hundred Years of Experience', *JRAHS*, 71, 1985, pp. 3–27; S Blair et al., 'Davidson's Whaling Station at Twofold Bay', *Heritage Australia*, spring, 1987. For a celebratory approach to Aboriginal involvement in the whaling industry see Roland Robinson, Percy Mumbulla and B. Bancroft, *The Whalers*, Angus & Robertson, Sydney, 1996; D Davidson, *The Davidsons of Kiah*, self-published, 1990.

34 H Wellings, *The Imlay Bros*, pp. 6–7. For the Kudingal name for Mount Imlay (Ballun) see Robinson's Journal, 27 August 1844, p. 180; Dymphna Clark (ed.) *Baron Charles von Hugel: New Holland Journal November 1833–October 1834*, MUP, 1994, pp. 317, 321.

35 Wakefield, *Adventures in New Zealand 1839–1844*, vol. 2, pp.187–8.

36 *Bega Gazette*, 19 December 1872; Vicky Small, *Kameruka*, Kameruka Estates, 1989, p. 14. The fact that a man named Nelson worked at Kameruka is also evidenced by a reference in a Bega Paper, the *Southern Star*, 8 March 1922: 'the district was first settled by the Walkers who placed a man by the name of Nelson in charge'.

37 Joshua Higgs, in *Bega Gazette*, 7 July 1883. This same account is also in the *Southern Star*, 13 March 1920. For further evidence of violence and conflict see Wesson, *An Historical Atlas*. In EJ Brady's papers (NLA MS 206 Series 9), Brady claims that remains on Gabo Island indicate relations were 'at times acrimonious'. For other references to violence see Oswald Brierly, Journal, 19 December 1842; L Neal, *Cooma Country*, Cooma–Monaro Historical Society, 1976, pp. 12, 25, quoted in G Monaghan, *Visions for a Valley: Catholic people in the Bega Valley 1829–1985, a History*, self-published, 1985, p. 2; *Bega Gazette*, 12 December 1872; JA Perkins papers, Box 1 Folder 1 NLA (George Day); Robinson, Journal, 30 August 1844, p. 186; Bayley, *The Story of the Settlement and Development of Bega*, pp. 13–14; DG Parbery, *Fabric of a Family*, self-published, 1992, p. 27; *Mallacoota Memories*, Merimbula and District Historical Society, 1980, pp. 13, 16, 61; PD Gardner, *Gippsland Massacres: the destruction of the Kurnai Tribes 1800–1860*, Ngarak Press, Ensa, Vic. 1993, p. 13. See also Sue Wesson, *Australian Alps Oral History Project 1994*, p. 54; H Wellings, *Eden Magnet*, 8 August 1931. For Wellings' articles on various aspects of Twofold Bay history see *Eden Magnet*, 23 May, 20 June, 4 July, 11 July, 18 July, 25 July 1931, 16 January, 30 January 1932, *Pambula Voice*, 6 March, 13 November 1931, *Bega District News,* 4 December 1924. See also *Australian Childhood*, 20 November 1930; JP Townsend, *Rambles and Observations in NSW*, pp. 103, 107, 109, 112, 114, 116, 119–21, 191.

38 Sue Norman, interview with Pat Whalan 1979. Sue Wesson, *South Coast Place* (available only from Wesson), quotes from interviews with the Badgerys at Cooma. On shootings of Aboriginal people see Laurie Platt, *Bygone Days of Cathcart*, self-published, 1989, pp. 156–7; L Gardiner, 'Eden–Monaro to 1850: A Regional History', MA thesis, University College, Canberra, 1951 (Menzies Library, ANU) p. 59, footnotes. See also the interview with Dan Bray, an early settler, at Rocky Hall, recorded by Judy Satchwell in 1977 and obtained from Sue Norman. Bray claims that on Cann River Flat at Pericoe stories survived that Aboriginal people were cleared out with a gun. He also refers to the killing of blacks at Bega after Badgery's hutkeeper, Dunn, was murdered. See also Harry Wellings' reference in an unfinished historical novel, 'The Story of Yankee Campbell', in which Wellings claims the Imlays wrote to the Governor (most probably

in June 1839) requesting permission to mount a punitive expedition. I have been unable to find this letter, but I have little doubt that Wellings saw it in the 1930s. I quote now from the Wellings novel (obtained with the kind permission of Betty Buckland): '[Members of the Twofold Bay tribe in the Imlays' employ] had been killed and their bodies taken away by the Maneroo natives. The Imlays made a strong appeal to the Governor of the colony for investigation into the affair and pressed for the despatch of a punitive party. The Imlays also offered £50 reward for their capture'. Wellings then claims a police inquiry found it was an internal dispute between the tribes over stolen women'. Given that every other historical reference Wellings uses in the novel comes from Howitt, Bulmer, Robinson or the Sydney papers, this story probably has some basis in truth. Also, it is worth remembering Wellings' statement in his Twofold Bay pamphlet that relations between settlers and Aboriginal people were 'more or less good'. In the *Eden Magnet* of 8 August 1931, Wellings is again fairly blunt about the acts of 'deeper dreadfulness' that went unrecorded.

39 My discussion with Sue Norman of Kiah, 25 May 1999 and my interview with Jack Burgess, May 1999. See also Brierly, Journal, 10 February 1847. Similar stories concerning Nungatta can be found in Kate Clery, *The Forgotten Corner Interviews*, Eden Killer Whale Museum, 2000, pp. 19–20.

40 H Wellings, *Bombala Times*, 1 July 1932.

41 *BDN*, 12 February 1938. See also Judy Satchwell's interview with Dan Bray, which corroborates the Pambula milk pan story and the use of strychnine, placing it most probably in the 1840s. But it adds that the bodies of Aboriginal people were placed on a bullock slide and thrown into the sea at Haycock Point.

42 Wesson, *An Historical Atlas*, pp. 98–9, 129–31.

2 Did the NSW Government and the Colonial Office intend that the rights of Aboriginal people in south-eastern New South Wales be protected?

1 Reynolds is not the only historian under attack. Richard Broome, Lyndall Ryan, Roger Millis and others have also been attacked. However, the public representation of the debate is often framed as Reynolds v Windschuttle. See for example Robert Murray, 'The Truth About Our Past', *Age*, 13 July 2001; Reynolds in *SMH*, 25 September 2000; Debra Jopson, 'Sunday Bloody Sunday', *SMH*, 13 November 2000.

2 Henry Reynolds, 'Aboriginal–European Contact History', paper given at ANZAAS Congress, Hobart, 1976, pp. 19–21. *The Other Side of Frontier* had then already appeared in *Historical Studies*, 17(66) 1976, pp. 50–63. See also 'Reynolds v Blainey', *Australian*, 11 November 1973; Reynolds' 1976 article was published in *Journal of Australian Studies*, 3, June 1978 and republished in Richard White and Penny Russell (eds) *Pastiche I: Reflections on 19th Century Australia*, Allen & Unwin, Sydney, 1994, pp. 45–62.

3 I also came across this paper in Manning Clark's library. Reynolds had sent the paper to Clark.

4 Henry Reynolds, *Dispossession*, Allen & Unwin, Sydney, 1989, p.vii and *Frontier*, Allen & Unwin, Sydney, 1987, p. 3.

5 Henry Reynolds, *Why Weren't We Told ?* Viking, Melbourne, 1999, p. 205.

6 Ibid., p. 215.

7 Peter Cochrane, 'Hunting not Travelling', *Eureka Street*, 8(8) 1998, pp. 32–40.

8 Henry Reynolds, *The Law of the Land*, Allen & Unwin, Sydney, 1992, p. 194.

9 H Reynolds and J Dalziel, 'Aborigines and Pastoral Leases: Imperial and Colonial Policy 1826–1855', *UNSW Law Journal*, 19(2) 1996, p. 363.

'What might have been'

10 From Eliot's 'Burnt Norton', the first poem in *Four Quartets*. TS Eliot, *The Complete Poems and Plays*, Faber & Faber, London, 1987 [1969], p. 171.

11 Bernhard Schlink, *The Reader*, Phoenix, London, 1997, p. 89.

12 Barbara Dawson, 'Holding selectors at bay: an analysis of the Robertson Land Acts on the property of Bibbenluke in the Southern Monaro', MA thesis, ANU, 1996, p. 16.

13 Claire Schofield, *Bombala: Hub of Southern Monaro*, Bombala Shire Council 1990, pp. 31–2.

14 *Illawarra Mercury*, 28 July 1856, Editorial.

15 G Haydon, *Five Years Experience in Australia Felix*, vol. 2, Queensbury Hill Press, Melbourne, 1983 [1840s], p. 7; L Gardiner, 'Eden–Monaro to 1850: a regional history', MA thesis, quotes from J Dixon's diary published in Edinburgh in 1822. For other evidence see Alexander Weatherhead, *Leaves From My Life 1834–1892*, Eden Museum, 1988. In the preface, Weatherhead remarks that 'the land on my arrival was in a state of nature and inhabited *only* by aborigines'. Also WA Brodribb, *Recollections of an Australian Squatter*, Queensbury Hill Press, Melbourne, 1976 [1883], p. 7. WK Hancock, in *Discovering Monaro: A Study of Man's Impact on his Environment*, CUP, 1972, p. 46, claims that in 1844 Boyd possessed fourteen Monaro runs totalling a quarter of a million acres, for which he was paying in total, for four licences, £40 per annum, roughly a rental of 1d for every 1000 acres. Marion Diamond, *Ben Boyd of Boydtown*, MUP, 1995 [1988], p. 56, says the rent was £80 and later revised to £140. She also points out the vagaries of squatting runs; the postage stamp comment is on p. 58. W Bayley, in *The Story of the Settlement and Development of Bega*, Brooks, Sydney, 1942, p. 13, claims the squatters in Bega area ignored Governor Bourke's rents in the 1830s and took the land; there was little policing.

16 Darwin to Covington, 23 November 1850, in J. Ferguson, *Syms Covington of Pambula*, Merimbula–Imlay Historical Society, 1981 [1971], p. 25. In another letter to Covington dated 21 October 1853, Darwin mentioned that he had had dinner with Mr Septimus Martin, former minister at Twofold Bay, and he had 'told me a little about it'.

17 *BDN*, 26 April, 10 May 1928.

18 *Bega Standard*, 7 August 1875.

19 Darling's margin notes on a letter from A Gibson to Alexander McLeay, 13 October 1830. Noted by Sue Wesson. NSW State Archives, Colonial Secretary Correspondence 2/8020.4, 'Aboriginal Outrages'. The complaints were investigated but no action was taken.

20 *HRA* Series I, vol. 28, p. 157. Bourke to Glenelg, 10 October 1835.

21 Glenelg to Bourke, 13 April 1836 and Glenelg to Bourke, 26 July 1837, in *House of Commons Papers*, vol. 7, 1837; 'Despatches relative to the massacre of various aborigines of Australia in the year 1838'.

22 AGL Shaw, 'Orders From Downing St', *JRAHS*, 54, Part 2, 1968, p. 118; AGL Shaw, 'British Attitudes to the Colonies, *ca.* 1820–1850', *Journal of British Studies*, 9(1) 1969, p. 76. Shaw details political pressures on civil servants in the colonial office.

23 *House of Commons Papers*, vol. 7; Gipps to Glenelg, 27 April, 2 May 1838. See enclosure A-I to minute no. 24 of 1838; Gipps to Glenelg, 21 July 1838 (squatters' petition included, as is the resonse of Colonial Secretary Edward Deas Thompson, 23 June 1838.)

24 Glenelg to Gipps, 31 January 1838, *HRA* Series I, vol. 19, pp. 254–5.

25 Shaw, 'British Attitudes to the Colonies'; Heather Goodall, *Invasion to Embassy: Land in Aboriginal Politics in New South Wales, 1770–1972*, Allen & Unwin, Sydney, 1996, pp. 46–7; Samuel Clyde McCulloch, 'Sir George Gipps and Eastern Australia's Policy Toward the Aborigine 1838–1846', *Journal of Modern History*, 33, 1961, p. 261.

26 Governor George Gipps to Lord John Russell, 14 September 1841. *HRA* Series I, vol. 21, p. 509; Claire Schofield, *Bombala: Hub of Southern Monaro*, Bombala Shire Council, 1990, pp. 7, 24–5.

27 Lambie, 7 May 1848 in *HRA* Series I, vol. 26, pp. 402–3.

28 Jonathan Fulcher, 'Sui Generis History? The Use of History in Wik', in G Riley (ed.) *The Wik Case: Issues and Implications*, Butterworths, Sydney, 1997, pp. 51–6; David Ritter, 'The Rejection of Terra Nullius in Mabo: A Critical Analysis', *Sydney Law Review*, 18(1) 1996, pp. 5–33.

29 Reynolds, *Why Weren't We Told?* p. 214.

30 Ritter, 'The Rejection of Terra Nullius', pp. 7, 11, 13, 28–33.

31 Dymphna Clark (ed.) *Baron Charles von Hugel: New Holland Journal*, MUP, 1994, p. 138.

32 Louis De Freycenet, *Reflections on New South Wales 1788–1839*, Horden House, Sydney, 2001, p. 295.

33 See Goodall, *Invasion to Embassy*, p. 53. Earl Grey's despatch of 1846, which allegedly insisted on the right of Aboriginal native title to coexist on pastoral leases, was never drafted by the Government'. See also Don Watson, 'The War on Australia's Frontier', *Meanjin*, 41, 1982, p. 145.

34 Reynolds and Dalziel, 'Aborigines and Pastoral Leases', pp. 321, 327, 328. Reynolds points out the difference between frontier practice and official policy.

PART TWO: FORGETTING

3 'A cult of disremembering'?

1 Geoff Page and Pooaraar, *The Great Forgetting,* Aboriginal Studies Press, Canberra, 1996, p. 3.

2 WEH Stanner, *After the Dreaming: Black and White Australians — An Anthropologist's View*, ABC, Sydney, 1968, pp. 24–5.

3 Bernard Smith, *The Spectre of Truganini*, 1980 Boyer Lectures, ABC, Sydney, 1980, pp. 10, 17, 22.

4 'Early 20th century history was self consciously nationalistic ... racial violence was an embarrassment': Henry Reynolds, *The Breaking of the Great Australian Silence: Aborigines in Australian Historiography 1955–1983*, Trevor Reese Memorial Lecture 1984, Australian Studies Centre, London, p. 2. See also Reynolds, *Why Weren't We Told*, pp. 91–2.

'This wonderful invasion'

5 Lieutenant HW Breton, *Excursions in NSW, Western Australia and Van Diemen's Land 1830–1833*, London 1833, p. 243.

6 Tom Griffiths, *Hunters and Collectors*, CUP, 1996, p. 108.

7 *Candelo and Eden Union*, 30 June 1887. See *Eden Propeller*, 17 July 1903. In the previous edition, they had asked readers to explain the origins of Eden's name; finally someone writes in on 21 July with the correct explanation.

8 W Bayley, *The Story of the Settlement and Development of Bega*, Brooks, Sydney, 1942, p. 16. In the EJ Brady papers (NLA MS 206 Series 9) Brady states that after contact with whites, the 'black man of Mallacoota is no more'. *SMH*, 21 July 1868, quotes the *Monaro Mercury* reporting that Aboriginal tribes of the Monaro and Twofold Bay districts are 'dying away year by year'; also *SMH*, 15 May 1871. Local histories sometimes blame the decline of the Aboriginal population on disease alone. See for example Norm Evans, *Roads to Water: The History and Story of Tathra Kalaru Wallagoot*, self-published, 1994, pp. 66–7. There were also laments for the disappearance of genuine Aboriginal artefacts, for example *Bega Gazette*, 7 May 1884, which reports on the loss of the Australian Museum's Aboriginal artefacts in a fire in the Garden Palace in Sydney.

9 D Moye (ed.) *Historic Kiandra: A Guide to the History of the District*, Cooma–Monaro Historical Society, 1959, p. 2.

10 Letter to the editor on the general subject 'the Australian Aborigines', *Bombala Herald*, 18 September 1875.

11 *Bega Gazette*, 7 May 1884

12 *SMH*, 27 September 1856

13 Sue Wesson, *An Historical Atlas of the Aborigines of Eastern Victoria and Far South Eastern New South Wales*, p. 9.

14 *Eden Propeller*, 13 November 1903 editorial. Another more general feature on the dying race of Australia's Aborigines in *Eden Propeller*, 17 April 1908.

15 G Haydon, *Five Years Experience in Australia Felix*, vol. 2, Queensbury Hill Press, Melbourne, 1983 [1840s], p. 35. K Howe and J Byrne, *Mallacoota Reflections*, Mallacoota and District Historical Society, Mallacoota, 1990, p. 12. For stories on cannibalism see *Monaro Mercury and Cooma and Bombala Advertiser*, 28 November 1862. In this issue there is a story on the 'bloodthirsty blacks' on the Burdekin Downs in Queensland, and another on 20 February 1863, and on 13 March 1863 the paper carries a story on Aboriginal people 'preparing for war in Armidale'. See also BDN, 'Reminiscences of Old Tanja Days violent cannibals', 6 May 1940: 'My heart stopped beating when one day walking along a Tanja bush track I met about thirty

Aborigines. They were making to Bega to collect their annual supply of blankets ... I ... recalled the stories I had heard of plump little boys being devoured by the blacks ... On two occasions I saw corroborees at the old mill flat, Bega, now part of the present showground ... Among these niggers were Blooah, Nelbar, Binyah, Haddigaddi, and later the original Pickalla'. For general references to tribal violence see Sister Bernice Smith (foundation secretary of the Bega Historical Society), Bega 1966, transcripts of interviews available at AIATSIS. Her memories of Aboriginal culture focus on 'tribal boundaries and battles' territory, disputes and war. For example, 'there was a great battle [at Broulee] ... there were two survivors'. See also *Bemboka Village in a Valley: A History of Education and Life in Bemboka 1840–1996*, Bemboka School Centenary Book Committee, 1996, p. 169. Harold Tarlinton, *The Story of Cobargo*, in *Tales of the Far South Coast*, vol. 3, Kingfisher, Bega, 1986 p. 2: 'Generally speaking the natives were friendly ... however tribal quarrels did occur'. As always, Aboriginal people disappear from the narrative as soon as the skirmishes are over. In *Childhood Reminiscences of Wilfred Alexander Watt de Beuzeville 1884–1954, ca. 1950* (NLA), he remembers his time near Bombala, mostly around the 1890s. 'Blacks' from the Delegate tribe would often visit his father's station. Charlie the King 'waddied his gin to death in a gunyah near the river', just below Bombala. Again the black violence is remembered, though the following detail is also recorded: 'I remember when the blacks came [to our station] the piccaninnies would feast on the scrapings from the molasses casks, getting their hair full of it, [until] their hair would stick out around their head like pegs, then an old gin would place the piccaninny between her knees and contentedly suck away at each peg of hair until the treacle had all vanished'.

16 See W Bayley's manuscript on the history of Cobargo in the manuscripts collection of the Mitchell Library. Bayley took notes from AS Wallace's *History of Cobargo* (1926), which retold the Tarlinton story. See also *Bega Gazette*, 18 October 1893; AB Jauncey, 'A History of Bega 1833–1916', *JRAHS*, 4, Part 6, 1918, p. 309; *BDN*, 6 March 1979; Laurie Platt, *Bygone Days of Cathcart*, self-published, 1989, pp. 156–7, details a tribal battle at Cathcart in the 1840s. The Tarlinton battle is also recounted in Frank Allen, *A History of Bibbenluke 1835–1971*, self-published, 1971, p. 3. See also DG Moye, *Historic Kiandra*, Cooma–Monaro Historical Society, 1959.

17 W Bayley, 'Notes on the History of Bega and Moruya 1770–1943', collected 1942–43 (NLA). In an interview I conducted with Jack Burgess in Bega in 1999, he insisted that there were 'not many Aborigines to begin with' in the Bega area. See also Jauncey, 'History of Bega', p. 309; Michael McGowan (ed.) *The Tarlintons in Australia 1791–1991: a Bicentennial History*, self-published, 1991, p. 15; W Bayley, *The Story of the Settlement and Development of Bega*, p. 10; *Bega Standard*, 20 August 1920.

18 For an example of conflict being admitted when pioneers are anonymous, see *Bega's Century of Progress 1857–1957*, *BDN* 1957 (NLA) p. 4, which refers to the Aboriginal people as 'often hostile' and the Bega Valley as 'dangerous'.

19 *BDN*, 27 January 1970, 'Australia's Cook Bicentenary'.

20 *Bega Gazette*, 21 July 1886; *Bega Standard*, 20 August 1920; *Illawarra Mercury*, 9 March 1857; *SMH*, 7 May 1872; NLA MS 5704, *Notes on the Early History of Bombala and the Monaro District*, collected by Thomas Fleming from HT Edwards, p. 2.

21 Celia Ann Rose, 'Recollections of the early days of Moruya', *JRAHS*, 7, 1923, Journal and Proceedings Supplement, pp. 375–6.

22 Edwards, *Notes on the Early History* ... Remarkably, after detailing numerous examples of Aboriginal people spearing the settlers' stock, Fleming claimed that Aboriginal people were 'not very fierce or hostile'.

23 David James, *Kindly Light: The Life and Times of Adolphus Summer Cloud James*, self-published, Sydney, 1999 (NLA), p. 20.

24 *Candelo and Eden Union*, 3 December 1885.

25 *Eden Magnet*, 25 June 1932, 2 July 1932; Wellings in *Eden Magnet*, 25 June 1932.

26 *Bega Gazette*, 19 December 1872. See also Album of cuttings on Bega History, NLA MS 5912, 'Bega 70 years Ago' (*Southern Star* 1922): Aboriginal people were 'numerous' but 'not of a hostile nature'. But one early resident claims Bega was 'uninhabited' and 'nothing but a

kangaroo run'. See also *Cooma Monaro Express*, 12 February 1945, JA Badgery, a trip to Monaro in 1845, where there is no mention of Aboriginal people.

27 *Bega Gazette*, 12 December 1872.

28 F Mitchell (ed.) *Back to Cooma Celebrations 20 February–27 February 1926*, Direct Publicity and Back to Cooma Executive Committee, Sydney, 1926, p. 34; 'Bega's Century of Progress 1857–1957', *BDN* 1957 (NLA), p. 6, refers to King Billy as the person 'whose ancestors had the distinction of being the first into the district'. *Bega Gazette*, 23 April 1874, refers typically to Aboriginal people as the 'sable sons of the soil'. *SMH*, 1 January 1859, in a report from Cooma, states that 'the Aboriginal owners of the soil are mustering around the township'. See *Sydney Times*, 6 February 1835, regarding proposed settlement of Irish emigrants at Twofold Bay.

29 *Bega Gazette*, 12 December 1872: the 'Imlays were the sole owners of the Twofold Bay district'. See Haydon, *Five Years Experience in Australia Felix*, p. 7; JP Townsend, *Rambles and Observations* in NSW, London, 1849, p. 107: 'The truth is where the country is closely occupied by farmers, they [the blacks] are thrust out altogether'. See also *Back to Cooma Celebrations 20th February–27th February 1926*, Back to Cooma Executive Committee, 1926, p. 34: The early settlers speak of the Aboriginals as existing in great numbers on the Monaro ... the country, in those days, was 'practically owned by them'.

30 *Bega Standard*, 3 April 1889, *Bega Gazette*, 18 October 1893. See also '50 years of Balmain Bros', Supplement to the *Bega District News*, 29 May 1959, p. 3.

31 Most of these recollections are to be found in the transcripts of interviews held at AIATSIS with Sister Bernice Smith (foundation secretary of the Bega Historical Society), Bega 1966. See also *Cobargo Chronicle*, 19 May 1933, 'natives were plentiful and several axes have been found on various occasions'. For more evidence, especially on the image of Aboriginal people as warlike, see the following sources. Bayley's *History of Cobargo*, pp. 111–15 (Mitchell Library) includes notes from AS Wallace, *History of Cobargo*, 1926. See also *BDN*, 11 December 1930: a letter from HB mentions the 'old remnants of these tribes' by name, where they camped, dozens appearing in Bega for their annual blanket gift, and also that 'an occasional corroboree took place on the showground where the present pavilion is'. In *Eden Propeller*, 23 June 1905, a traveller walks to the south head of Twofold Bay from the south: 'here and there evidence is seen of the swarthy race of long ago ... judging by the numbers of trees from which shields were taken the bygone inhabitants of Eden must have been a fighting race, or else had to protect themselves against the onslaughts of other warlike tribes'.

32 *Monaro Mercury and Cooma and Bombala Advertiser*, 3 April 1863.

33 *Bombala Times*, 7 August 1875. *Cooma Gazette*, 7 August 1875. The *Bega Gazette*, 5 August 1875 says, selfishly, that the Americans shouldn't think of coming to the Bega Valley — 'though there is much Crown land available, the eyes of this part of the colony have been well and truly picked out'.

34 *Candelo and Eden Union*, 30 June 1887; *Candelo and Eden Union*, 26 January 1888, editorial; *Illawarra Mercury*, 26 January 1856.

35 JLA Lhotsky, *Journey from Sydney to the Australian Alps*, Sydney, 1835 pp. 19, 44. See also John Lhotsky, *Illustrations of the Present State and Future Prospects of the Colony of NSW*, Sydney, 1835 p. 12.

36 Dymphna Clark (ed.) *Baron Charles Von Hugel: New Holland Journal November 1833–October 1834*, MUP, 1994, p. 417.

37 Robinson Journal, 7 August 1844. See also JP Townsend, *Rambles and Observations* in NSW, London, 1849, pp. 119–20.

38 *Moruya Examiner*, 26 January 1888. The Eliot quote is from 'Burnt Norton' (*Four Quartets*) in TS Eliot, *The Complete Poems and Plays*, Faber & Faber, London, 1987 [1969], p. 187. See also a poem by 'Eucalyptus', 'From Mumbulla', a lament for the passing of the natural environment and traditional Aboriginal culture, in *Southern Star*, 22 June 1901; District of Monaro, newspaper cuttings, Mitchell Library Q991/N vol. 44.

39 *Eden Magnet*, 1, 8 August 1931.

40 *Bega Standard*, 24 May 1898; *Bega Standard*, 16 March 1920, obituary of the pioneer William Bartley.

41 District of Monaro, newspaper cuttings, Mitchell Library Q991/N vol. 44. 'Veritas' interviews the old Monaro pioneer Bernard O'Rourke on his verandah. Also *Braidwood Despatch*, 17 November 1933, reports on the memorial unveiled to Thomas Braidwood Wilson, 1792–1843.

42 *Monaro Mercury and Cooma and Bombala Advertiser*, 6 January 1865. For pushing back the past see the following: *Southern Star*, 9 May 1906, which reports the death of Daniel Gowing, one of the most 'ancient' citizens of New South Wales. He first came to Bega in the 1830s or 'as he very appropriately called it, the Garden of Eden'; also *Candelo and Eden Union*, 28 December 1893; *Bega Gazette*, 18 October 1882: '[unlike the lakes of Scotland,] when we float on the surface of Merimbula Lake … history has no record of its past'. See also W Bayley, *The Story of the Settlement and Development of Bega*, Brooks, Sydney, 1942, p. 10. Bayley deals briefly with 'primeval Bega'. In *BDN*, 12 February 1938, an obituary of George Keys refers to 'the early days' as around the 1860s, when Keys first came to the area. On the same day the term 'far distant past' is used for the Aboriginal past. In *Bega Gazette*, 2 May 1868, the Eden correspondent laments the decline of whales compared to 'olden times' (i.e. only thirty years ago!). In *Bega Gazette*, 31 July 1873, the history of Australia was compared to Europe and America: 'unwritten, its pages of a virgin whiteness'. The *Candelo and Eden Union*, 23 June 1887, reported the unveiling of the statue of Henry Wren at Kameruka: 'In a young colony where the scene changes so swiftly and where the past is forgotten so easily', it is a good idea to erect monuments'. See *Bega District News*, 12 February 1938, where a report on the Burragate show lauds Tommy Stevens, an old pioneer. The *Bega Standard*, 31 May 1912, in 'On Dr George Mountain', speaks of 'years ago when the names of Boyd and Imlay were great on the South Coast. The Imlays now lie under vine clad stones in a little cemetery on the hills above the Bega river' … at night the glare of gas lamps has taken the place of the blacks' camp fires'.

43 *Candelo and Eden Union*, 28 December 1893.

44 'Those first convicts and exiles who were part of the workforce on the lonely Monaro runs played a major role in the destruction of a proud and independent people': L Neal, *Cooma Country*, Cooma–Monaro Historical Society, 1976, p. 35.

45 Bain Attwood, *The Struggle for Aboriginal Rights: A Documentary History*, Allen & Unwin, Sydney, 1999, p. 6.

4 Emily's story

1 *SMH*, 14, 16 May 1870, *Bega Gazette*, 14, 24 April, 26 May 1870.

Making settler history

2 Geoff Page and Pooaraar, *The Great Forgetting*, Aboriginal Studies Press, Canberra, 1996, pp. 61–5. The 'classic text' of the title is Stephen H. Roberts' *The Squatting Age in Australia, 1835–1847*, a book which signally failed to acknowledge even the presence of the Aboriginal people.

3 *Bega Gazette*, 7 March 1885.

4 Joshua Higgs, *Bega Gazette*, 7 July 1883: 'I killed the first fresh beef the Imlays had'. *Moruya Examiner*, obituary of Margaret Weatherhead, 5 December 1885: 'First white woman to cross the river … in a log canoe'. *Bega District News*, 25 January 1932: The 'first white born on the southern side of Bega river'. *Bega Standard*, 14 January 1888: 'First white man who trod foot on Pambula flat'. *Bega Standard*, 24 May 1898: 'First man to put bells on cattle and horses'. W Bayley, *The Story of the Settlement and Development of Bega*, p. 14: First white child. Bayley on Thomas Underhill, *History of Bega*, p. 89: 'First white man to travel through the district in that direction'. See also *Bega Gazette*, 24 March 1888; *Bega Standard*, 11 March 1898; *Bega Standard*, 25 November 1898; *Bega Standard*, 19 April 1901; *BDN*, 7 June 1928. See also Graeme Davison, *The Use and Abuse of Australian History*, Allen & Unwin, Sydney, 2000, p. 200: 'the endless list of firsts' in pioneer history.

5 *Bega Gazette*, 14 June 1882. See also obituary of WD Tarlinton, *Cobargo Watch*, 20 October 1893; *Cobargo Chronicle*, 19 May 1933; Rev. G Monaghan (ed.) *Visions for a Valley: Catholic People in the Bega Valley 1829–1985, A History*, 1985; W Bayley, *W.D. Tarlinton*, Mitchell Library B1049.

6 *BDN*, 25 January 1932 and *Bega Gazette*, 12 November 1874 report on the death of 'Big Jack'.

7 *Further Glimpses of Tathra's Past*, Tathra Historical Society, 1980, NLA.

8   *Bega Gazette*, 5 April 1928.

9   Laurie Platt, *Bygone Days of Cathcart*, self-published, 1989, p. 1;Vicky Small, *Kameruka*, Kameruka Estates, 1989, p. 12; *Bega's Century of Progress 1857–1957*.

10 Davison, *The Use and Abuse of Australian History*, p. 197. On pp. 202–3 he speaks of the difference between pioneer history and that which succeeded it, patriarchal history. The shift, he says, 'was from a story of origins to a story of generations, from recollection to recording, from celebration to commemoration, from testimony to chronicle'. In Eden–Monaro at least, the shift was not as neat and tidy as Davison suggests.

11 *BDN*, 13 October 1967; *BDN*, 29 January 1965: Bega's School of Arts was demolished for the building of 'a new chain store' in Carp Street; see Davison, *The Use and Abuse of Australian History*, p. 80.

12 *Magnet Voice*, 29 February 1968, p. 7. Crawford is supporting the claim of the Imlay District Historical Society. See also *BDN*, 28 July 1967: 'History in Eden to mark the spot where the first Imlay Shire Council met'.

13 Leslie H Sullivan, *From Cardboard Box to Courthouse: The First Ten Years of the Bega Valley Genealogy Society*, 1997 and *Monumental Inscriptions in the Bega Valley Shire*, Book 1, Bega Valley Genealogy Society, 1989. See also *Imlay Magnet*, 7 January 1988, p. 27. Davidson's whaling station was acquired by the NPWS in 1986 as a 'historic site'.

14 *Delegate Argus*, 30 July 1914, report of a 'burning fatality' at Craigie on Monday, 27 or 20 July; *Eden Propeller*, 13 July 1906: report of death of girl by fire.

15 Centenary Supplement, *BDN*, 1 December 1964. *Bega Standard*, 7 August 1875, lauds the creation of a 'yeoman class' in the 1860s.

16 NLA MS 5912, Album of cuttings on Bega. *Bega Standard*, 8 March 1922. Bega show report in Davison, *The Use and Abuse of Australian History*, p. 204. The interwar years were the heyday of 'back to' celebrations, but they had waned by the 1950s. See also TH Kerrison, *A History of the Bombala RSL Sub Branch*, Bombala RSL, 1981, p. 6.

17 *Southern Star*, 8 March 1922, report on Back to Bega movement.

18 *BDN*, 21 October 1969.

19 *Southern Star*, 22, 25 February 1922.

20 See for example Margaret Evans, *History of the Bega Show*, Bega AP & H Society, 1998; S Codrington, *Gold From Gold: A History of Dairying in the Bega Valley*, Mercury Research Press, Sydney, 1979; Beatrice Gallo and Ray Barnett, *A Dairy Tale*, Inkwell Publishing, Candelo, NSW, 1994.

21 GF Phillips, *The Founding of the Eden Killer Whale Museum*, 1981 (NLA); A Trip to Eden, South Coast, NSW, Voyager, 1917 (NLA); *Eden Propeller*, 6 November 1903, again refers to Boyd's time as 'long ago'; the *Propeller* was the first paper in Eden to circulate the stories of Boyd and whaling. See 27 November, 11 December 1903, 25 August, 1, 15 September, 10 November 1905. *Eden Propeller*, 26 May 1905, speaks of the 'haunted stillness of Boydtown'. See *BDN*, 21 August 1942. *Eden, Twofold Bay, NSW, Its Beauty Spots and Places of Historical Interest*, Eden Tourist Association, 1907 (Petherick, NLA) attempts to attract tourists to the area by telling them of the whaling history and Boyd, who in this pamphlet is something of a founding father, 'the Cecil Rhodes of Australia' — 'how few know of the ancient history of Ben Boyd and Boydtown, and the interesting relics and ruins he left behind' (p. 11).

22 *Eden Propeller*, 18, 25 December 1903. See also *Magnet*, 18 December 1997, reprinting an article from the *Eden Observer*, 18 December 1903.

23 *BDN*, 27 January 1970.

24 *BDN*, 17 April 1970, *BDN* 27 January 1970. In Bombala, little interest was displayed in the Cook celebrations (or in the Tent Embassy in 1972) but there was a call to turn the old Cathcart public school into a historical museum. *Bombala Times*, 22 May 1970, reports on a school centenary procession held in Cathcart, historical costumes, transport parade, drovers and cowboys and bushrangers but no Aboriginal people.

25 *BDN*, 19 April 1937.

26 Platt, *Bygone Days of Cathcart*, p. 156.

27 For stories of settler suffering at the hands of Aboriginal people see Platt, p. 239.

28 For denial see *Bega Standard*, 11 November 1876, 'Foundation of Bega'. There is no mention of Aboriginal people; pioneers simply 'opened up' the country. Also WA Smith, *A Walk down Memory Lane and the Red Bull Story* (NLA). For blaming indigenous deaths on the lower classes see G Haydon, *Five Years Experience in Australia Felix*, vol. 2, Queensbury Hill Press, Melbourne, 1983 [1840s], pp. 11, 48. For trivialising indigenous resistance, see W Bayley, *The Story of the Settlement and Development of Bega*, Brooks, Sydney, 1942, p. 13. See also S. Codrington, *Gold From Gold: A History of Dairying in the Bega Valley*, Mercury Research Press, 1979, p. 27; Beatrice Gallo and Ray Barnett, *When the Mill Came to Merimbula*, Inkwell Publishing, Candelo, NSW, 1993, p. 2: 'The traditional life of the aboriginal people was *disturbed* as early as the 1830s with the arrival of white settlers who squatted in the area to graze their sheep and cattle'.

29 WEH Stanner, *After the Dreaming: Black and White Australians — An Anthropologist's View*, ABC, Sydney, 1968, pp. 24–7.

30 BJ Ferguson, *A Short History of Merimbula*, Imlay District Historical Society, 1970s, pp. 3–5.

31 Laurie Neal, *Cooma Country*, Cooma–Monaro Historical Society, 1976; *Back to Cooma*, Back to Cooma Celebrations Committee, February 1926, pp. 34–5.

PART THREE: ABANDONMENT

5 The architecture of grace

1 Rev. EG Pryce, Account of the Mission of Maneroo, Addressed to the Lord Bishop of Australia, 1 January 1844, in *The Church in Australia*, Part II, *Two Journals of Missionary Tours in Districts of Maneroo and Moreton Bay, New South Wales, in 1843*, Society for the Propagation of the Gospel, London, 1845. For Broughton see *The Church in Australia*, Part I, *Two Journals of Visitation to the Northern and Southern Portions of his Diocese by the Lord Bishop of Australia 1843*, Society for the Propagation of the Gospel, London 1845, p. 47: extract from the letters of Bishop Broughton 3 July 1843, 3 April 1844, 22 June 1844.

2 *The Church in Australia*, Part III, *A Journal of Visitation by the Lord Bishop of Australia, in 1845*, Society for the Propagation of the Gospel, London, 1846. In February 1845 Broughton journeyed south through the Monaro as far as Cooma where he met EG Pryce and the Commissioner for Crown Lands, John Lambie. See Broughton's entry on 13 February, pp. 16–17.

'Waiting for civilisation — longing for home'

3 'A Drum for Ben Boyd', in Francis Webb, *Collected Poems*, Angus & Robertson, Sydney, 1979 [1973], p. 17.

4 Dymphna Clark (ed.) *Baron Charles von Hugel: New Holland Journal November 1833–October 1834*, MUP 1994, pp. 314–15.

5 Rev. EG Pryce, Account of the Mission of Maneroo, Addressed to the Lord Bishop of Australia, 1 January 1844, in *The Church in Australia*, Part II, p. 10. See also *SMH*, 11 September 1860: complaints of 'lamentable lack of public worhip' in Eden; WK Hancock, *Discovering Monaro: A Study of Man's Impact on his Environment*, CUP, 1972, pp. 84–5.

6 JL Lhotsky, *A Journey from Sydney to the Australian Alps*, Sydney, 1835, pp. 51–2, 67, 83, 106.

7 *Monaro Mercury*, 15 April 1864.

8 *Bega Gazette*, 2 June 1866. See also Lang on his visit to the area in *The Empire*, 31 May 1866; *The Church in Australia*, Part III.

9 Sue Wesson, *South Coast Place*, quotes from a speech written by John Jauncey in 1894.

10 *Candelo and Eden Union*, 18 May 1882. See also W Bayley, *The Story of the Settlement and Development of Bega*, Brooks, Sydney, 1942, p. 97.

11 Journal of Farquar Mackenzie (Mitchell Library). Another example of the squatter's approach to

boredom — shooting pigeons for sport — can be found in *Eden Magnet*, 26 May 1932.

12   Imlay Bros Accounts Book MS CY A 3031 (Mitchell Library) (most probably Alexander Imlay). See also *SMH*, 11 January 1847 for a report on George Imlay's death.

13   Dymphna Clark (ed.) *Baron Charles von Hugel: New Holland Journal November 1833–October 1834*, MUP, 1994, pp. 316–19; Robinson, Journal, 4 July 1844, p. 129, remarks on the 'miserable' state of one of Boyd's huts on the Monaro, 'the hutkeeper a dirty cursing character'.

14   H Wellings, *The Imlay Bros: Peter Alexander and George Imlay*, Sydney, 1966 (NLA), p. 17.

15   *Cooma Gazette*, 7 August 1875. The *Bega Gazette*, December 1866, draws on Spaniard Don Henrique Mantano's travels in Australia 1854–55. Mantano described the squatters as the most 'thoroughly selfish lot of men on the face of the earth'. A letter to the *Sydney Gazette*, 19 May 1832, eagerly anticipates the opening up of land at Twofold Bay.

16   L Neal, *Cooma Country*, Cooma–Monaro Historical Society, 1976, p. 13, quotes from Lhotsky's journal.

17   *Australian*, 31 October 1839, reports on bushrangers attacking Imlay's station at Bega. A Weatherhead, *Leaves From My Life 1834–1892*, Eden Museum 1988, on travelling in the Monaro in the 1830s: 'women got very scarce the further we went along'. *SMH*, 1 August 1845: Monaro squatter claims squatters were 'driven to a state of depression from the paucity of marriageable ladies'. A letter in *SMH*, 24 June 1839 from Maneroo refers to 'cattle stealing' and 'retailers of poisoned spirits'. See also *Bathurst Free Press*, 23 August 1856: report from Eden states that bullock teams drink their wages for two days in the public house and leave their bullocks tethered outside without food or water. See also letter in *SMH*, 27 December 1839: 'In the Southern districts … there is no such thing as a border police'. *Sydney Gazette*, 23 May 1839, reports that the Monaro region 'teems' with 'outrages and robberies'. A letter to *SMH*, 6 October 1846, says the Monaro 'is in a most lawless state, there being as many cattle stealers as licensed settlers'. Alan EJ Andrews, *Earliest Monaro and Burragorang 1790 to 1840*, Tabletop Press, Canberra, 1998, pp. 94, 99.

18   *Illawarra Mercury*, 20 October 1856. Also Thomas Wilson's letter in *Australian*, 31 October 1841.

19   *Pambula Voice*, 21 July 1899; H Wellings, *Benjamin Boyd in Australia 1842–1849*, Sydney, 1956 (NLA), pp. 11, 17, 23–4; *Candelo and Eden Union*, 12 August 1886.

20   Oswald Brierly went on board the *Velocity* when the ship arrived at Twofold Bay and immediately condemned Boyd's scheme. For more on Boyd's labour scheme see Captain J Watson, 'Benjamin Boyd', *Navy League Journal*, 4(10) 1924: 26; Marion Diamond, *Ben Boyd of Boydtown*, MUP, 1995 [1988], pp. 126–40, 192–3. The *Australian*, 21 September 1848, reports on the fate of the islanders taken back to the Coral Islands by Boyd. See Wellings papers, NLA: Box 3 Book 6, Boyd's letter to SB Daniels, station master at Upper Murray; Box 4, Boyd folder. See the letter from Thos Bullen to the Colonial Office, 15 November 1847. Bullen describes Boyd's scheme as a 'foul blot over the English name and reputation'. See also K Hartig and G Waitt, 'The lost metropolitan centre of New South Wales: resolving the unfulfilled claims about Eden, 1843–1920', *JRAHS*, 83, Part 2, 1997, pp. 118–35; Wellings, *Benjamin Boyd*, p. 29.

21   Parbery, *Fabric of a Family*, p. 28. James Walker sold up in 1852 and died in France in 1881. Parbery, p. 27, quotes Robinson, Journal, 5 July 1844, p. 130: 'Boyd [has] bought all the land at Twofold Bay and monopolises the timber; squatters [are] obliged [to] buy off him and at his prices; he will not bring them supplies from Sydney … The squatters or men are at his mercy'. By 1844, the Imlays owned a total of 960 000 acres between Twofold Bay and the Clyde River. Vicky Small, *Kameruka*, Kameruka Estates, 1989, p. 14: in 1848 the *Government Gazette* listed Walker's Kameruka run purchased from the Imlays at 192 640 acres.

22   Wellings, *The Imlay Bros*, p. 24; JAS McKenzie, *The Twofold Bay Story*, Eden Killer Whale Museum, 1991, p. 12; *Daily Telegraph*, Historical Supplement, 14 April 1969; H Wellings, 'The Brothers Imlay' *JRAHS*, 17, Part 4, 1931, pp. 209–14. On boiling down see Wellings, *The Imlay Bros*, p. 24 and W Bayley, *The Story of the Settlement and Development of Bega*, p. 17.

23   Letter from Tim Bobbin to *Bega Gazette*, 22 July 1865; reply 29 July 1865.

24   Alice Otton, 'The Simple Pleasures', in *Tales of the Far South Coast*, vol. 1, 1982, p. 103. Lhotsky in *Sydney Gazette*, 2 December 1834, arranges a traditional song of the Monaro people for pianoforte: 'The music and words … for majestic and deep melancholy would not dishonour a

Beethoven or a Handel'. Also my interview with Jack Warren (born 1904), 27 May 1999. Warren worked in the 1920s with the Davidsons for two seasons and claimed he didn't like killing the whales. He could hear the whales moaning at night from his home. See CE Wellings, 'The Killer Whales of Twofold Bay NSW: Australia Grampus Orca', *The Australian Zoologist*, 10, Part 3, 1944, pp. 291–3. See also HS Hawkins and RH Cook, 'Whaling at Eden', *Lone Hand*, 1 July 1908, p. 267. For various reactions to the natural environment see the following: *Bega Gazette*, 12 September 1868, which tells the story of Jabez Lapstone, the legend of the Mount Imlay cobbler; *BDN*, 12 February 1938. CH Darragh writes explaining how he 'discovered' Mt Darragh: *Bega Standard*, 14 January 1888. See also John Hayden ('Big Jack') in *Bega Gazette*, 18 October 1882; *Twofold Bay and Maneroo Telegraph*, 14 September 1860; *Bega Gazette*, 7 and 4 March 1885. Howe's journey up coast in 1797 is in *HRNSW*, vol. 3, Government Printer, Sydney, 1895. p. 762.

25   Joseph Lingard, *A Narrative of the Journey to and from NSW*, 1846 (Mitchell Library).

26   *Regional Histories of NSW*, Heritage Office and Department of Urban Affairs and Planning, NSW Government, 1996, pp.167–8, 172–4; Jauncey, 'History of Bega'. p. 305, Gibbney, p. 17; Laurie Platt, *Bygone Days of Cathcart*, self-published, 1989, p. 92; Michael Pearson, *A Brief History of Settlement: Ben Boyd National Park*, NPWS, 1979.

27   *Bega Standard*, 11 January 1888. See also *Eden CRA Region*, p. 28, quoting Lucy Ann Marks who travelled from Twofold Bay to Pollacks Flat in 1852, and wrote in a letter to her parents of the poor roads: 'I can see nothing nor no boddy only trees hills and mountings [sic]'. *Pambula Voice*, 12 July 1901: an old resident of Bombala returns after twenty years away: 'the streets ... were wide and clean — no little crooked lanes or dirty flagstones anywhere'. *Pambula Voice*, 31 December 1901, reports on a dinner held in Eden to commemorate the discovery of Twofold Bay by Bass in 1797. In his speech, the president of the Eden Progress Association said, 'since then a century has passed, and instead of the native wilderness of that long past day we now have British homes and homesteads all around us'. CW Holgate, Diaries, 1884, NLA MS 7539: Holgate visits Eden in April 1884 by steamer. He ends his journal entry after his first day in Eden, as he does for every day, 'the end of 163 days from home'. See also *Bega Standard*, 7 August 1875; *Illawarra Mercury*, 13 November 1857, 1 April 1858.

28   *Braidwood Review*, 27 June 1922, repeating a report from the Sydney *Chronicle* in the 1840s.

29   Obituary of William Rixon in *Southern Star*, 26 December 1916. Report on Balmain Bros car in *Southern Star*, 8 January 1919. See also Rev. WB Clarke, *Researches in the Southern Goldfields*, p. 228, quoting from a letter of TS Townsend, 16 March 1846. Samuel Sidney, *The Three Colonies of Australia: New South Wales, Victoria, South Australia: their pastures, copper mines and gold fields*, London, 1852, p. 347: As he leaves Twofold Bay and passes Cape Howe, Sidney speaks of 'the imaginary line' dividing the provinces of New South Wales and Victoria. On naming, see W Bayley, *Notes on the History of Bega and Moruya 1770–1943*, collected 1942–43, NLA. He says one paper in Bega in the 1950s tried to establish that the name Bega went back to the seventh century. See also letter from Monaro re Aboriginal pronunciation of names, *SMH*, 29 May 1858; letter to *Illawarra Mercury*, 27 May 1858; Joshua Higgs in *Bega Gazette*, 7 July 1883.

30   SJ Rea, *I Sought Adventure*, Blackie & Son, London, 1940, pp.196–8.

31   *Southern Star*, 24 January 1903; *Gippsland Times*, 6 June, 27 April 1883; M Walker (ed.) *Come Wind Come Weather: A Biography of A. Howitt*, MUP, 1971. See especially John Mulvaney's chapter, 'The Ascent of Aboriginal Man: Howitt as Anthropologist', pp. 285–312 . See also J. Mulvaney, 'The Anthropologist as Tribal Elder', *Mankind*, 7(3) 1970, pp. 205–17. The editor of the *Bega Gazette*, 16 May 1883, expresses his hope that Howitt will soon be able to publish 'a book of reference for all questions concerned with a race soon to be extinct'.

32   *Bega Gazette*, 10 October 1872. Transcription of Parkes' speech at Armidale.

6   Agent of civilisation

1   A map of the County of Auckland in the 1850 edition of *The Church in the Colonies, No. XXIV, Australia, a letter from the Lord Bishop of Melbourne, 1849*, Society for the Propagation of the Gospel, London, 1850, shows 'Boyd' (Boydtown), 'Twofold Bay' (Eden), 'Towamba River', 'Mt Imlay or the Peak', and a 'Mt Brierly', at the source of the next river to the north of the Towamba, 100-odd kilometres inland, which must be the Bega River.

'This black mother earth': The journals of Oswald Brierly

2   Marion Diamond, *Ben Boyd of Boydtown*, MUP, 1995, pp. 31–3. For biographical details on Brierly see *Australian Dictionary of Biography*. In an interesting anecdote in the *Eden Propeller*, 3 November 1905, JM Sinclair wrote in a Melbourne paper that he was told the following by his uncle, James McInnes, who knew both Brierly and Boyd. Boyd was walking along Fenchurch Street in London, and stopped to admire a sketch of the *Wanderer* in a picture dealer's shop. On being told it was painted by Brierly, Boyd sought him out and Brierly agreed to come with him. His uncle recalled Brierly as 'an enthusiast' and remembered him as a young man sketching on the deck of the *Wanderer*.

3   The phrase 'colonial earth' is taken from the title of Tim Bonyhady's *The Colonial Earth*, MUP, 2000. Oswald Brierly, *Journal of a Visit to Twofold Bay December 1842–January 1843*, A535, Mitchell Library, 15 December 1842.

4   Brierly, Journal, 16, 20 December. See also Robinson, Journal, August 1844, p. 163: 'Cut my name on tree GA Robinson 10 August 44'.

5   H Wellings, 'Twofold Bay in 1842', *Eden Magnet*, 14 November 1931.

6   Brierly, Journal, 19 December 1842. Brierly reflects on the hardships experienced by the founders. A537 contains the comparison with American Indians.

7   A535 is by far Brierly's best journal.

8   All quotes from Brierly's journal, A535. Worthy of note is Brierly's observation that when Toby was sent to shoot a duck and instead came back with a platypus, he claimed never to have seen one before and at first 'seemed afraid of it'. This is crucial because it shows that the coastal tribes were indeed separate from those of the Towamba Valley, which were in turn separate from those on Monaro. It also demonstrates the multi-lingual nature of Aboriginal society. Wellings describes part of this journey in the *Bombala Times*, 18 November 1932, and remarks how 'Toby proved invaluable'.

9   H Wellings, *Eden Magnet*, 14 November 1931; Brierly, Journal, A535, 16, 18, 20 December. In Brierly's Journal, 14 August 1844, Monaro blacks perform a corroboree, which he describes in detail. Robinson, Journal, 19 August 1844, describes the funeral for 'Teapot'. See also Robinson, 15, 16 August 1844, p. 171, 30 September 1843, 26 September 1844.

10   Brierly, Journal, 20 December 1842, A535.

11   'This evening Toby and crew came on board gave him the Governor's card and by his directions wrote on back "Toby King of Nullerker, Beemere, Toormeryun, Coxswain, Twofold Bay, B. Boyd Esquire and guide to the Maneroo Country. by G. A. Robinson J.P. C.P.A." and would not be satisfied until he wrote as I dictated: he was proud of the card. Toby furnished me with a number of words of the Twofold Bay vocabulary': Robinson, Journal, 14 August 1844, p. 165.

12   Brierly, Journal, 20 December 1842.

13   Brierly, Journal, A549. Also quoted in Wesson, *South Coast Place*.

14   Brierly, Journal, January 1843, especially 5 and 10 January. Brierly mentions he will caution Toby about liquor: 28 September 1843.

15   Brierly, Journal, A535.

16   D Davidson, *Davidsons of Kiah*, self-published, 1990, p. 25: 'On the dining room wall at Oswald Bloxsome's House "'the Ranger's" at Mosman Bay, Brierly painted his celebrated picture of H.M.S. Rattlesnake in a gale off the island of Timor in November 1848'.

17   Brierly, Journal, A533, p. 2. While in Sydney, Brierly met Miss D. See also 19 March 1843 and 16 August 1844 in Sydney. The horse and exercise line is in Brierly's Journal, A527. See 19 March 1843, A533, for 'Miss D'.

18   Brierly, Journal, 24 December 1843. See also 25 March 1845 A539, which contains abstracts of earlier journals written up on the *Wanderer* in a small and excruciatingly neat hand, displaying extraordinary diligence. Robinson was no different; see for example Journal, 29 August 1844, p. 185: 'busy all day writing vocabulary, collecting information'. Brierly notes his meeting with Robinson on 12 August 1844 and is very impressed with him. But he also quips, 'I have seen some of his notes here and there illustrated by very crude attempts at sketches'. A good example of the scientific endeavour that pervaded British colonisation can be seen in the instructions

given to Captain Phillip P King, *Narrative of a Survey of the Intertropical and Western Coasts of Australia 1818–1822*, John Murray, London, 1827.

19   Brierly, Journal, August 1844, 13 August 1843: 'Faults most liable to'; 5 June 1843 chess metaphor; March 1845, A539, also contains exhortations to self-improvement and is one of the most revealing in terms of Brierly's personality.

20   Brierly, Journal, 21 August and 5 June 1843 on board *Wanderer*: 'My studies lately have been reading and making abstracts of the most celebrated Romans and Athenians — Caesar, Cicero Demosthenes and Pericles'.

21   In a plan for making a whaling journal, Brierly (Journal, 25 March 1845) lists details he should record: 'detail number of men in whaling party, preparations, tryworks, measurements of boats worth of oil and bone ... Secure these particulars and this with your daily journal and the sketches will make a work that will at once give you position — but whatever you do make it complete let nothing divert you from this one object and do not tell others'.

22   Brierly, Journal, 7 August 1843.

23   Brierly, Journal, 9 August 1844 (anchored at East Boyd).

24   Brierly, 'Cetacea', A546, p. 19; Brierly, Journal, 11 August 1844. On Aboriginal relationship with the killer whales, see 5 June 1843 where Brierly remarks on the expertise of Aboriginal crews. Brierly also notes the Aboriginal people's disquiet when one of the Killers is killed — 'King Toby a good whaler' — as he does in 'Cetacea', p. 4. For another example of Brierly's ability to appreciate the beauty of the bush, see Journal, 15 September 1844.

25   Brierly, Journal, 24 December 1843.

26   For Brierly and Boyd, see Brierly, Journal, 5 January 1847: 'Boyd is tired of Boydtown. Says he is tired of the people ... [but the truth is] I rather think that he has succeeded in making himself so disagreeable to the people that they are tired of him'. This is very different from the entry on 5 June 1843 when he described Boyd in glowing terms as raising towns and fitting out fleets like Pericles. See also Journal, 20 June, 22 August 1847, 25 March 1845. On 1 January 1847, Brierly writes out a large section of a letter from Boyd. This letter followed shortly after George Imlay's death and it reveals Boyd's greed: 'See Peter Imlay and get all George's runs on the South side, ask what are his views about the Bigga country ... In the meantime quietly drive the sheep upon Mowera ... if any words should take place you can say that Dr. George had once told you that you might drive sheep and cattle upon it and that you always considered it part of my run ... [Also] it would be as well to secure Batangaby [*sic*] ... but this must be done judiciously otherwise he will be pasturing with it'.

27   Brierly, Journal, 11 February, 26 September 1844.

28   David R Moore, *Islanders and Aborigines at Cape York: An ethnographic Reconstruction based on the 1848–1850 Journals of O.W. Brierly and information he obtained from Barbara Thompson*, AIAS, Canberra, 1979. Brierly, Journal, A509, 17 October 1849; M Bassett, *Behind the Picture: HMS Rattlesnake's Australia New Guinea Cruise 1846–1850*, OUP, Melbourne, 1966; J Huxley (ed.) *T.H. Huxley's Diary of the Voyage of HMS Rattlesnake*, Doubleday Doran & Co., New York, 1972.

29   Brierly, Journal, 18 April 1848; July 1847: 'my heart and feelings are so wedded to the place'.

30   Brierly, Journal, 18 April 1848.

31   Marian Hutcheon, *A Little Piece of History*, NLA, n.d., pp. 15–16: Edrom Lodge, a reincarnation of the Logan family estate south-east of Edinburgh in Scotland, now stands where Brierly's cottage once stood. See also Davidson in the *Davidsons of Kiah*, p. 110.

7   'Victims of singular neglect'

1   Ann Curthoys, 'Mythologies', in Richard Nile (ed.) *The Australian Legend and Its Discontents*, UQP, 2000, pp. 13, 37.

2   Henry Parkes was responsible for the phrase 'the victim of singular neglect'. He used the expression to describe Eden in 1891. See *Eden Observer*, 29 January 1909.

3   *SMH*, 13 September 1856.

4   *The Colonist,* 4 August 1836, describes Twofold Bay as 'a sort of halfway house between Sydney and Hobart Town'. See also *Bega Gazette*, 2 May 1868; *SMH*, 8 January 1960; Samuel Sidney, *The*

Three Colonies of Australia, London, 1852, p. 275; *The Empire*, 1 July 1861; *Sydney Mail*, 29 August 1963 on Kiandra gold rush; *Daily Telegraph*, 29 May 1911 on failed schemes for the development of Twofold Bay, 'the victim of singular neglect'; *Bombala Times*, 26 June 1942 on the history of local Railway Leagues; *SMH*, 7 October 1881, Eden–Bega–Cooma railway proposed; *SMH*, 28 November 1884; *SMH*, 19 May 1923.

5   *Eden Propeller*, 29 March 1907; AT Daplyn, *To Eden with the Government Tourists*, 1917 (NLA), p. 5. See also K Hartig and G Waitt, 'The Lost Metropolitan centre of New South Wales: Resolving the unfulfilled claims about Eden, 1843-1920', *JRAHS*, 83, Part 2, 1997, pp. 118–35, which posits Eden as the lost city and the failed metropolitan centre. See also *The South-Eastern Gate: Twofold Bay*, Twofold Bay Development League, 1926. The *Eden Propeller*, 4 December 1903, contains an article on Eden–Bombala entitled 'A neglected corner'. See also the continuation of this theme in Kate Clery, *The Forgotten Corner Interviews*, Eden Killer Whale Museum, 2000.

6   RG Castle and JS Hagan, 'Aboriginal Work and Society on the Far South Coast 1920–1975', paper presented to the Labour History Seminar, Canberra, February 1978 (AIATSIS), p. 2.

7   DW Rawson and SM Holtzinger, *Politics in Eden–Monaro*, Heinemann, London, 1958, p. 1.

8   *Eden Propeller*, 19 December 1902.

9   *Colonist*, 4 August 1836, describes Twofold Bay as 'a sort of halfway house between Sydney and Hobart Town'. *SMH*, 13 September 1856, speaks of Boyd's hotel and lighthouse as 'very early monuments of decay in so new a country'. See also K Hartig and G Waitt, 'The Lost Metropolitan centre of New South Wales: Resolving the unfulfilled claims about Eden, 1843–1920', *JRAHS*, 83, Part 2, 1997, pp. 118–35; *Bega Gazette*, 2 May 1868; *SMH*, 8 January 1960; Sidney, *The Three Colonies of Australia*, p. 275; *The Empire*, 1 July 1861; *Illawarra Mercury*, 16 March 1857; *SMH*, 8 June 1868.

Waiting for Eden

10   LT Carron, *A History of Forestry in Australia*, ANU Press, Canberra, 1985, p. 41; *BDN*, 10 March 1967; *Magnet Voice*, 28 November 1968.
BDN, 18 April 1967, editorial, 'Conservation Urgent'.
BDN, 8 August 1969, editorial refers to the 'growing ranks of conservationists'.

11   *Magnet Voice*, 24 April 1969, 12 June, 10 July 1970. For much earlier arguments for conservation see for example *BDN*, 6 December 1949, p. 2, where W Dickinson of Bermagui writes that he is apalled by 'the scarring of the natural beauty of Mount Dromedary, and flora and fauna habitat destruction'. He writes to the Premier requesting the creation of the Dromedary National Park.

12   Daniel Lunney and Chris Moon, 'The Eden Woodchip Debate 1969–1986', *Search*, 18(1) 1987, p. 12; D Quarmby, *Eden Woodchipping — A Review*, National Parks Association, Canberra, 1986, p. 2; RG Bridges, *Integrated Logging and Regeneration in the Silvertop Ash–Stringybark Forests of the Eden Region*, Research Paper No. 2, Forestry Commission of NSW, 1983.

13   Helen Hannah, *Forest Giants: Timbergetting in the NSW Forests 1800–1950*, Forestry Commission of NSW, 1986, p. 27. See also *The South-Eastern Gate*, p. 43; Daniel Lunney and Chris Moon, 'An Ecological View of the History of Logging and Fire in Mumbulla State Forest on the South Coast of NSW', in KJ Frawley and N. Semple, *Australia's Ever Changing Forests: Proceedings of the first National Conference on Australian Forest Industry May 1988*, Department of Geography and Oceanography, University of New South Wales.

14   *The Voice*, 22 May 1969; Lunney and Moon, 'The Eden Woodchip Debate', p. 15. For similar arguments see John Formby, *No Garden of Eden: The Eden Woodchip EIS*, CRES Working Paper 1986/24 ANU, July 1986.

15   Harris Daishowa, *An Environmental Impact Statement for the Eden (NSW) Export Woodchip Operation*, prepared for the Commonwealth Government, March 1977, pp. 5, 85; John Dargavel, *Fashioning Australia's Forests*, OUP, Melbourne, 1995, p. 163; Lunney and Moon, 'The Eden Woodchip Debate', p. 16.

16   Lunney and Moon, 'The Eden Woodchip Debate', pp. 16, 45; Manning Clark, National Library Oral History Cassette tape TRC 501 (my transcript).

17   *Mumbulla, Spiritual Contact*, Research School of Pacific Studies, ANU, 1980.

18 *Canberra Times*, 16 September 1979.

19 *BDN*, 10 August 1978.

20 D Byrne, *The Mountains Call Me Back: A History of the Aborigines and the Forests of the Far South Coast of New South Wales*, NSW Ministry of Aboriginal Affairs Occasional Paper No. 5, June 1984, pp. 25–6. In December 1978, the Forestry Commission of NSW agreed to halt logging while the anthropologist Brian Egloff investigated the Aboriginal people's claims on Mumbulla Mountain. For the emergence of nineteenth-century religious involvement in Aboriginal protection see *Bega Gazette*, 26 September 1885. Denis Byrne, in *The Mountains Call me Back*, reprints the letter of Jean Draper, Secretary of Trees.

21 *BDN*, 3, 10, 17, 28 August. Byrne, *The Mountains Call Me Back*, pp. 25–6; Brian Egloff, *Mumbulla Mountain: An Anthropological and Archaeological Investigation*. Occasional Paper No. 4 1981, NPWS, Canberra, 1981.

22 *BDN*, 28 August 1979.

23 *BDN*, 10 August 1979.

24 DJ Mulvaney, *Encounters in Place: Outsiders and Aboriginal Australians 1606–1985*, UQP, 1989, pp. 220–4.

25 Harris Daishowa, *Draft Environmental Impact Statement for the Eden (NSW) Export Woodchip Operation for the Period 1989–2009*, 1986, p. 33 (Mitchell Library).

26 John Dargavel, *Fashioning Australia's Forests*, OUP, Melbourne, 1995 pp. 153, 170.

27 *South East Forests Campaign Handbook*, June 1989.

28 *Imlay Magnet*, 2 February 1988, pp.1, 23; *Imlay Magnet*, 4 February 1988: Mr Peter Went, the general manager of Harris Daishowa, informed Carr by stating that the company 'had never taken sides in elections until now'. Public meetings were held and there were front-page photographs of the distraught wives of timber workers clutching their children. See the new national anthem in *Imlay Magnet*, 9 February 1988; see also *Imlay Magnet*, 17 March 1988. For examples of local debate see the letter from a timber worker in *BDN*, 20 February 1998: 'Today's greens are yesterday's reds in another guise, what they really want is the breakdown of the capitalist system'; 'when our backs are against the wall we have to fight back … [against] the greenies [and] inner city electorates'. *Imlay Magnet*, 13 July 1993, contains a letter making it clear that decent folk, unlike the greenies, 'cannot rely on social security payments to live – some of us have to work for a living'.

29 *The New Forests of Eden*, Forestry Commission of NSW, 1987, p. 2; Dargavel, *Fashioning Australia's Forests*, pp. 192–3. Eden and Monaro Survival Group established: *Imlay Magnet*, 3 March 1988.

30 S Bochner and L Parkes, *The Psychological Effects of the Timber Industry in the Eden Region of NSW*, A Report Prepared for the NSW Forest Products Association, January 1998; *Local Impacts of Forest Industry Expenditure in the Eden CRA Region*, A Report Undertaken for the NSW CRA/RFA Steering Committee, project no. NE30/ES, Rush Social Research, December 1997. Also *Imlay Magnet*, 2 September 1999; *Regional Forest Agreement for the Eden Region of NSW between the Commonwealth of Australia and the State of NSW*, August 1999.

31 *Structural Adjustment and Mitigative Processes in the Eden CRA: A Social Assessment*, A Report Undertaken for the NSW CRA/RFA Steering Committee, Rush Social Research, December 1997, pp. 3, 13, 18, 19, 18–24, 33, 34, 39, 40, 41, 43.

32 Geoffrey Stokes, 'One Nation and Australian Populism', in Michael Leach, Geoffrey Stokes and Ian Ward (eds) *The Rise and Fall of One Nation*, UQP, 2000, p. 23; Murray Goot, 'Hanson's Heartland; Who's For One Nation and Why', in Tony Abbott et al., *Two Nations: The Causes and Effects of the Rise of the One Nation Party in Australia*, Bookman Press, Melbourne, 1998, pp. 51–74. Drawing attention to the grievances felt by some residents is not to say that there is no sympathy and understanding in the community for Aboriginal culture. In one survey conducted in 1998, 48 per cent of respondents said that Aboriginal sacred sites in local forests should be protected, 32 per cent said they should not be protected and 20 per cent claimed to be undecided: *Social Values of Forests Eden CRA Region*, Social Assessment Unit, DPIE, A Report Undertaken for the NSW CRA/RFA Steering Committee, Project no. NE02/ES, April 1998, pp. 42–3.

33 Bochner and Parkes, *The Psychological Effects of the Timber Industry*, pp. 8–9; *Social Values of Forests Eden CRA Region*, Social Assessment Unit, DPIE, A Report Undertaken for the NSW CRA/RFA Steering Committee, Project no. NE02/ES, April 1998, p. 56 (Bombala), pp. 63–5 (Eden).

34 Rhonda Gallagher and Denis Peters, *Greenseas: The Way We Were*, Excel Printing, Eden, 1999 (NLA); *Imlay Magnet*, 26 June 1997.

35 *Imlay Magnet*, 6, 13 May, 8 July 1999. In 1995, workers at the cannery had accepted a four-day week rather than lose 20 per cent of their workforce.

36 *Imlay Magnet*, 13, 20 May 1999. Signs still line the streets: 'don't close the gates of Eden'. *Imlay Magnet*, 27 May 1999, p. 3: Bega Valley Shire Council reps to meet with Carr. *Imlay Magnet*, 3 June 1999: Carr claims he will work towards the new 'Gateway tourist information centre'.

37 *Imlay Magnet*, 8 July 1999.

38 *Imlay Magnet*, 15 July 1999, 30 March 2000.

39 Graeme Davison, *The Use and Abuse of Australian History*, Allen & Unwin, Sydney, 2000, p. 219.

40 *Imlay Magnet*, 9 March 2000: Public rally protests against cuts to Pambula hospital. *Imlay Magnet*, 20 April 2000: Westpac at Eden closes down.

PART FOUR: CONFRONTATION

8   New history, new politics

1 Bernhard Schlink, *The Reader*, Phoenix, London, 1997.

2 Ibid., pp.156, 168.

3 *SMH*, 30 April.

4 *Age*, 30 April, p. 2. For a similar expression of guilt regarding the shooting and poisoning of Aboriginal people on the frontier, see John Pringle's article in the *Age* on 29 April, p. 6.

5 *Australian*, 7 February.

6 See for example *Churinga*, May 1970, p. 29; *Age*, 2 February 1970.

7 *Australian*, 7 February 1970.

8 *Australian*, 30 April 1970.

9 *Age*, 29 April 1970.

10 *Australian*, 7 February 1970; *Age*, 11 February 1970; *SMH*, 29 April 1970.

11 *Age*, 30 April 1970.

12 *Australian*, 29 April 1970.

13 Lynn Spillman, *Nation and Commemoration: Creating National identities in the United States and Australia*, CUP, 1997, pp. 111–16.

14 *Age*, 30 April 1970.

15 Graeme Davison, *The Use and Abuse of Australian History*, Allen & Unwin, Sydney, 2000, p. 72.

16 *SMH*, 26 January, 31 December 1988.

17 Anna Haebich, *Broken Circles: Fragmenting Indigenous Families 1800–2000*, Fremantle Arts Centre Press, Fremantle, WA, 2000, p. 568; Human Rights and Equal Opportunity Commission, *Bringing Them Home: National Inquiry into the Separation of Aboriginal and Torres Strait Islander Children from their Families*, April 1997. See also Robert Manne, 'In Denial; The Stolen Generation and the Right', *Australian Quarterly Essay*, 1, 2001. Also *SMH* and *Australian*, 27 May, 27 August 1997. For international coverage see *New York Times*, 27 August 1997, p. A10.

'We are all one': Aboriginal people in Eden–Monaro, 1860–1960

18 Lee Chittick and Terry Fox, *Travelling With Percy: A South Coast Journey*. Aboriginal Studies Press, Canberra, 1997, p. 163.

19 'Bowral to Bega on foot', handwritten exercise book notes, 1904, by W Lunney, Bega Museum.

20 D Horton (ed.) *The Encyclopedia of Aboriginal Australia: Aboriginal and Torres Strait Islander History, Society and Culture*, Aboriginal Studies Press, Canberra, 1994, vol. 1, p. 430. See also Ossie Cruse in Kevin Gilbert, *Living Black*, Penguin, Melbourne, 1977, pp. 55–62. For details on Wallaga Lake and Lake Tyers see J Long, *Aboriginal Settlements: A Survey of Institutional Communities in Eastern Australia,* ANU Press, Canberra, 1970; Heather Goodall, *Invasion to Embassy: Land in Aboriginal Politics in New South Wales, 1770–1972,* Allen & Unwin, Sydney, 1996. See also Long, p. 17: Lake Tyers was established in 1861–62 and handed over to the Protection Board by the Church of England in 1908. For an example of how Aboriginal people were forcibly removed see NSW State Archives Aborigines Protection Board minute books, Minutes for 8 January 1891; in the first week of 1891 police at Eden suggested to the Board that the Adgery family be removed to Wallaga Lake. Wellings Papers, NLA Box 2, black exercise book no. 3, p. 103, quoting *Twofold Bay Observer*, 5 February 1861, p. 99: 'Remnants of a tribe of Aborigines camped not far from Chandos St.'

21 *Bega Standard*, 9 March 1887.

22 *Bega Standard*, 15 August 1888, reports on 'the death of an old Aboriginal', Jimmy Queero, who died at Cohen's Lake off the Tathra Road. Queero was buried at 'the selection set apart for the Aboriginals at Cohen's Lake, alongside his old comrades Georgie Cohen, Charlie and Tall Boy'. See also *Bega Standard*, 22 December 1905, where there is a photograph of Queero. The article claims he fished up and down the coast, 'leading whites to places where they would catch schnapper'. See also *Cobargo Chronicle*, 20 April 1900: report on corroboree at Wallaga Lake; NSW State Archives, Aborigines Protection Board minute books, 8 January 1891: police at Eden suggested the Adgery family be moved to Wallaga Lake; *Bega Gazette*, 26 September 1885: Bega Council meeting on 'how best to deal with the Aborigines'; Sue Wesson, *An Historical Atlas of the Aborigines of Eastern Victoria and Far South Eastern NSW*, Monash Publications in Geography and Environmental Science No. 53, Monash University, 2000.

23 Peter Read, *A Hundred Years War: The Wiradjuri People and the State*, ANU Press, Canberra, 1980; Sue Wesson, PhD thesis, Monash University (draft).

24 Haebich, *Broken Circles*, pp. 156–64. Haebich discusses the national exclusion of Aboriginal people, and exercise of control, especially through the intrusion into family life, by the new white Commonwealth and the variations in state policies. On p. 203 she quotes *Bringing Them Home*: between one in three and one in ten indigenous children were forcibly removed from their families between 1910 and 1970. Haebich concurs with *Bringing them Home* that this policy continued the pattern of genocide (p. 207).

25 JPM Long, *Aboriginal Settlements of Institutional Communities in Eastern Australia*, ANU Press, Canberra, 1970, p. 62; Sue Wesson, *An Aboriginal Whaling History Project*, NPWS, Sydney, 2001, p. 9.

26 Chittick and Fox, *Travelling with Percy*, p. 164: many Aboriginal people speak about how the manager at Wallaga Lake wouldn't allow them to speak their language. See also Goodall, *Invasion to Embassy*, p. 347, on the strong knowledge of traditional customary law and history at Wallaga Lake.

27 Wesson, PhD, pp. 199, 254–6.

28 Ibid. On numbers of children removed see *1994 Aboriginal and Torres Strait Islander Survey: Queanbeyan ATSIC Region*, ATSIC and Commonwealth Bureau of Statistics, Commonwealth of Australia, 1996. *Bega Gazette*, 29 June 1867, includes a piece from the *Braidwood Despatch*. *Bega Gazette*, 24, 28 April, 16 May 1883, on Howitt's visit; Aboriginal people come from Monaro, Bega and Bermagui and Moruya.

29 Michael Young, Ellen and Debby Mundy, *The Aboriginal People of the Monaro*, NSW NPWS, Sydney, 2000, pp. 235–47. Young includes the NSW Protection Board reports from 1891 to 1932. See also Long, *Aboriginal Settlements*, p. 29.

30 RG Castle and JS Hagan, 'Aboriginal Work and Society on the Far South Coast 1920–1975', paper presented to the Labour History Seminar, Canberra, February 1978 (AIATSIS), pp. 3–6. By 1948 Aboriginal children could attend government schools without needing a medical certificate, though they could still be expelled without notice. *BDN*, 5 February 1965: Wallaga Lake school closed and twenty-three Aboriginal children started at Bermagui. See also Haebich, *Broken Circles*, pp. 185, 503.

31 Haebich, *Broken Circles*, pp. 181–6. See also Sue Wesson's thesis for details of the Stolen Generations in south-east New South Wales.

32 Chittick and Fox, *Travelling with Percy*, p. 41. Guboo Ted Thomas speaks of HJ Bate's farm at Tilba, where Aboriginal people would be paid in tucker for clearing the land. His father had worked for Bate.

33 Sue Norman, interview with Ozzy Cruse and Beryl Cruse 1996 and interview with Rodney Hyde, 1985.

34 Castle and Hagan, 'Aboriginal Work and Society', pp. 3–11; *Canberra Times*, 12 June 1973. Also Sue Norman, interview with Rodney Hyde in 1985. Hyde said an Aboriginal family was living in the bush at Nadgee behind Newton's Beach, south of Eden, in the 1940s. Aboriginal people would come to Eden to trade fish for bread.

35 Heather Goodall, 'New South Wales', in Ann McGrath (ed.) *Contested Ground: Australian Aborigines Under the British Crown*, Allen & Unwin, Sydney, 1995, pp. 89–90.

36 *BDN*, 3 February 1954.

37 Chittick and Fox, *Travelling With Percy*.

38 Ibid., p. 36.

39 Ibid., p. 113.

40 Chittick and Fox, p. 7. See also Bain Attwood, 'A Tour of Duty in Australia's History Wars', *Australian Financial Review*, 1 June 2001, pp. 8–9.

41 Chittick and Fox, pp. 29–31.

42 Ibid., p. 44. See also pp. 89–92, 138–9.

43 Ibid., p.136. The generosity of the Otton family is also mentioned here.

44 Ibid., p. 30 (Doris Kirby), pp. 125–6 (Max Harrison).

45 Castle and Hagan, 'Aboriginal Work and Society', pp. 9–11. See also Goodall, *Invasion to Embassy*, p. 182.

46 Chittick and Fox, *Travelling with Percy*, pp. 136–7; pp. 31–2 (Doris Kirby), p. 55 (Eileen Pittman).

47 Ibid., p. 166; pp. 50–2 (Cyril Parsons), p. 103 (Sharon Thomas).

48 For examples of Aboriginal resistance in the early twentieth century see Goodall, *Invasion to Embassy*, pp. 117, 147, 160.

9 'Friendly but firm discrimination': The fight for Aboriginal housing in Bega, 1960–1970

1 E Witton, *Aborigines on the South Coast* (AIATSIS PMS 2037), 1965.

2 *BDN*, 2 June 1967.

3 Lee Chittick and Terry Fox, *Travelling With Percy: A South Coast Journey*, Aboriginal Studies Press, Canberra, 1997, p. 55.

4 South Coast Labour Council, Aborigines Advancement League, *Survey Into Living and Social Conditions of Aboriginal People from Wollongong to the Victorian border*, 6–12 December 1961 (AIATSIS); Heather Goodall, *Invasion to Embassy*, Allen & Unwin, Sydney, 1996, p. 309.

5 In 1949, the Aborigines Welfare Board regazetted a section of the eastern foreshores of Wallaga Lake, for use as holiday cottages. See Goodall, *Invasion to Embassy*, pp. 307–8.

6 For a similar report see Witton, *Aborigines on the South Coast*. Witton, vice-president of the 'Aboriginal Australian Fellowship', visited Bega and Wallaga Lake in January 1965. At Wallaga Lake, he and his wife were forced to wait in the car, while his friend Ken Brindle, who had come to visit relatives, was allowed only ten minutes to see them. Witton described the 'impossible situation, that Aboriginal people on reserves may not invite white friends into their homes while often being subjected to the indignity of police entering their houses without warrant of any kind'. Aboriginal people working as pickers told him they were chased off the farmer's property and their houses pulled down if they dared to take up a job with the Council. He was also shocked by the conditions in which many Aboriginal families were living and working. They worked under no award, with no legal minimum conditions, and

were forced to live in shacks in conditions that only 'breed despair and apathy'.

- Charles Rowley, *Outcasts in White Australia: Aboriginal Policy and Practice*, vol. 2, ANU Press, Canberra, 1971, p. 254. Another 'perceptive neighbour' remarked that the Aboriginal people actually came to believe the white stereotypes and that they were 'bodily offensive' — 'squalor is the final state of self-condemnation'.

- Ibid., pp. 250–8.

- *Canberra Times*, 2 September 1964: Geoffrey Sawyer on American race politics; 4 and 5 September: race riots in New York, background to US election; 7 September: Kenyan Minister for Justice. See also *Canberra Times*, 16 September: the Nigerian journalist Olabisi Alala writing on racial discrimination in Papua New Guinea; Kim Beazley Snr, 17 September 1964.

0 Ann Curthoys, 'The 1965 Freedom Rides', paper delivered in the History seminar series in the Research School of Social Sciences, ANU, October 2001.

1 *BDN*, 19 March 1965, p. 1.

2 Rowley, *Outcasts in White Australia*, pp. 254–6.

3 *Canberra Times*, 25 August 1964. See also *BDN*, 1 January 1988, on Jauncey.

4 *Canberra Times*, 27 and 29 August 1964.

5 *Canberra Times*, 28 August 1964.

6 Ibid.

7 Ibid.

8 Quoted in Rowley, *Outcasts in White Australia*, p. 258. See also *Canberra Times*, 29 August 1964.

9 *Canberra Times*, 3 September 1964.

20 Rowley, *Outcasts in White Australia*, p. 256.

21 *Canberra Times*, 1 September 1964.

22 *Canberra Times*, 4 May 1967, p. 26.

23 Anna Haebich, *Broken Circles: Fragmenting Indigenous Families 1800–2000*, Fremantle Arts Centre Press, Fremantle WA, 2000, p. 505.

24 *BDN*, 21 April 1967.

25 *BDN*, 26 April, 12 May 1967.

26 *BDN*, 28 April 1967.

27 *Canberra Times*, 3 May 1967, pp. 1, 17.

28 *Canberra Times*, 4 May 1967, p. 26.

29 *BDN*, 19 May 1967.

30 *BDN*, 26 May 1967. See also M. Rayner, *A Study of Housing for Aborigines within Bega NSW 1967–1970* (AIATSIS PMS 3324), p. 5.

31 *BDN*, 16 June 1967.

32 *BDN*, 30 June 1967, p. 11.

33 For Holt's appeal see *SMH*, 27 May 1967. See also the *Age* editorial on 22 May 1967, which again placed the referendum in an international context, fearing that a No vote would label Australia as 'a country addicted to racist policies ... [a] label [that] would have a millstone's weight around the neck of Australia's international reputation'.

34 Witton, *Aborigines on the South Coast*. See also Ozzie Cruse interviewed in the *Imlay Magnet*, 28 August 1990; Nicholas Brown, 'A Place at the Coast', *Eureka Steet*, 6(9) 1996, pp. 42–4.

35 *BDN*, 30 May 1967.

36 *BDN*, 16 June 1967 (Michael Sawtell).

37 *BDN*, 25 August 1967. The paper conducted its own survey of Bega residents' views on the proposed housing scheme and found that the majority of residents were strongly opposed to the settlement of Aboriginal people 'in a concentrated group': *BDN*, 2 June 1967. The Mayor seized on the result of the survey and claimed it was proof of the community's fear 'as to the possible creation of an undesirable colony in the area': *BDN*, 6 June 1967.

38 *BDN*, 25 August 1967: Report on public meeting. *BDN*, 22 September 1967: Council votes to oppose the Welfare Board's scheme. *BDN*, 26 September 1967: BVAAA and editorial warning against rushing one family into a cottage. *BDN*, 29 September 1967: Euphoric headline 'No Mass Housing Scheme, One Aboriginal Home for Bega's Glebe'.

39 *BDN*, 11 July 1969, p. 6.

40 *BDN*, 20 May 1967; ABC, *Four Corners*, 19 May 1967.

41 *Canberra Times*, 6 March 1969; *BDN*, 25 May 1969. On Walgett see Goodall, *Invasion to Embassy*, pp. 282–3.

42 *BDN*, 25 February, 23 September 1969. For more on the housing issue see *BDN*, 18 July 1967: reports that Mumbulla Shire Council is to move nineteen Tarraganda Aboriginal people, on 'health and hygiene grounds'. *BDN*, 26 September 1969: Mumbulla Council refused farmers permission to erect tents for seasonal workers and demanded huts with showers and toilets. ED Otton, a local farmer, complained that 'huts are a blot on the countryside … tents are more hygenic for these people'. See also *BDN*, 3 October 1969, 23 January 1970. Even when William Wentworth agreed to send prefabricated houses from the Snowy to the south coast, Mumbulla Shire Council complained to the federal office of Aboriginal Affairs that it had difficulty in obtaining sites for the housing.

43 *BDN*, 10 October 1969.

44 *BDN*, 24, 27 October 1967.

45 'Aboriginal Housing Project Launched': *BDN*, 20 March 1970. *Voice*, 20 March 1970, describes the caravans as a 'Big Effort to Help Aborigines'.

46 RG Castle and JS Hagan, 'Aboriginal Work and Society on the Far South Coast 1920–1975', paper presented to the Labour History Seminar, Canberra, February 1978 (AIATSIS), pp.16–18. See also Ozzy Cruse interviewed in the *Imlay Magnet*, 28 August 1990.

10 Raising a different flag: The struggle for Aboriginal rights in south-eastern New South Wales in the 1970s

1 Lee Chittick and Terry Fox, *Travelling With Percy: A South Coast Journey*, Aboriginal Studies Press, Canberra, 1997, p.14.

2 Ibid., pp. 1, 177. On the term Yuin see Sue Wesson, *An Historical Atlas of the Aborigines of Eastern Victoria and Far South-eastern New South Wales*, Monash Publications in Geography and Environmental Science, No. 53, Monash University, 2000, p. 129.

3 M. Rayner, *A Study of Housing for Aborigines within Bega NSW 1967–1970* (AIATSIS PMS 3324), p. 12. Gunyah Aboriginal Housing Cooperative formed in 1972. See also Castle and Hagan, 'Aboriginal Work and Society', p. 20.

4 Castle and Hagan, 'Aboriginal Work and Society', p. 23; Chittick and Fox, *Travelling with Percy*, p. 194.

5 Chittick and Fox, *Travelling with Percy*, p. 194.

6 *BDN*, 10 July 1978.

7 The Whitlam government funded the South Coast Aboriginal Legal Service in 1973.

8 Chittick and Fox, *Travelling with Percy*, pp. 168–9, 177, 180–1.

9 Quoted in Kevin Gilbert, *Living Black*, Penguin, Melbourne, 1977, p. 59.

10 *The House of Representatives Standing Committee on Aboriginal Affairs*, Transcript of Proceedings Taken at Eden NSW, Sunday, 30 September 1973, p. 624.

11 Ibid., p. 637.

12 Goodall, *Invasion to Embassy*, p. 351.

13 Ibid., p. 671; Chittick and Fox, *Travelling with Percy*, pp. 194–6.

14 Ibid., pp. 175–6. For evidence of the Tent Embassy being important in the local sphere, see for example *BDN*, 10 August 1979. At a public meeting on Mumbulla, Brian Egloff pointed out that 'there is a tent on Capital Hill to draw attention to land rights'. See also Haebich, *Broken Circles*, pp. 570–7 where she discusses the shifts in Aboriginal politics in the 1970s, the greater

prominence of the UN, the stress on cultural pride and assertiveness, the influence of black power, and the crucial importance of the Tent Embassy.

15 Whittick and Fox, *Travelling with Percy*, p. 130.

16 See Terry Fox, 'A South Coast History', in the appendix to *Travelling With Percy*, p. 191.

17 Ibid., pp. 175–82; D Byrne, *The Mountains Call Me Back: A History of the Aborigines and the Forests of the Far South Coast of New South Wales*, NSW Ministry of Aboriginal Affairs Occasional Paper No. 5, June 1984. Merriman Island in the centre of Wallaga Lake was the first Aboriginal site of significance in New South Wales to be declared an Aboriginal place under the National Parks and Wildlife Act. The campaign was also led by Guboo Ted Thomas.

18 *BDN*, 9 February 1979, p. 3.

19 *Joint Volumes of Papers Presented to the Legislative Council and Legislative Assembly. NSW Parliament, Third Session, 1980–81*, vol. 4, *Minutes of Evidence Taken Before the Select Committee of the Legislative Assembly upon Aborigines at Wallaga Lake on Wednesday 7 February 1979* (pp. 581–613 in the Joint Volumes), p. 3.

20 Ibid., pp. 594–8.

21 Ibid., p. 599.

22 Ibid., p. 605–6.

23 Fox's evidence can be found in ibid., pp. 609–13.

24 Ibid., pp. 1449, 1447–50.

25 Ibid., pp. 588–9.

26 See for example ibid., p. 1033; Cruse as chairman of the NSW Aboriginal Lands Trust is on p. 1439. Cruse notes the change in the assertiveness and pride of Aboriginal culture. Stanner is quoted on p. 1128 on the historical causes of socio-economic deprivation; Kenneth Maddock is interviewed on pp. 583–619. A letter to Wran from Guboo Ted Thomas (pp. 585–7) compares the situation at Wallaga to that of Aboriginal people in Queensland. For further evidence of historical work being referred to, see *Aboriginal Land Rights and Sacred and Significant Sites, First Report from the Select Committee of the Legislative Assembly on Aborigines, NSW Parliament*, 1980. For historical background, this report relies on Rowley, for prehistory on Berndt. Other historians employed included Jean Woolmington (*Aborigines in Colonial Society*, Cassell, Melbourne, 1973) and David Denholm (*The Colonial Australians*, Penguin, Melbourne 1979).

11 'A very hurting thing': Apologising for history

1 Brierly, Journal, 5 January 1847; *HRNSW* Series I, vol. 25, p. 559.

2 Dan Weeks in *BDN*, 26 May 1967.

3 Laurie Neal, *Cooma Country*, Cooma–Monaro Historical Society, 1976, pp. 34–5.

4 *Bombala Times*, 10 February 1988; *BDN*, 31 December 1987, 26 January 1988.

5 Klaus Hueneke, *People of the Australian High Country*, Tabletop Press, Canberra, 1994, p. 1. The Aboriginal people (Wolgal) 'were the discoverers and first explorers of the [Snowy] mountains. None of them are left now'. 'The history of the Aborigines of the Snowy Mountains region is part of the Australian tragedy. Under the impact of white settlement their numbers dwindled and in less than one hundred years they were gone' (p. 2). See also Kate Clery, *The Forgotten Corner Interviews*, 2000, Eden Killer Whale Museum; Jack Loney, *Yambulla Gold*, self-published, 1987, p. 7. See also *Cooma–Monaro Time Walk: A Mosaic record of the History of the Monaro from 1788–1988*, Cooma–Monaro Historical Society, 1988. During the bicentenary the history of Cooma–Monaro was represented by the society through a Mosaic Time Walk made of forty tiles, each with an image symbolic of an aspect of the area's history, funded by a grant from the Bicentennial authority. The first two tiles show images of the Aboriginal tribe the Ngarigo. The text on p. 4 reads: 'being generally friendly to the white man they fell victim to European diseases and became extinct in a very short time'. No mention is made of conflict over land under the section on the first squatters. See also *Cooma 150 Years On*, Cooma–Monaro 150 Years On Committee, 1999, which includes a substantial historical overview on the occasion of the town's 150th anniversary. This publication addresses the issue of the Aboriginal people's loss of land but still dodges the issue. Aboriginal people are given

two pages under the heading 'Early Days of Cooma and Monaro', then they disappear from the story.

6   *Imlay Magnet*, 13 April 1993

7   *Imlay Magnet*, 17 June 1993; *BDN*, 7 November 1997, p. 1: 'All Crown Land in Shire Claimed'.

8   *BDN*, 13 July 1993; *BDN*, 27 November 1992. The council fails to support an Aboriginal land claim to two vacant blocks of Crown land at Bournda and Wolumla. The land, it said, was needed for 'essential public services'. For positive stories on Aboriginal people see *Imlay Magnet*, 28 January 1993. On Ozzie Cruse, see *BDN*, 29 January 1993: Aboriginal Land Council opens in Bega, funded by the NSW Aboriginal Land Council: *BDN*, 8 June 1993: Colour spread, 'students celebrate Aboriginal day': *Imlay Magnet*, 13 April 1993: Year of Indigenous People. *Imlay Magnet*, 8 June 1993.

9   *BDN*, 20, 27 December 1996.

10 Bain Attwood, 'Learning About the Truth', in *Telling Stories*, Bridget Williams Books, 2001, pp. 199, 206.

11 *BDN*, 15 August 1997, p. 1.

12 *BDN*, 20 August 1997. See also 19 August 1997.

13 *BDN*, 20 August 1997.

14 For details of the Council for Aboriginal Reconciliations declaration in 2000 see their website.

15 John Howard in the *Australian*, 24–25 February 2001.

16 *BDN*, 10 February, 3 March 1998.

17 *BDN*, 27 February 1998.

18 *BDN*, 24 March, 29 May 1998.

19 *BDN*, 20 August, 17 September 1999.

CONCLUSION

Looking for Blackfellas' Point III

1   *BDN*, 23, 30 October 1998, 6 November 1998.

2   *BDN*, 5 September 2000.

3   *BDN*, 8 September 2000, p. 3, 12 September 2000.

4   For positive stories see *Magnet*, 8 July 1999: 'Our Aboriginal Community celebrates NAIDOC week'. *Merimbula News Weekly*, 19 May 1999: the Federal Government provides funding of $100 000 dollars for Jigamy Farm (Keeping Place) to provide training in hospitality, indigenous tourism, eco-tourism and visual performing arts. *BDN*, 7 July 2000: local Koori women's choir sings in the opening event of NAIDOC week, and the Aboriginal flag is raised. *BDN*, 6, 17 March 1998: report on a reconciliation lunch at Bega as part of International Women's Day activities. See also celebration of NAIDOC week. *BDN*, 31 March 1998: Bega High students organise a 'dance, smile and reconcile' dance, Guboo Ted Thomas present, front page coverage. *Magnet*, 8 July 1997: NAIDOC Week celebrated in Eden, Aboriginal flag is raised in the main street. *Magnet*, 5 August 1997: Towamba school students paint mural for NAIDOC week. For evidence of the increased sensitivity to indigenous culture in political negotiation since the 1980s in south-eastern New South Wales; see *Social Assessment with Indigenous Aboriginal Communities in Eden CRA Region: A Report Undertaken for the New South Wales CRA/RFA Steering Committee*, May 1998.

5   *Magnet*, 1 June 2000.

6   See for example the 1994 ATSIC survey of the indigenous poopulation in Eden–Monaro, which revealed a familiar story of Aboriginal disadvantage. One in eight Aboriginal people over 25 years of age had been taken away from their families as children. Although 70 per cent of the indigenous population identified one area as their homeland, only 1.1 per cent claimed that they could speak an indigenous language. School retention rates were low, with nearly half of those over 15 years of age having left school without gaining a school certificate and few going on to complete Year 12 and tertiary studies. The unemployment rate was 30 per cent and over 80 per

cent of households had an annual income of less than $25 000. The Queanbeyan ATSIC region is essentially the federal seat of Eden–Monaro, an area of 57 600 km. It has the smallest indigenous population of any ATSIC region in New South Wales. See *1994 Aboriginal and Torres Strait Islander Survey: Queanbeyan ATSIC Region*, ATSIC and Commonwealth Bureau of Statistics, Commonwealth of Australia, 1996, pp. 9, 11, 13, 39, 45, 51.

7   Vivienne Mason was interviewed in Narooma in 1992 by Trisha Ellis, and Brenda Ardler by Trish Ellis at Wreck Bay in 1991. Transcriptions are by Trisha Ellis. The tapes are held at AIATSIS Film and Sound Archives, Canberra.

8   Helen Swinbourne and Judy Winters, *Pictorial History: Bega Valley Shire*, Kingsclear Books, Sydney, 2001, p. 8.

9   Ken Inglis, *Sacred Places: War Memorials in the Australian Landscape*, pp. 21, 23, 26 and, quoting Henry Reynolds, pp. 448, 450–1.

10 For details on Reconciliation Place see the Minister's Explanatory Statement Tabled in Federal Parliament in September 2001 for approval by both Houses. See also Minister Ruddock's letter to the *Canberra Times*, 5 December 2001.

11 Quoted in *Sharing History*, Key Issues Paper No. 4, Council for Aboriginal Reconciliation, 1994, p. 9. For a different view, which emphasises the need for white Anglo-Celtic Australians to be given the space to mourn the passing of their traditional identity, see Miriam Dixson, *The Imaginary Australian: Anglo-Celts and Identity: 1788 to the Present*, UNSW Press, Sydney, 1999, pp. 43–4.

12 Ken Inglis, 'Media Amnesia', *Eureka Street*, 9(1) 1999, p.10 (see also pp. 11–12); Henry Reynolds, *The Other Side of the Frontier*, Penguin, Melbourne, 1981, p. 201.

13 My interview May 1999 with Jack Burgess, a descendant of Thomas Underhill; *BDN*, May 1962.

14 District of Monaro Newspaper cuttings, Mitchell Library Q991/N vol. 44 (most probably 1890s); Robinson, Journal, 25 August 1844, p. 176.

15 *SMH*, 29 May 1851. On the history of Aboriginal cooperation with settlers see Robinson, Journal, 25 August 1844, p. 176; *Moruya Examiner*, 26 September 1942. WK Hancock, *Discovering Monaro: A Study of Man's Impact on his Environment*, CUP, 1972, pp. 69–70, recognises the contribution of Aboriginal people to settlement, especially as guides. P Bateman, *The Story of the Heffernans from Clonbonane, Aranda*, Canberra, 1990, p. 100, mentions that Catherine Tarlinton was saved from bushrangers by Aboriginal people armed with guns. There is a similar story in Hetty Laws, *Thalia's Way*, Boolarong Publications, Brisbane, 1987 p. 5. *Bega Gazette*, 23 April 1874, reports on the death of William Roohan, 'The Pioneer Mailman', 'the first to carry the mails overland from Monaro to Twofold Bay, procuring the service of the blacks to mark the trees along his route for his guidance'. *Bega Gazette*, 12 December 1872: John Campbell first came to Bega in 1832 'accompanied by black guides'. He had heard of the area from blacks to the north. *Sydney Gazette*, 16 February 1806: an open boat party from the *Contest* (left for repairs at Twofold Bay) travelled up the coast and was probably saved by Jervis Bay Aboriginal people who gave them six eels in exchange for clothing. See Celia Ann Rose, 'Recollections of the early days of Moruya', *JRAHS*, 7, 1923, Journal and Proceedings Supplement. p. 375; at the age of 4 Rose came to Broulee (near Bateman's Bay) when her father was appointed overseer. 'Aboriginals saved the settlement several times from starvation by supplying fish and oysters'.

16 On the Chinese see W Bayley, *Notes on the History of Bega and Moruya 1770–1943*, collected 1942–43, NLA. *Bega Budget*, 23 November 1910: the last of the Chinese stores closes down in Bega. *Bega District News*, 26 August 1929, speaks of 'quite a colony of Chinese gardeners' in Bega 'years ago'. See Marian Hutcheson, *A Little Piece of History*, self-published, Eden, 1989, pp. 25–7. In the 1880s, her grandfather came to Twofold Bay, purchasing land adjoining the Boydtown estate and employed fifty Chinese men to clear the land. See also *Candelo and Eden Union*, 14 June 1883; Eileen Morgan, *The Calling of the Spirit*, Aboriginal Studies Press, Canberra, 1994. *Bega Gazette*, 1 August 1885, reports on the honesty of Chinese labour in bushwork such as 'clearing and burning off'. See also the unpublished work of Sue Norman at Kiah, who has written on the relationship between Aboriginal people and the Chinese, especially in the abalone trade. For German settlers at Twofold Bay in 1855, see Vicky Small, *Kameruka,* p. 15; typed notes by Norman Librihien held at Bega Museum; *BDN*, 10 December 1931 (death of Andrew Koeller). Barbara Dawson, in *Sheep and Shepherds, Sheepwashers and Shearers on Bibbenluke*

1851–1867, Bombala and District Historical Society, 1996, p. 9, lists five Aboriginal people working on Bibbenluke as sheepwashers in 1851. As late as the 1850s, the list of employees included one Tahitian, thirteen men of French or Belgian descent, eight of German descent, and the remainder Greek, Irish, Scottish or English. See also *Childhood Reminiscences of Wilfred Alexander Watt de Beuzeville 1884–1954, c.* 1950, which speaks of Aboriginal people, a Jewish auctioneer, a Chinese storekeeper and fossickers, and a Syrian market gardener in Bombala in the late nineteenth century (NLA).

17 Peter Read, *The Stolen Generations: The Removal of Aboriginal children in New South Wales 1883–1969*, NSW Department of Aboriginal Affairs, Sydney, 1998. Peter Read, 'Aborigines Making History', in W Hudson and G Bolton (eds) *Creating Australia*, Allen & Unwin, Sydney, 1997; Tom Griffiths, *Hunters and Collectors*, CUP, 1996, esp. Chapter 5; Tom Griffiths, 'Legend and Lament', *The Australian's Review of Books*, March 1999, pp. 11–13.

18 Sue Wesson, PhD thesis, Monash University (draft), p. 175.

19 Brierly, Journal, 13 August 1843.

20 Wellings papers, NLA.

21 *Bega Gazette*, 22 November 1882. See also W Bayley, *The Story of the Settlement and Development of Bega*, Brooks, Sydney, 1942, p. 91 on James Manning: 'it was he who found the road from Merimbula to the top of Tantawangalo'. *Sydney Gazette*, 16 November 1839 reports on a road being 'discovered' in the county of St Vincent leading to Batemans Bay. *Mallacoota Memories*, Merimbula and District Historical Society, 1980, p. 23: Aboriginal people followed 'Genore' River on their trek up to Monaro for moths. 'Much the same route was used by the white settlers'.

22 *Age*, 14, 16 May 1902

23 J Liston, *The Thaua Language: An Aboriginal Pictionary from the NSW Far South Coast*, Canberra, n.d. (AIATSIS); Nicholas Brown, 'On the Margins of the Littoral Society: The New South Wales Coast Since 1945', *Environment and History*, 4, 1998, pp. 209–37; Brian Egloff, *A Report on an Investigation of Places of Cultural Significance to Aboriginal People in the Southern Portion of the Eden Woodchip Agreement Area*, NPWS, Canberra, 1987; *A Survey of the Cultural History of Biamanga (Mumbulla Mountain) and the Biggah (Bega) Area May 1999*, Conservation and Restoration Certificate II Course, Coast Train Bega. Conclusions of report, p. 27.

select bibliography

During the four years I spent researching and writing *Looking for Blackfellas' Point*, I found the work of local historians particularly helpful. For the Bega area, W Bayley's *History of Cobargo* (Mitchell Library) and his *Story of the Settlement and Development of Bega*, Brooks, Sydney, 1942, provided me with important leads, especially newspaper articles. Bayley's *Notes on the History of Bega and Moruya 1770–1943*, held in the National Library, also contain valuable material. One of the most useful and interesting collections for the Eden–Bombala area is the papers of Harry Wellings, also held in the National Library. Wellings produced a large body of newspaper articles in the 1930s on the history of south-eastern New South Wales, some containing important details of indigenous oral history. By far the most credible and well-researched history of the southern Monaro is Claire Schofield's *Bombala: Hub of Southern Monaro*, published by Bombala Shire Council in 1990. For Ben Boyd, the best work is easily Marion Diamond's *Ben Boyd of Boydtown*, MUP, 1995. The few 'academic' histories that focus on the south-eastern corner of New South Wales lean towards 'environmental' history. Chief among them are WK Hancock's flawed but landmark history of the Monaro, *Discovering Monaro: A Study of Man's Impact on His Environment*, CUP, 1972. Hancock drew much of the material for this book from the papers of JA Perkins held in the National Library. Perkins' papers are an invaluable source for the history of the Monaro. The historian Nicholas Brown has published two valuable articles which focus on the social, economic and environmental history of the far south coast of New South Wales in the latter half of the twentieth century: 'On the Margins of the Littoral Society: The New South Wales South Coast since 1945', *Environment and History*, 4, 1998, pp. 209–37, and 'Everyone Who Has Ever Done a Tree Sit Always Says that the Tree Talks to You', in Tim Bonyhady and Tom Griffiths, *Words for Country*, UNSW Press, Sydney, 2001. Another useful article on the history of Eden during the same period is K Hartig and G Waitt, 'The Lost Metropolitan centre of New South Wales: Resolving the unfulfilled claims about Eden, 1843–1920', *JRAHS*, 83, Part 2, 1997, pp. 118–35.

For indigenous history in south-eastern New South Wales, both before and after 1788, I have drawn on Sue Wesson's *An Historical Atlas of the Aborigines of Eastern Victoria and Far South-eastern NSW*, Monash Publications in Geography and Environmental Science No. 53, Monash University, 2000. I owe a great debt to Sue, and her work now offers the most authoritative guide to Aboriginal societies in south-eastern New South Wales. Sue's PhD should be available through Monash University Library by the end of 2002, and will I hope be published in due course. Other useful and reliable sources relating to indigenous history are Michael Young, Ellen and Debby Mundy, *The Aboriginal People of the Monaro*, NSW NPWS, Sydney, 2000; Denis Byrne, *The Mountains Call Me Back: A History of the Aborigines and the Forests of the Far South coast of NSW*, Occasional Paper No. 5, NSW Ministry of Aboriginal Affairs and NSW NPWS, Sydney, June 1984; Michael Organ, *A Documentary History of the Illawarra and South Coast Aborigines 1770–1850*; and Brian Egloff's two reports, *Mumbulla Mountain: An Anthropological and Archaeological Investigation*, Occasional Paper No. 4, NPWS, Canberra, 1981, and *A Report on an Investigation of Places of Cultural Significance to Aboriginal People in the Southern Portion of the Eden Woodchip Agreement Area*, NPWS, Canberra, 1987. Egloff has also published on the subject of Aboriginal fishing. See his 'Sea long stretched between': perspectives of Aboriginal fishing on the south coast of New South Wales in the light of Mason v Tritton, in *Aboriginal History*, 24, 2000, pp. 20–211. Finally, for the participation of Aboriginal people in the rural economy, see RG Castle and JS Hagan, 'Aboriginal Work and Society on the Far South Coast 1920–1975', paper presented to the Labour History Seminar, Canberra (AIATSIS) February 1978. This article also appeared in A Curthoys and A Markus (eds) *Who are our Enemies: Racism and the Australian Working Class*, Hale & Iremonger, Sydney, 1978.

Much of the primary material gathered for this book comes from newspaper sources, the details of which appear in the notes (but see the list of local papers below). A small amount is drawn from the interviews I conducted with local residents, both Aboriginal and non-Aboriginal, and I am indebted greatly to those who gave freely of their time and memories. The remainder comes from the journals and recollections of three men in particular. The journals and sketches of the artist Oswald Brierly, held in the Mitchell Library in Sydney, often provided me with the inspiration to continue, as did the journals of George Augustus Robinson, now transcribed and held in AIATSIS in Canberra. The last and most personal source was the journals of the Austrian Baron Charles von Hugel, written in the 1830s and translated and edited by Dymphna Clark: *Baron Charles von Hugel: New Holland Journal November 1833–October 1834*, MUP, 1994. I use the word 'personal' because I came to know Dymphna Clark in the last three years of her life. Through the Clark property at Wapengo, north of Bega, Dymphna had a close relationship with the south coast of New South Wales. I still remember the day she handed me a copy of von Hugel's journals and said in her wry and understated way, 'I think you'll find this interesting'. One of my few regrets is that she is not here to share the book that she helped to inspire.

Looking beyond regional histories to works that focus more on national history and politics, I have
referred frequently to the following books and articles: Bain Attwood and Andrew Markus, *The Struggle
for Aboriginal Rights: A Documentary History*, Allen & Unwin, Sydney, 1999; Ann Curthoys, 'Mythologies',
in Richard Nile (ed.) *The Australian Legend and Its Discontents*, UQP, 2000; Graeme Davison, *The Use and
Abuse of Australian History*, Allen & Unwin, 2000; Heather Goodall, *Invasion to Embassy: Land in Aboriginal
Politics in New South Wales, 1770–1972*, Allen & Unwin, Sydney, 1996; Anna Haebich, *Broken Circles:
Fragmenting Indigenous Families 1800–2000*, Fremantle Arts Centre Press, Fremantle, WA, 2000; Peter
Read, *Belonging: Australians, Place and Aboriginal Ownership*, CUP, 2000; Henry Reynolds, *Why Weren't We
Told? A Personal Search For the Truth About Our History*, Viking, Melbourne, 1999; Don Watson, *Caledonia
Australis: Scottish Highlanders on the Frontier of Australia*, Vintage, Sydney, 1997 [1984].

The process of writing history, at least for myself, is enriched constantly by my reading of literature.
The work of several writers has sparked ideas and connections that might have been otherwise left unex-
plored. In writing this book I drew on images and ideas found in the poetry of TS Eliot, the work of
Australian novelists Murray Bail and Rodney Hall, and the German novelists Bernhard Schlink and
WG Sebald. I also drew inspiration from the powerful meditation on history and forgetting by the
Australian poet Geoff Page and the Aboriginal artist Pooaraar in *The Great Forgetting*, Aboriginal Studies
Press, 1996.

The following newspapers are cited in the notes.

The Age (1854–present)
The Australian (1824–48 and 1964–present)
Bathurst Free Press (1851–1904)
Bega District News (1923–present)
Bega Gazette (1864–1900)
Bega Standard (1870–1923)
Bombala Herald (1863–1911)
Bombala Times (1863–present)
Braidwood Review (1915–58)
Canberra Times (1926–present)
Candelo and Eden Union (1882–1904)
Cobargo Chronicle (1898–1951)
Cooma Gazette (1873–75)
Cooma Monaro Express (1879–1949)
Daily Telegraph (1879–1990 and 1996–present)
Delegate Argus (1895–1943)
Eden Magnet (1919–40)
Eden Observer (1903–10)
Eden Propeller (1902–03)
Gippsland Times (1861–1981)
Goulburn Herald (1848–1927)
Illawarra Mercury (1855–present)
Imlay Magnet (1971–93)
Magnet (1993–present)
Moruya Examiner (1863–1964)
Monaro Mercury and Cooma Bombala Advertiser (1860–1931)
Merimbula News Weekly (1996–present)
Magnet Voice (1940–69)
Pambula Voice (1893–1938)

LOOKING FOR BLACKFELLAS' POINT

Southern Star (1900–23)
Sydney Gazette (1803–42)
Sydney Mail (1860–1938)
Sydney Morning Herald (1831–present)
Sydney Times (1834–64)

index